Swamp Songs

Swamp Songs

THE MAKING OF AN UNRULY WOMAN

Sheryl St. Germain

The University of Utah Press
Salt Lake City

LIBRARY OF CONGRESS CATALOGING-IN-PUBLICATION DATA

St. Germain, Sheryl.
  Swamp songs : the making of an unruly woman / Sheryl St. Germain.
    p. cm.
  ISBN 0-87480-743-3 (hardcover : alk. paper)
  1. St. Germain, Sheryl. 2. St. Germain, Sheryl—Homes and haunts—
Louisiana. 3. Poets, American—20th century—Biography. 4. New Orleans
(La.)—Social life and customs. 5. Louisiana—Social life and customs.
6. Women—Louisiana—Biography. 7. Family—Louisiana.   I. Title.
  PS3569.T1223 Z47 2003
  811'.54—dc21

                              2002014256

    Printed on acid-free paper
    07 06 05 04 03 02
    5 4 3 2 1

    ISBN 0-87480-743-3

The Defiance House Man colophon is a registered trademark of The
University of Utah Press. It is based upon a four-foot-tall Ancient
Puebloan pictograph (late PIII) near Glen Canyon, Utah

Tell me the landscape in which you live,
and I will tell you who you are.

—Jose Ortega y Gassett

CONTENTS

ACKNOWLEDGMENTS / xi

Lakeshore Drive, New Orleans / 3

Eye of the Storm / 6

Bodies of Water: A Suite from the South / 17

The Story My Mother Told Me / 35

Trying to Sing / 40

Controlling François / 57

Sweets and Shiny Things / 78

Swamp Songs / 95

Disappearing Bodies: Fishing for a Brother and a Land / 110

Communion / 128

Looking for Light / 140

The Sound of Planes / 161

Whips and Unruly Women   / 185

AFTERWORD: *Bring Me a Dream*   / 219

ABOUT THE AUTHOR   / 228

ACKNOWLEDGMENTS

Some of these essays were published in the following journals: *Ascent, Black Warrior Review, Chattahoochee Review, Crab Orchard Review, Event, Flyway, Fourth Genre, ISLE, Louisiana Literature, Louisiana Studies, Mid-American Review,* and *Southern Humanities Review.*

I would like to thank Barry Ancelet, Paul Griffiths, and Greg Guirard, who read and commented on drafts of some of the essays and allowed me into their lives. Steve Pett edited the essay "Swamp Songs" and suggested that title to me, and I thank him. I've been inspired and befriended by many who have, in individual ways, helped me to understand something fundamental to the writing of this book. These include, most important, the members of my family, both living and dead. Rainer Schulte and Galway Kinnell encouraged me when I first began to take myself seriously as a writer, and I doubt I would have gotten very far without their support in those tender days. Tim Gautreaux, my first creative writing teacher, suggested once that someone should write about Kenner, and I thank him for that suggestion as well as for his early lessons. Darrell Bourque, Alexis Levitin, Debra Marquart, Joni Palmer, Derek Smith, and Ruth Schwartz have been steadfast in their friendship and support, and I thank them from the swampy recesses of my restless heart for all their kindnesses.

I have changed the names of some of my family members as well as the names of some of the other people mentioned in this book to protect their privacy. For the same reason I have left out some family members altogether, have sometimes obscured place locations, and in one case changed a location. This book is as true as I can make it, but it is, in the end, only one person's translation, or version of a truth. My mother, my father, or my siblings would have told different stories, and my choice of stories, and the weight I have given to particular parts of the stories, says as much about me as it does about my family. Any factual errors or lapses in memory are my own.

Iowa State University supported the writing of this book by granting me course releases and travel grants, which gave me time to write and allowed me to travel to Louisiana for the 2001 Mardi Gras.

My editor, Dawn Marano, suggested the shape of this book, and believed in my ability to complete it. Without her unflagging support and guidance this book would not exist.

Swamp Songs

Lakeshore Drive, New Orleans

It snakes into a kind of desperate embrace of Lake Pontchartrain. At one end are the seafood restaurants with their familiar fish smells that rise up from the waters when you arrive, smells that always preceded the good fried seafood we ate there. It was a kind of profound twinning I came to understand as a child, that something bad was always connected to something good. The restaurants themselves floated on the lake; you could almost say they extended the drive into it with their creaky wooden piers that ended abruptly above deep waters, as if the lake itself were an answer to a question you hadn't yet asked.

Pontchartrain Beach, before its demise, occupied the far end of Lakeshore Drive. Its flying horses were run by bearded men who hobbled and grimaced like ill-tempered dwarves, but I loved them; this was the first ride I got to go on alone. The best was to be on the outside horse so that you could pretend you were really flying into the night. I can still remember the thrill of the horse's inevitable movements up, then down, up, then down, the small fear I came to love when the horse rose, and the feeling of safety when it came back down. And my parents were always there, waving as I passed by, always, always there—no one had gone yet.

When we were older we'd go on the faster, louder rides that pounded their music into our bodies like a drug, hurled us out over the lake, then pulled us back just when we seemed at the brink of death. The white wooden roller coaster was our favorite because we loved having our hearts in our mouths, the blood rushing everywhere, our eyes wide open, never had we felt so alive. I loved the Wild Maus ride, too, which had a car rumored to have once derailed and actually flung a child into the lake. Even my father was frightened the only time we rode it together; the guy who loaded the cars muttered, as he pushed us off, that there just might be too much weight in our car. I could see the uncertainty in my father's eyes, and felt a fearful bonding with him.

And the freedom of it, later, to run from one end of the beach to the other alone, from the Haunted House to the Toboggan ride; and, much later, to feel the first clammy hand of a boy creep around my breast as we were thrown close on some swirling ride.

We used to swim in the lake even then, warm as blood it was, choppy and dirty; you'd be covered with peppery specks of who-knew-what when you got out. It smelled sour, but it was the only smell we'd ever known the lake to have, so it seemed normal to us, like our lives, like the wild heart of this city the lake stains like some original sin.

Farther down, past the beach, were the long grassy beds where, later, we would lie burning in the sun with our new breasts, proud of the whistles of boys, wanting more.

And even farther down, past more expanses of grassy beds and polluted waters, at the far end of the drive was my grandmother's house, its gardens of petunias and four-o'clocks that lit the outside of it, hiding its shabbiness. Fig and magnolia trees grew next to and sometimes over the house, making it dark and cool inside. This was the house where Mere, my great-grandmother, had died, the house where I lay on her bed, surrounded by her collection of jars filled with formaldehyde and small dead creatures, and first dreamt of death. Accidentally locked in her room, I dreamt that night gathered into a shape above me there, on her deathbed, took on the breath of the lake, and whispered into my ears.

Every major hurricane would close Lakeshore Drive, and the angry, whitecapped waters would rise up under the floors of the restaurants, the wooden supports of the roller coaster, the foundation of my grandmother's house, and the grass would swell with the heaviness of the water, the drive itself become just more lake bottom.

We weren't really afraid of hurricanes as children, though. I think we believed them to be like flying horses, or roller coasters; there would be a fear, a lifting up that we welcomed, then a coming back down to ground. We reveled in the thrill of the fear because we always believed the ground would show itself again, the way our parents did when the rides were over.

When we were much older, weekend nights we'd park along the drive next to the Mardi Gras Fountain, almost the halfway mark between the seafood restaurants and my grandmother's house, the fountain with its public waters that lit the night gold, purple, and orange, and we'd look up at it between kisses and breaths, spraying higher than we could ever reach. We'd lie in those cars, music turned up high, and the first sex was as hard and fast as the rides at the beach, as garish as the colors of that fountain, of this city that is my mother, this city that taught me to love hard and fast, to love all that is wild and dark and feels good.

The beach is torn down now, the rides gone. My father and brother are dead. They died young, their deaths typical of many others in this city. A new sign announces that Lakeshore Drive is *one way,* the way to my grandmother's house, and even that one way closes at dusk, so no more kissing and fumbling goes on there at night, no wolves will eat little girls on this shore, nor will wolves suckle them, and I have to say I miss it. I loved and still love everything that was wild and dirty about this place, even though I know it led some of us to rides we drank and sniffed and swallowed and smoked and some of us died of. This drive and the wolves that lived here are family. It's hard to say good-bye.

Eye of the Storm

It was 1965 when Hurricane Betsy hit the Bahamas, then banked off the coast of Florida into Louisiana. Almost one and a half billion dollars worth of damage and close to a hundred lives lost—but I was only eleven years old at the time and didn't learn these facts until much later. All I knew was that Betsy had ripped the roof off our house, flooded it with the lake's dark waters, spawned tornadoes that destroyed the houses around us, and made a river of our street. The evidence of Betsy's power was inescapable, but it was into the very eye of that power I chose to walk, as a child, in search of my father.

Today, more than thirty years later, I'm visiting my mother; we're sitting in the small living room of the house that was rebuilt after Betsy, drinking jasmine tea, halfheartedly watching television, and talking. It's early fall, and it's warm and windy outside: high hurricane season. We've just finished watching the weather report about a new tropical storm called Georges that's gathering strength and heading this way, so our talk has turned to hurricanes, and the first one I remember. My mother, who is recovering from heart surgery she had a few months ago, still can't quite catch her breath when she talks, so that everything she says sounds weak, wounded.

She remembers two things about Betsy. First, that we had to move out of our house for almost a year while they repaired it after Betsy was done with it; she stresses how difficult this move was with three young children, coming, as it did, at the beginning of a school year. And second:

"I still don't know *why* you walked outside, Sheryl." She's breathing heavily. "I told you children I don't know how many times about the eye of the hurricane. But you, you had to go out in the middle of it and get lost. You never would listen."

It's funny that I remember those times of evacuation so clearly, though other childhood memories have long since faded. I think the undeniable presence of a thing we couldn't control wrote itself into me deeply and indelibly, like a tattoo I didn't ask for. At any rate my mother has her version, and I have mine:

We are under mandatory evacuation orders. My father has driven us from our small house near swelling Lake Pontchartrain in the middle of a rainy night to a big, sterile-smelling army building, part of the Jackson Barracks complex. Because my father is a sergeant in the Louisiana National Guard, we always evacuate to the barracks of the guard. We are in our pajamas, and except for the weather, we could have been going on our regular Friday-night trip to the drive-in.

The children are put to bed in a large room on the second story of one of the buildings with our pillows, blankets, and stuffed animals and a small television that flickers on and off. Pillows on the cold floor, blankets piled around us like shed skins, my brother and sister and I press against one another for warmth and safety. Electricity has long since been lost, and the blank television screen is as frightening to us as the storm outside. Only the weak light from a hurricane lamp burns in a far corner. Mother is somewhere downstairs with the other adults. My father and the other men are out sandbagging the levee.

We are two girls and a boy. The boy, my younger brother, will kill himself before he reaches his midtwenties, a crazy husband will lock my sister in a closet and kill himself before she is twenty, and I, the oldest, not having the emotional strength to handle these catastrophes, will leave this place. But for now I sing them to sleep, for now I make the stuffed animals talk, though the hurricane is eating our house, though the windows begin to shatter one by one, as if being shot out by snipers surrounding the building, and the air rushes in, warm and wet and full of desire; it doesn't matter, I sing on. The mouthless bears chatter, *We are safe, we are children and stuffed bears, nothing can harm us.*

I sang the others to sleep, the singing punctuated by the shattering of each window, a sound that affected me the way my father's belt did— more damage to heart than body. I couldn't sleep myself. The wind out- side sounded like some giant's breath, or the wolf who huffed and puffed and blew the house down. Though I closed my eyes and tried not to feel the shattered air around me, or listen to that tunnel of a voice, it seemed as if that 150-mile-per-hour thing were laughing at us. I couldn't have understood it then, but I think I was feeling, viscerally, the utter indifference of nature. All I could think about were other times when nature, or God, had seemed unfathomably indifferent—the times, for example, when my father, drunk, would throw my brother down the entrance hall to our house, and slam his head on the front door over and over.

Then, suddenly, quiet. Again, like my father, who would awake, sud- denly, from his rampage, look at his hands as if appalled, and order us all to bed. A stillness, a calm, a strange not-to-be-trusted quiet, a gray clar- ity—I was seduced by them to walk outside into the wet night to look for my father. Though it was my father I was most afraid of, he was also the one I felt could do something about the shattered windows. I think I wanted something I can only describe as male, some kind of protection or nurturing that felt harder than what my mother gave. I also knew I could trust my father's feelings, or thought I could. What you saw was what you got: playfulness, straightforward anger, or clear drunkenness. Every gesture of love from my mother, sober as she was, seemed to me to be hiding something—guilt, anger, frustration, regret. I know I felt this as a child, though I could not have expressed it.

I had no idea where the levee was, but I thought that's where my father was, and I thought I could ask someone. I walked downstairs and outside into that silence. It was a full silence, like the silence after an astonishing poem, or a horrible thing said that one can never take back, a silence that wasn't really a silence, but a kind of disembodied presence, a stunned recovery from insight, the cocoon where one considers, safely, the implications of tragedy. The storm's eye.

Meteorologists will tell you that a hurricane is composed of a circular pattern of storm clouds and torrential rains that is whipped around by winds that can be as high as 180 miles per hour. At the center of the storm within a curved "wall" of high-velocity winds is the eye, a circular cloud-free area of relatively light winds whose diameter may be from six to sixty miles. A sinking motion in the eye causes warming and drying. Surface pressure reaches its minimum in the eye. Though these facts were often explained to me as I was growing up—by my parents, schoolteachers, and the meteorologists we watched every year when hurricane season came around—they never really spoke to me as a child.

The term *eye* as it is used in describing the center of a hurricane is, of course, a metaphor. And though my understanding of the eye was in many ways purely metaphoric, it was also absolutely literal. Despite what my mother had told me about the eye of the storm, as a child I really thought the eye was an eye; I believed that the storm could see, and that if I were in the eye of it, I could see what the storm saw. So that even though I did want to find my father, I believe I also wanted to be able to see with that Cyclopean Eye. I had the audacity to think that I too could possess the storm's knowledge. Today, each time I pick up a pen to write about my family I feel like that girl who descended those stairs to walk into the eye in search of her father.

A volunteer found me later, after the other side of Betsy had passed, huddled under an outside stairwell. I'd gripped the concrete stairs above me until my fingers bled while the storm blew around me. Moments after I had reached the bottom of the stairs the wind had started up again, and I'd run under the stairs, clinched my eyes shut, and held on tight. Before I closed them I saw that the sky, which had been strangely clear during the moments of the passing of the eye, had become infected with clouds again. The clouds, like the cataracts that prevented my grandfather from seeing well, ensured that I would not see, or at least not see well, with the eye of the hurricane. The wind became immediately more muscular and aggressive; the smell of something horribly wrong floated in the air, the salty smell of ocean in the wrong place, the smell of dying fish on a beach. The wind began to bellow and roar, and sound like it had when I'd been upstairs with my siblings. I closed my eyes to the smell, I closed my eyes to the sound, and went deep into the pitiful darkness of my own small soul and prayed to that abstract God the nuns had promised me existed.

My eyes have always been bigger than my stomach, my idea of what fright I could stomach always larger than the reality. The volunteer, a Cajun National Guardsman who worked with my father, found me shivering, eyes so tightly closed I wouldn't open them for him at first. "Oh, cher," he said, "pauvre petite, what you doing out here in this weather? Where's your papa? What you doing going out in the eye of dis bete?" He gathered me in his arms, talking in his gentle voice that was like a lullaby to me, until he had me safely inside.

But I'm getting too far away from the story I want to tell. I am not in the midst of a hurricane now; I'm visiting my mother. We're sitting in her small living room drinking jasmine tea, watching television, and talking. The threat of Georges is not yet real, only a thing to watch, and plot. It's a line on a page like the red line on your skin that would make its way to your heart, my grandmother used to tell me, if you had an infection and didn't take care of it.

Instead of the splendid displays of leaves turning colors, a display I've come to love since moving to the Midwest several years ago, New Orleans has splendid displays of winds that have the potential to become hurricanes. In fact, the wind's voice, angry and insistent as it whips up the weeping willow on the north side of the house, mixes with the voice of the television, so it almost seems as if they sing as one—the voice of something ancient and powerful married to the newer power. We know the gusts outside are due to some localized disturbance, nothing serious—yet—though the threat of Georges on the horizon makes us both a bit nervous. In fact, Georges will miss New Orleans, but not until after it frightens New Orleanians with several threatening nights. My mother will not leave her small house, dangerous because it is located so close to both Lake Pontchartrain and the Mississippi. My sister, her children, and her dog will come to stay with her because the shelters will not take pets, and my sister refuses to leave her dog alone. The shelters will not hold everyone, and it's those who have the least money who will be affected the most. Those who can afford it will fill the hotels and motels north of here in a line following the major highways inland, but not everyone can afford three or four days in a hotel—most of which also won't take animals—to wait out a storm that may or may not come. My sister is not the only one who refuses to leave an animal.

But right now things just feel comfortable and normal. It's like old times, other late nights when we'd sit together on this same sofa, my mother with a pile of clothes to fold, and I, curled up in a gangly curve next to her in my flannel nightgown, the sweet-flowered scent of the jasmine tea, the clarity of the black-and-white images on the screen, and, often, the sound of the wind's bluster outside binding us together like some sad, haunting song. I've heard all about the evils of television, but some of the most intimate moments I spent with my mother were spent watching television with her, as if the television protected us from speaking too much, and we could just be together.

When I was a child, there were only two situations when she'd let me stay up later than my usual bedtime. One was when there was the threat of a hurricane; she'd let me listen to the weather forecasts late into the night with her, tracking the course of the storm on the hurricane map I'd been given from school. The other times she'd let me stay up late were Saturday nights, when there wasn't any school the next day. She'd let me watch *Morgus the Magnificent* with her, a show that started at ten and ended at midnight. "Morgus" was Sid Noel, a New Orleans weatherman, who by day predicted and charted the heat, hurricanes, and flooding rains. By night he donned a dirty smock and wig, marked up his face, and became Momus Alexander Morgus, otherwise known as Morgus the

Magnificent, a mad scientist who introduced and commented on the grade-B horror movies that made up the bulk of his show.

During the breaks he would be shown trying some experiment or other, experiments that usually blew up or failed in some profound way, like love gone bad in his face. These disasters often involved preposterous inventions, such as the BUBA machine, the Bio-Ultronic Body Analyzer, a medical home appliance supposed to stop sickness before it happened. The funny thing was that his experiments, though darkly comic, usually made sense in some way; who *wouldn't* want a machine that stopped sickness? But Morgus treated his machines as if they were home appliances, giant toasters or blenders or food processors that processed anything but food. His was a peculiarly American solution: the deepest, most profound societal problems would be solved by a machine that could be turned on and off with the flick of a switch, a machine you could purchase at the corner store, a machine that would fit on or under the counter in the kitchen, a machine that made alteration of human behavior unnecessary.

These are my fondest memories of Mother, sitting with her, drinking tea, and watching the *Morgus* show. Even though I was small, and probably shouldn't have been watching horror movies, I wasn't afraid because my mother was there; I was calmed by her quiet presence and the repetitive movement of her hands as she bravely and surely folded towels and shirts and pants and dresses through all the horrors Morgus showed us, as if the only response to horror was to fold clothes, folding as humans turned into insects, folding as insects turned giant and started to feed on humans, folding through inanimate matter come alive and carnivorous, folding through madmen with axes and chain saws, folding through women and men come back from the grave to feed off living flesh and blood.

My brother and sister and father in bed, the quiet was like a bandage for us both, gathering us in its walls as it had other nights when we had wished for silence. And strangely enough, even the horror of Morgus's movies seemed comforting, familiar, somehow. Those evenings with Morgus would prepare me for my adolescence, where drugs, alcohol, and

*

violence would transform and then take the lives of several members of my family. The litany of events that were to come, a litany not *too* unusual for a middle- or lower-class family from New Orleans—brother jailed at eighteen, dead of a drug overdose not long after being released from jail; brother-in-law dead of suicide at nineteen; nephew killed at eighteen by a drunk driver; father dead at fifty-four of cirrhotic liver; cousin turned prostitute and junkie dead at thirty of drug and alcohol overdose—is one that would seem unbelievable in a work of fiction. This is the dark side of the love of drama, the cultivation of intensely felt experiences, whether through music, food, or drink, the passions that define many who call themselves New Orleanians. These are the blood storms that could destroy a home just as surely as recurring hurricanes. But as a young child watching Morgus, I didn't know these family horror movies were to come, and though there was surely some sense in which I felt the rumblings and understood the beginnings of the slide to those disasters, it was not yet something I had to face. Indeed, the worry I feel now at the prospect of Georges reminds me a little of the feeling I always carried in my gut as a child; I knew there was disaster ahead, but I couldn't quite predict when and where it would hit.

The horror movies Morgus introduced, though scary, seemed safe: not only was my mother there folding clothes, but the TV screen separated us from the horror and made it feel *other*—as long as those things were happening behind that screen, they couldn't bleed into the house or the sofa where we were sitting. When François, the oldest of my two brothers, lay in a coma for a week before he died, and Jules, my younger brother, couldn't bear to come into the intensive-care room to visit him, but instead went to see *Halloween* on the big screen, I understood. There is something primal in us that needs to be scared to death occasionally, but having the movie screen or television screen there gives us some measure of control: we can walk out.

The *Morgus* show has long since gone off the air, and I am now a grown woman who has folded her own clothes through calamity. A peace comes to you after so many things have happened and you have survived them; I notice, for example, that my mother seems almost unflappable now. You could tell her just about anything, and she would respond with great calmness. Hurricanes, or the threat of them, still make her nervous, but drugs, alcoholism, sex, murder, suicide—give her any kind of family tragedy—she'll chew it up and spit it out. And I have learned that all you need are a few good people to hold on to; if they're strong enough, you can ride out almost any storm.

Instead of Morgus, my mother and I are watching the *Emeril Live* show on the Food Network tonight, although we occasionally flip back to the local channel for updates on Georges. Emeril Lagasse, one of the great chefs of New Orleans, is the star of a live cooking show where his food experiments, unlike those of Morgus, always turn out successfully. But the two share a flair for the dramatic; instead of sedately adding pepper to his dishes, Emeril fists it at them—freshly ground black, red, and white—shouting BAM as he does, often getting the audience to shout it with him. Each time he shouts BAM I'm reminded of Morgus's explosions, and I smile, also remembering my mother's explosively hot dishes, her love of cayenne pepper and Tabasco sauce, her legacy to me. She put pepper, and lots of it, in everything; even her eggs in the morning looked riddled with the bloody stuff. When we were really young, she kept the foods for us fairly mild, but used the pepper to punish us; both she and my father would make us stick out our tongues when we'd done something wrong, and they'd splatter hot sauce or put a pinch of pepper on them. Eventually, I got used to it. I remember clearly the day when my father put pepper on my tongue as punishment, and I closed my mouth and it didn't burn or hurt: I liked it.

Mother says the Food Network has shows twenty-four hours a day, but that Emeril's is the most popular in New Orleans, as popular as the *Morgus* show used to be, and I wonder what that means, from horror to cooking, I wonder if there's some kind of pattern, or connection, I'm not fully understanding between the two. Is it something in the water here— the mud-colored, slow-moving Mississippi, the brackish, polluted Lake Pontchartrain—that makes us so love the thing that hurts us?

It's during one of the commercial breaks that my mother, out of the blue, tells me something I think she's wanted to for years. I don't know why she chooses just this moment. We had been looking at old photo albums earlier that day, and an old journal my Maw-Maw, her mother, had kept as a child, which certainly contributed to her mind-set. Maybe watching Emeril cook the kind of food she can't eat now since her heart attack earlier this year also reminded her of her mortality and things that needed to be said, to be set right—

"Paw-Paw was unfaithful to Maw-Maw," she says.

Both of them dead for some years now, I look at her blankly. She knows how I worshiped my Paw-Paw. I'd written several poems about him, how I loved watching him make spicy hogshead cheese, how I loved the Crackerjacks he'd bring us on Sundays, how I loved running to get him at the local bar, Fanks, where he'd be singing or reciting in his blustery voice some poem he knew by heart. He was one of the good things I'd been holding on to, some uninfected blood I had hoped to pass down to my son.

"Many times," she continues. "He gave her gonorrhea," she says. "And later, syphilis."

I can see there's nothing I can do to stop her, so I turn without response and pretend to watch television. The last time I saw my grandfather alive was the Christmas Eve of my seventeenth year, a few months before he died of stomach cancer.

"He was mean to her," she says. "Maw-Maw said he trampled her like a flower."

Now she's crying.

"She had such a sad life," she says. "She never had anything, and nothing I did could ever change her life."

I hear her words, and take them in like some food I dislike intensely, food I can't quite get down without gagging, like the horrible canned spinach she used to force me to eat. Or maybe food that has just too much of that pepper I love. Somewhere in me I can hear, like a mournful whisper, my mother's almost unbearable grief for a mother she couldn't save, but I am a selfish child, and mostly what dominates is my own howling.

My heart is a gallows as we both turn back to the screen, seduced by

Eye of the Storm

Emeril's voice. I feel heavier than I did moments ago, heavy with knowing I can never love my grandfather again in the old way. I want Morgus back, I want his Bio-Ultronic Body Analyzer to work, and I want him to invent one for the soul. I want him to go back in time and use it on my Paw-Paw and Maw-Maw. I want to believe, I *do* believe in Morgus, *I do, I do.*

As Emeril shouts his next BAM for another fistful of pepper, an intense gust of wind rattles the shingles of the house and rubs the willow tree up against the windows behind us. The lights flicker, dim, and almost go out, an electrical problem somewhere in the heart of the house. We're used to this; but when I turn to my mother in the flickering light for a moment she seems transformed, her dress peppered with dark spots, her hair false, failure in her face, a kind of regret there I've never seen before at having served up this black weather, this blistering food.

The lights go out, the screen goes dark, and we sit in silence for a moment. It is in that speechless silence, when I can't see my mother's face, that I feel again some understanding for the eye of the storm, that quiet where no one speaks and no action is necessary.

A strange music repeats itself outside the window, three low whistles, two long and one high. It is an empty music, a fatherless music. I don't know what it is, or where it comes from, if it is bird, or wind, or terror.

I hear Mother fumbling for the matches to light the hurricane lamp, and I pray she will not find them. I pray to stay a few moments longer blinded.

Bodies of Water

PRELUDE

I was born in New Orleans and spent most of my childhood in Kenner, a city that is almost a suburb of New Orleans. We lived about a quarter mile from Lake Pontchartrain, the shallow urban estuary that, along with the Mississippi, links and dominates the landscapes of both cities. I used to walk to the lake frequently as a child because it was so close by, and it is that body of water that first helped shape my voice and character in ways I could have hardly guessed then. I remember its surface always looking oily and black, as if the bile of some huge beast had been let loose into it. Though the lake is much cleaner these days, when I was growing up it was always polluted. Gray foam mouthed the shore. Fish floated, belly-up, along the banks. If you swam in the lake, its oily, decaying smell became yours, and you were sure to be sick sometime later in the week from the swim—perhaps just an earache or sore throat, maybe an eye infection, but always some consequence for having dipped your body into its waters.

I didn't dislike the lake or avoid it because it was polluted. I grew to feel as close to it as I was to my family. I didn't hate my father because he was an alcoholic; neither would I abandon the lake, poisoned as it might be. We swam in it, skied on it, fished in it, got sick from it, and drank our first alcohol on its shores. I spent many summers as a child on its levees where I could look out on the large expanse of its black body. Sometimes I'd bring a book to read, and was comforted by the lake's brooding presence as I explored all manner of questions in the poems and novels I read lying near it. Sometimes I brought a pen and wrote my own stumbling poems, and sometimes, bookless and penless, I stared into its waters and found a blacker version of my own face staring back. Other times, when winds whipped the face of the lake into a frothing monster I saw in its disturbed surface a reflection of the rage I felt when hurricanes twice ravished our house.

I remember being astonished at what still could live in that lake: crabs and catfish, for example, scavengers who fed on decaying and putrid flesh, scavengers whose own meat was paradoxically so sweet. I wondered how they were able to transform the shit of the lake into such exquisite nourishment, and I remember the moment it occurred to me that perhaps I needed to learn this transforming act.

My first poems, bad as they were, were all poems of transformation that searched for insight and epiphany. I was scavenging, like the crabs and catfish, but my meat took the shape of poems. I learned to search for ways to honor even the dirt, to transform it into something nourishing. And I came to understand failures of writing as failures of transformation.

Years later, after writing a couple of books of poems and struggling with my first job teaching writing, I realized that not all writers care as much as I about transforming experience into insight or epiphany. In fact, for many, it was love of language, rhythmic expression, music, or the desire to express an idea or feeling lyrically that drew them to poetry. I loved language and music too, but for me the poem always failed if some alchemy had not been performed. If shit had not been transformed to gold in some way the poem was not as interesting to me, though I might be drawn to its language or cadence, or admire its form or the weave of whatever linguistic tension might be at its core.

ALLEMANDE

NEW ORLEANS WAS BUILT about three hundred years ago on an island of cypress swamp teeming with snakes and alligators at the spot where the Mississippi River comes closest to Lake Pontchartrain. By the early eighteenth century, when the first of the French and German immigrants who would start our family in the New World made their homes here, New Orleans, drained, was a city bounded on three sides by swamps, and on the fourth by a river. At high tide the river would flow through the streets as naturally as blood does through veins.

As a result of the swampy soil, all houses to this day must have pilings driven seventy feet to reach bedrock before construction can begin. Our cemeteries are aboveground, since we learned early on that floods would simply cause coffins to rise and drift away like some macabre flotilla. Not all the rural areas surrounding New Orleans can afford to bury their dead aboveground, though, and just a few years ago I saw footage on the local news of coffins from a cemetery near Sunset, Louisiana, floating down flooded streets. One of the coffins housed my friend's uncle Louis, a jovial, hard-drinking man who had died of cirrhosis. My friend remarked, after watching his uncle's coffin bob across his television screen amidst a backdrop of half-flooded homes and trees, that he was sure Uncle Louis would've liked the ride.

The soggy ground was called "flottant" or "floating land" by the settlers, whose shovels struck water at eighteen inches' depth. Because of the waterlogged land, it is extremely rare to find any cellars in New Orleans. Perhaps because we've learned you can't hide or store anything in the ground, not our vegetables or even our dead because the water will bring them up again, we've also learned to put everything on the table. We're not like westerners, laconic, reticent, never speaking of how we feel. We say everything. We tell everything. Within five minutes of meeting people from here you may know more than you ever wanted to know about their personal lives, details about divorces, sexual intrigue, abortions, deaths, just tossed off like they're talking about the weather. I've sometimes embarrassed myself in a conversation with a nonsoutherner by getting excited about something and revealing too much about myself. You can tell by the subtle movement in a person's eyes that you've gone too far, and there's no way for you to retreat and unsay what you've said. This is a quality of openness—of flooding, if you will—I find impossible to change in myself, and I've come to understand this nakedness as a mask of sorts, nakedness a shield for nakedness. After all, if it appears you have revealed all, no one will be curious about what you have not revealed. This condition—I'm not sure I'd want to call it a *quality*—of openness also leads to a love of that condition in others, and I've found myself drawn to those who can respond to that openness with openness. Another way of saying this would be to say I value the condition of intimacy, and in that I am not unlike many other southerners.

I'm also drawn to art and writing that cultivate a sense of deep intimacy. In writing this kind of intimacy can be seen most clearly in memoir, where if the reader doesn't feel something akin to intimacy with the narrator, the work fails to move. In art, the luminous self-portraits of Frieda Kahlo are beautiful examples of the excruciating power of intimacy. In music, Bach's *Suites for Solo Cello*. One cannot listen to Bach's *Suites* without the feeling that the cello is singing to you alone, the single, richly varied cello a whisper, the confidential song of a dark angel. The stylized dances that make up the movements of the Suites offer a stout form within which that sometimes terrifying, sometimes joyous intimacy might be contained.

MENUETT

SOUTHERNERS ARE NOTORIOUS for their love of drama and exaggeration. There's so much drama to the land here—not only flooding, but also recurring hurricanes, heart-stopping heat and humidity, schizophrenic muddy land that can't decide whether it's land or water—that we've developed an appetite for it. Scheherazade and her fantastic tales would have flourished in New Orleans where tall tales and exaggeration in everyday talk abound. And, in the popular imagination, a love for the sentimental and melodramatic. Opera and blues, the most emotionally charged musical forms, are big favorites in New Orleans. My grandfather August Frank, a typical New Orleanian whose father immigrated to America from Germany, loved sentimental poetry. My grandmother would often send me to fetch him from the neighborhood bar he used to frequent, and I'd find him, more often than not, standing tall and stiff (and usually half-crocked), reciting, for the umpteenth time, "The Face on the Barroom Floor" as if it were the most profound poem he'd ever had the privilege to encounter.

Just as it's more important for our politicians to be interesting than to be honest (Edwin Edwards is a case in point), it's more significant that our life stories be interesting than literally true. That's not to say there's no truth in our stories, though, only that we've fixed them up because no one here will listen to you unless what you're saying is engaging or otherwise entertaining. That's why my mother distorted the truth—whether consciously or not—when telling me the story of how my great-grandfather accidentally shot his eye out. She insisted for years that the accident occurred when he learned his wife had given birth to an eighth daughter; he was upset because he had wanted a son to help him in the fields. Each time his wife had gotten pregnant he had prayed for a son, and each time his wife had given birth to a girl. This last girl had been too much, the last straw, my mother said. And so he shot his eye out in anger, and cursed his wife's womb, and the family, while doing it. In fact, I found out while doing genealogical research that there had been a son early on, and the son had been a great help to his father, had probably been in the fields helping him when they received the news about the eighth daughter. My mother neglected to tell me about the son because it just wasn't as interesting a story if you knew about him.

ONLY 10 PERCENT OF THE land in south Louisiana's coastal zone is more than three feet above sea level. The Mississippi River flows above sea level, but much of New Orleans is below, and half of it is also below the storm level of Lake Pontchartrain. The city still wants to be a swamp, and it takes a prodigious effort to deter it. New Orleans has the largest drainage system in the country, and engineers from all over the world come to study it. We have twenty-two pumping stations, one of which is the largest pumping station in the world, and more than 240 miles of canals (Venice has only 68). One thousand five hundred miles of drainage pipes lie under the city.

It is, in some ways, an impossible task to keep this city properly drained, but through heroic feats of engineering we've managed to transform a large, thriving swamp into a large, thriving urban area. It takes constant surveillance, though. Look away for a moment, let one levee deteriorate or one pumping station go out, and we're on the way to becoming a swamp again.

Eight generations of my family have lived and worked this land and harvested these waters. Jean Fleuren Cossé and Marie Laisaine were the first of my ancestors to make the trip from France in the mid-1700s, along with hundreds of other immigrants, the ones who would be the parents of those who would come to be known here as Creoles. My French ancestors built an orange plantation along the banks of the Mississippi in Buras Settlement, sixty-four miles south of New Orleans, where most of what was not river was Gulf or coastal marsh or swamp. The land they found themselves on—now Plaquemines Parish—was nothing like the land they had known in France. The "land" that lined the natural levees along the Mississippi where they had to build their homes wasn't really land, but swamp. Some of them drained the swamps or dug canals to try to control the water; others built homes on stilts on top of the swamps.

Propaganda posters from the time advertise Louisiana as a tropical paradise; the soil, the posters claim, will bear two crops a year without cultivation; Indians adore the white man and work for him—for nothing. There are gold mines, pearl fisheries, a pleasant climate, no diseases. Of course, there was nothing of the sort. In fact, the air was damp, the waters stagnant, the ground marshy. Tidal waves from hurricanes brought saltwater into the orange groves and destroyed the roots or drowned the trees. The moisture in the climate encouraged disease. Cholera and yellow fever claimed more lives in south Louisiana than anywhere else in the country at the time. Even in the nineteenth century when piped drinking water was available, it was too expensive for most. Some drank river water, and some drank water from their backyard cisterns, not knowing they were breeding grounds for the *Aedes aegypti* mosquito, the carrier of yellow fever. The outbreaks of malaria, cholera, yellow fever, and typhoid in New Orleans through the latter part of the nineteenth century occurred at twice the rate and intensity of other large urban areas. Many immigrants died soon after landing from some waterborne disease. In one six-year period alone twelve thousand people died of yellow fever.

Meanwhile, the hurricanes came every year, bringing with them floods. Those who chose to live, as my relatives did, on the wiry peninsula on which Buras is situated were (and still are) most affected by hurricanes. The Mississippi runs thick down the whole length of the peninsula to its mouth, and is prone to flooding even without any help from hurricanes because there's so little land, and what's there is below sea level. Most of the land surrounding the Mississippi as it pours itself for its last miles to its mouth is coastal marsh, with some forested wetland and a thin strip of development and farms along either side of the river. It is along this thin strip that my maternal ancestors lived for close to three hundred years. In the early twentieth century their orange plantation, their home, and even the cemetery where some of them were buried were washed away in the aftermath of a hurricane. Where they lived and worked and loved and died was claimed by the river. And the rest may yet be claimed by the Gulf. Because of coastal erosion, much of Plaquemines Parish will be open water in fifty years.

Those of my ancestors who survived the 1915 hurricane moved to New Orleans and tried to get on with their lives.

The waters come, the waters recede, we respond by rebuilding or relocating; hurricanes come, hurricanes leave, again we rebuild or move. We answer the weather as we do partners in a dance, following, holding them close, and trying to respond to their moves—even as they step on our feet.

SARABANDE

NEW ORLEANS REGULARLY takes the honors for being first or second in obesity in the nation. You are more likely to see the profoundly obese—one hundred pounds or more overweight—in New Orleans than perhaps anywhere else in America. Paul Prudhomme, the famous chef who popularized Cajun food, is so obese he has to be moved about in a wheelchair. And not for nothing is the infamous suburban version of the French Quarter, located in Metairie, called "Fat City." The Friday before Mardi Gras is called "Fat Friday," and Mardi Gras itself is known as "Fat Tuesday."

One of my relatives, who recently had a heart attack, weighed about a hundred pounds more than what he should have. In a session designed to educate the family about good eating habits so that we could help our relative as he recovered, the nurse (not a native) said to us, in a disgusted voice she did not try to disguise, "This has happened because of what you people [meaning New Orleanians] eat. Do you have any idea how much cholesterol is in crawfish? Or shrimp?" she queried. We had to admit we didn't.

A study done in 1997 by the Coalition for Excess Weight Risk Education concluded that New Orleans was the fattest major city in America, with 38 percent of the population weighing in as obese. The study found that cities like New Orleans, with high unemployment rates, low per-capita income, a high number of food stores per capita, large numbers of black residents, and, interestingly enough, high annual precipitation rates, had the highest rates of obesity. I'm not sure how much our rainfall rate actually contributes to our rate of food consumption, but I do know that food, and a lot of it, is a vital element of the culture here. And we're not talking health food either: fried catfish, boudin sausage, roast beef po'boys slathered with mayonnaise, muffulettas, seafood gumbo, filé gumbo, jambalaya, fried oysters, baked oysters, oysters Bienville, oysters Rockefeller, oyster spaghetti, oyster soup, stuffed mirlitons, redfish courtbouillon, red beans and rice with ham hocks and Italian sausage, boiled crawfish, fried crawfish, stuffed crawfish, sautéed crawfish, crawfish pasta, crawfish étouffée, fried shrimp, boiled shrimp, sautéed shrimp, grilled shrimp, shrimp Creole, boiled crabs, crab salad, crab dip, fried soft-shell crabs, sautéed soft-shell crabs, trout amandine, bananas Foster, and sweet, sweet iced tea. We eat the fat in crabs, we eat the fat in crawfish, and we like our meat heavily marbled with fat—people expand out of their clothes, rounder and fuller than any human should be, until any discernable skeletal structure disappears. Where is flesh and where is bone? Where is water and where is land?

BOURÉE

THE IOWA LANDSCAPE, where I now live, is a no-nonsense one: straight lines of corn and soy beans, 90 percent of the land flat and planted. Midwesterners tend to have attitudes and temperaments to match. When I first moved here from Louisiana I couldn't help but notice the stark contrasts between the two regions. Consider just the differences in the way women dress in the South: more makeup, tighter, more revealing outfits. More jewelry, more perfume, more hair. They are, through cultural conditioning perhaps, more seductive, and those from New Orleans are the most seductive of all. In the Midwest what a woman wears is more aggressively determined by the weather. In Iowa, which has much longer and much more serious winters, women tend to care less about beauty and more about warmth and comfort. The winds, the snow, and cold lead to hats, mufflers, and coats Iowa women have to wear to protect themselves, which discourage fancy hairdos, sheer stockings, high heels, or see-through anything. The difference between the women of the two regions is not unlike the difference between the lush, full-leafed tropical flora that thrives in this semitropical climate and the more sedate, conservative flora one finds in colder climes.

Bodies of Water

If you were raised in New Orleans you learned early on that seduction and sex infuse everything, even something as innocuous as the weather report. Taking off your clothes is natural in a hellishly hot climate like ours. Remember, we have nothing to hide, not our vegetables, not our dead, not our stories, and, it seems, not even our bodies. The humidity, which often reaches 90 percent and stays there over the summer, is nothing like any humidity I have ever felt anywhere else. This humidity is like a presence, an animal that breathes on your shoulders, your thighs, your head and legs. The humidity's associate is the temperature, which can reach the hundred-degree mark through September. By then I believe some of us would even peel off our skin if we could.

What's the big deal about nudity? we ask. In New Orleans no one uses the euphemism *exotic dancing,* which for years I never understood (Asian dancers? belly dancers?). We call it what it is: stripping. Almost everyone raised in the city was exposed to the strippers on Bourbon Street in the French Quarter at some point, because weekend nights the Quarter, that sixty-six-square-block network of streets that in 1718 composed the entire city, was the place to go. In the midnight hours we'd walk from deep in the Quarter, where we'd parked our cars, up Bourbon Street past Esplanade Street and the Creole cottages, shotgun houses and two-story apartments with the signature French and Spanish wrought-iron grillwork, through the gay district where guys slumped against each other and danced in the streets to Donna Summers pumping from the second story of someone's apartment, toward Canal Street and the even wilder parts of the Quarter. We'd descend into its potent mix of blues and jazz clubs, past the tourist shops selling T-shirts, hot sauce, alligator heads, and hurricane mix, the sex shops where we giggled at cock rings and edible panties, past the swinging doors of strip club after strip club where hollow-eyed men shouted, *All girls, all nude, all the time.*

Maybe we'd stop for a drink in the Old Absinthe Bar, or have some raw oysters or a seafood platter at the Acme Oyster House on Iberville, or turn off into Pat O'Brien's for a hurricane. Then back onto Bourbon, back into the heat and humidity, the smell of the Mississippi in the air, and by now also the smell of piss, sweat, and vomit, the sour smell of warm beer and rotting seafood, by now plastic cups and straws and paper lining the sides of the streets, by now more and more people stumbling, or falling down. Eventually, we'd pass the strip club that had a second-floor window through which a naked mannequin swung. There were curtains in the window, and as the mannequin, in a sitting position, swung out into the curtains and over Bourbon, the curtains would gather into her crotch, hiding its nothingness from the audience below.

When we tired of walking we'd turn off Bourbon for good—at least for that night—away from the street and its colorful, smelly press of people that now make me think of lost spawning salmon. We'd turn toward the river, walking toward the heart of the Quarter—Jackson Square— where we'd soon see the spires of St. Louis Cathedral, the oldest continually active cathedral in the country, the cathedral where several of my ancestors were married in the eighteenth and nineteenth centuries. Walking alongside the cathedral we'd turn onto Pirate's Ally and pass by the house William Faulkner lived in during his sojourn in New Orleans, where he wrote *Soldier's Pay* in 1925. As we walked closer to the river the levee would rise to dominate the background, and the lights of Café du Monde, the open-air café just the other side of the levee from the Mississippi, would appear, twinkling and as seductive to me as the warm light from the countless votive candles that surrounded the Virgin Mary's statue in our church. The antidote for a stroll down Bourbon Street was always chicory coffee and beignets—hot rectangular doughnuts sprinkled generously with powdered sugar—at Café du Monde. We'd sit outside the café, the shadow of the cathedral on one side, the levee and the Mississippi on the other, and drink the drink the café was famous for: equal amounts of pungent chicory coffee and hot milk. The powdered sugar on the beignets stuck onto our lips and chins and dusted our clothes, but we didn't care. There was nothing like biting into one of those freshly fried sweet things, full of air and yeast and sugar; if the ritual walk through the Quarter had become a sort of mass for us, this was the communion.

Sex was everywhere as we were growing up, though, not just in the sleazy, packaged-up-for-tourists stuff on Bourbon Street. My father and mother radiated sexual energy, though not always toward each other; flirting, I came to understand, was something you were expected to do. Mardi Gras was an annual public celebration of sex on many levels. Even the statues of Jesus and Mary and the saints in our church were earthy and sexual. I remember Mary's most because I prayed to her most. Her robe was sky blue, edged in gold, and it clung to her closely, revealing all the curves we associate with being a woman. She even wore makeup (or so I used to think): her face was painted with flushed cheeks and peach-dark lips, her eyelashes were as dark as mine when I covered them with mascara, and her hair fell in thick waves around her face, the way mine did when I curled and blow-dried it. The face of Christ, in the throes of death on the cross, was painted with excruciating detail, and there was something deeply physical and gut-wrenching about the care the artist had taken depicting his near-naked body. I think we loved the statues in the church precisely because they were so lifelike and seemed so like us. The church soon began to worry about our attachment to the statues, though, and one day when we arrived for mass all of them had been replaced by nondescript, unpainted wooden statues. The priest explained to us that we had been taking the statues too seriously. They were symbols, he reminded us sternly, only symbols.

Our parish, our church, and school were named after Saint Lawrence the Martyr, one of the Roman Church deacons who fell victim to the persecution of Valerian in the year 258. The nuns told us different stories about how Saint Lawrence met his death, most of which involved eventual decapitation, but the one I liked best was the story about how, when commanded to surrender the church's treasures to Valerian, he distributed the wealth to the poor instead, and at the end presented those poor to Valerian as the wealth of the church. Valerian, infuriated, initiated a series of tortures, the last of which was to roast Saint Lawrence on a gridiron. It is said that during his roasting he joked with his torturer, saying, "One side has been roasted, turn me over and eat it."

In addition to teaching us the stories about the lives of the saints and having us memorize the appropriate answers to questions of faith, once we hit fifth grade the nuns also taught us about sex, or rather how to avoid it. Sister Gisela, a big red-faced nun of an indeterminate age, would lecture us on sex during religion class, pacing the hot, un-air-conditioned classroom, huffing, her face getting redder and redder, as she spoke, her black habit flying out behind her when she turned as if to whip into shape any kid who might have been behind her.

"Your body is the holy temple of the Holy Ghost," she'd say. She had a sometimes stiff way of speaking, and an accent I later learned was Cuban. "This means no kissing until you marry and no touching the holiest parts of your body until you marry!" At this point she would turn and glare at us, one by one, and I swear it seemed as if she could see right into my rotten, sex-crazed young soul. When she looked at me like that I knew that she knew those thoughts I had during mass while I was pretending to pay attention.

Sometimes she would separate the boys from the girls. Father Schutten, our pastor, would talk to the boys, and she would talk to us.

"No wearing of shiny shoes!" she proclaimed one day. "The boys are looking into the shine of the shoes and seeing what is under there, that which they should not see until you are married." She was sweating on the day she told us this, and I remember how flushed her face was, how drenched she was. She wiped her forehead with a handkerchief. "Jesus, Mary, and Joseph," she whispered under her breath.

"And girls, you must look before you walk down the stairs in this building. I have discovered that the boys are waiting underneath the stairs to look up the skirts of the girls as they descend. This is a sin, and it causes the Virgin Mary great sorrow when these sins are committed." We squirmed in our seats, and my friend Maggie whispered to me, "It's the boys' sin, not ours!"

Although I don't think it was the nuns' aim to teach us that our bodies are sinful—they meant to teach us they are holy—that was how we came to understand their lectures. The unclothed body was an unholy body, and anything we did with that body that felt good was probably a sin. We learned that lesson well, but that didn't mean we didn't still take pleasure in seduction. After all, sins of the flesh were not mortal sins.

My friend Maggie gave the first slumber party my mother ever

Bodies of Water

allowed me to attend. We were both in seventh grade. Saint Lawrence, not to mention Sister Gisela or Father Schutten, would have been displeased to know that we spent much of the night playing striptease music and undressing.

We spent the early part of the evening calling boys on the phone and hanging up. We made several calls to Brian Tizzard, the quiet dark-haired boy we all had a crush on. At one point we snuck out of Maggie's bedroom window and ran the few blocks down the street to Brian's house, where we threw rocks against a window we hoped was his bedroom window. When his mother's head appeared at the window we shrieked and ran back to Maggie's. By midnight Maggie's parents were asleep and we could begin our stripping. I had never seen my mother's naked body, or the unclothed body of any mature woman, for that matter. My breasts were just barely beginning to grow, but Maggie's were fully developed, and I wondered what they would look like.

Maggie went first; she had been practicing, she said. Setting the needle of her pink record player to the beginning of "The Stripper," which she had as a 45, she jumped up on top of her bed and threw her thick dark hair back, looking at us with a look that reminded me of Sister Gisela's look, but this one knew something else. As the music began she pranced around the bed, tossing her hair this way and that, slowly unbuttoning the buttons of her cotton pajama top, which had, as I recall, blue elephants on it. Her breasts bounced as she danced. She turned away from us, dropped her pajama top, looked back at us, and grinned, and with the music as loud as we dared (we didn't want to wake her parents) she jumped and turned toward us, revealing herself to us in all her bounty. Hair falling over her face, olive skin glowing in the lamplight, she grabbed her breasts and held them out to us, kicking her legs out from side to side to the music. She represented at that moment all I knew of desire and its mysteries, and all I wanted. With her full brown breasts and their darker areolas and even darker nipples, Maggie's body was both enticing and frightening. Her gutsiness infected us all, and soon we were all gyrating hips and waists, throwing our hair about and tossing off our pajamas.

We were fascinated with the strippers on Bourbon Street whom we'd only seen glimpses of thus far. During trips to the Quarter, set up by the church or our family to introduce us to its "history" and "architecture," we always wound up walking down Bourbon Street, which I guess the adults thought was okay as long as it was daytime. But the strip clubs rarely closed, and sometimes we'd get a peek when the men guarding the doors held them open briefly to entice passersby. The strippers, it seemed to me then, had a power over men I wanted to have. Years later, as a young woman, I would try to get a job as a dancer in a Fat City club, but when I learned stripping was expected I couldn't go through with it. By then I preferred a more intimate form of power and pleasure. I loved the way an orgasm would wash through my body like a flood, filling me, swelling me from my earlobes down to the very spaces between my toes. To reach orgasm was to reach that place so like a swamp, to be filled in that way with such a diversity of flora and fauna and still, still water, to be awash with desire—this was what it was to be alive, I thought. At once swamped and lifted up above it all.

GIGUE

WHEN I THINK OF THE waters of south Louisiana I am reminded of the attributes of the people who live there. I think of the turbulent Mississippi, which has wreaked havoc on the population with floods that wiped out entire cities and shifted or eliminated boundary lines, and I think of the flooding of emotions and desires I see in people who call this state their home, a state rated sixth in the nation for violent crimes and a state whose murder rate is twice the national average. Just as the Mississippi doesn't like being pinned by levees and must be given outlets for its annual swellings, so too do those who live here dislike being told what to do and seem to need to jump their banks regularly, to find outlets for their excesses. Unfortunately, though the Mississippi appears to be in check now, due to new techniques and engineering feats that have built seemingly impregnable levees, one cannot say the same for the people.

Bodies of Water

The love of drink in New Orleans—there are hundreds of drinking establishments in the city, and it is rated fourth in the nation in terms of alcohol-related fatalities—has much to do, of course, with the culture the early European settlers brought with them, a culture in which good wine was sometimes as important as good food, but one can't help but note the stark parallel between the flooding of the waters and the drunkenness of a people. We flood ourselves just as our waters flood us. We water ourselves as excessively as the rain waters the earth here (five feet annually).

It's said that the very idea of the cocktail was invented in New Orleans, but even if it wasn't we've invented enough of them to claim bragging rights: sazeracs, ramos gin fizzes, brandy milk punches, dripped absinthe, café brûlot, mimosas, to name only a few. Drinking and driving is de rigueur here; frozen daiquiri drive-through stands are everywhere, the alcoholic versions of the equally ubiquitous, but less intoxicating, snowball stands. Even our foods are often made with liquor: we put champagne on our oysters, rum in our omelets; we cook our steaks in brandy. And most of our desserts contain a healthy amount of alcohol: bread pudding with whiskey sauce, bourbon pecan pie, rum pralines.

One of our most famous and potent drinks, which has been the undoing of many a tourist, is the hurricane, a rum-based tropical fruit drink served up in a glass made to look like a hurricane lamp. The spirit of the actual hurricane, which some of us honor by evacuation to higher, safer ground, and others of us honor by hosting "hurricane parties," finds its metaphorical equivalent in its sweet but deadly namesake drink. If we cannot actually become a hurricane, we can at least symbolically ingest it, take it inside our bodies and hearts as some take the wine that represents Christ's blood. Thus do we assimilate its power, its chaos, and its potential for both transformation and destruction.

With respect to the excessive drinking and other forms of debauchery prevalent here, Lyle Saxton would write, only partly tongue in cheek, of New Orleans that "there seems to be an insidious chemical in the air which tends to destroy Puritanism." Indeed, some New Orleanians have suggested that it is the humidity or the heat itself that leads them to such a love of drink; others have claimed it is rather the foul flavor of the Mississippi water. Certainly, when the water you drink makes you sick (which it often did in the early years of the city), wine or liquor may seem a pleasant alternative. These days, however, the complaint is that the water, though "pure," still tastes bad because of all the chemicals we've put in it to get it that way. So we continue to feel ourselves absolved in choosing to drink anything other than water.

The importance of bodies of water to our very sense of orientation can be seen in the fact that designations of place here are always related to them: you don't go north or south, east or west (as you must in the Midwest, for example), but rather upriver or downriver, across the river or to the lakeside or the riverside. Even then it's not easy to know where you are; streets follow the river and curve around so that a street can run parallel to and perpendicular to itself. As a child I found it hard to figure out where the real edges of cities, parishes, or subdivisions were because they were all located between a shifty river and a shallow, expansive lake; land that wasn't marsh or swamp was cut up into pieces by canals and bayous. Because most of the borders I understood as borders were liquid, the concept of precision with respect to location often escaped me. Indeed, my relatives also often seemed without boundaries. Excessive drinking allowed them to "get out of their skins," so to speak. For a people who were already always ready to spill their guts, alcohol let it all flow out so that the walls between *self* and *other* were often utterly erased.

Louisiana was the landscape where I first learned to speak and to see, the landscape I first walked through, making my way into the world. What I want to understand is how this place gave breath to my voice and desire, and how it might have shaped (or altered) the character of a people, my people, those born and raised in New Orleans; how this place insinuated itself into us in ways that feel, sometimes, like infection.

Bodies of Water

I've come to understand Louisiana waters as the ink that gives my words body. It is the ink I was given at birth. When we write with this birth-ink, we are writing with waters that not only quench our thirst and feed our crops, but saturate our land and destroy our homes and bodies as well. Our words, our lines, and our sentences carry the weight of that water's penchant for both baptism and destruction.

The Story My Mother Told Me

It begins in the orange grove our ancestors owned for six genera-
tions. It is 1867, two years after the end of the Civil War. The
grove, now underwater, was then located on the banks of the Mississippi
River sixty-four miles south of New Orleans. A young woman is reaching
up to pull down a bright orange. Her hair is brown as roux, and long
enough to conceal her derrière, which is as full and ripe as the orange she
has just picked. She has a white cotton shift on and no shoes. She begins to
peel the orange. A breeze from the Mississippi blesses the grove, and pulls the
woman's hair back so that her eyes shine out like jewels. Her name is Juli-
enne Victoria Da Roca, she is fourteen years old, and she is your great-
great-grandmother.

It is at precisely this moment, when the breeze has lifted both her hair
and her dress, that Alfred Leopold Moizant, a French sailor, will see her.
Alfred has jumped ship and walked across the levee looking for work in
the orange groves that line the river. Perhaps it is the smell of oranges in the
air, or the massive flames of hibiscus surrounding the gallery where he is

*standing watching her; perhaps it is the Mississippi wind that carries some
passion he has never known, or even the humidity, which surrounds him
like an animal—whatever it is, he is struck by her.*

My mother will insist that it was the way her hair was flowing behind
her, her hair that she will never cut, her hair that I will remember years
later, white and silky, reaching her feet when she unrolls it like some
sweet, sexy surprise at night; my mother will say all the women in the
family get their beauty from my great-great-grandmother's blood, that it
is a gift for which we should be grateful. I think it was the foreign land,
so full of promise, the alluvial soil built by the river so black and moist
it seemed drunk with riches, that conspired to cast a spell on this French-
man. When Victoria looked up from the orange and met his eyes, he saw
all the richness of the land in her eyes.

My mother is losing her voice, and she looks up at me with the eyes
of a child. I take her hand, careful not to dislodge the IV, and continue
the story for her. Her eyes close, and only the occasional flutter of her
eyelids and pressure on my hand let me know she's still awake and listening. I think of all the years she read to me, how deeply her beautiful
voice with its dramatic inflections and pauses lies within me and shapes
my own voice.

Alfred and Victoria will marry within the year. She will move with
him to a small house not far from her parents. Alfred builds the house
himself on swampland his father-in-law helps him to drain. They will
inherit the orange grove, also built on drained swampland, that
belonged to Victoria's parents. She will give birth to a child every year for
the first eight years of their marriage. They are all girls, although Alfred
prays to God in the church of Notre Dame de Bon Port that he be given
a boy to help him with the work in the fields. God does not answer, and
each new birth means more toil, more despair. His heart grows hard. It
is a hardness not yet visible in the way he printed his last name on their
marriage certificate, which we found at the Plaquemines Parish Court
House, in large childlike letters: MOIZANT. He knows four languages and
has almost no formal schooling. But at least he can write. Victoria makes
an X, as do all the witnesses.

It is 1878 and Victoria is pregnant with their eighth child. By now her genteel ways, the slight touches of art and beauty in the small house, the oleanders, the sweet olive, the crepe myrtle, the hibiscus, azalea, camellia, and wisteria that cover the front, back, and sides of their home, are little but irritation to Alfred. To him her gardens are a garish mess that covers the simple lines of the small house he struggles to hold on to, part of this swampy jungle he must constantly fight to keep the orange grove alive. Every few years a tidal surge from a hurricane washes the roots of the orange trees with saltwater and he must irrigate with Mississippi River water. He continues to lose trees to saltwater damage. And then there's flooding from the Mississippi, which is just as bad. Every spring he spends time he should be cultivating shoring up the levee. And then there are the freezes, which no one can predict, and which often mean replanting more than half of the grove. There's the crawfish pond, the fishing and hunting needed to keep his large family fed. And though he has no feeling about slavery one way or another, he understands that it was his father-in-law's four slaves, free men now, that kept the grove alive all those years before the war. Now men must pray for sons to take the place of slaves.

Mother opens her eyes. *You got that part right, for once,* she says. She clears her throat. *I can finish it now,* she says, pulling herself up to a sitting position on her bed. I wait. She sips water from a glass on the side of the bed. Then she speaks, her voice low and musical.

The day Victoria gave birth to Dina, your great-grandmother, her eighth and last child, was hot. She looked out of the open side window where she could see the dark leaves of the camellia she had planted the first year they moved here. It was not in bloom; she knew it would bloom in the coldest months, January and February, and she liked what seemed like a slight perversion on the part of the flower. Her mother had insisted that she wear camellias in her hair when she married Alfred because she said camellias symbolize what you have to do in a marriage: bloom during the coldest times. Victoria closed her eyes, bore down, and imagined she was a camellia bush, blooming, blossoming, giving forth its lifeblood to the darkest time of year.

The Story My Mother Told Me

37

It was not a difficult birth; after so many the body knows what to do, and the mind is ready for it. The oldest girl, Delphine, sat with Victoria in the back bedroom where she lay on top of the sheets soaked with sweat. She fed her mother ice chips she'd made by using a hammer to smash a small block of ice wrapped in a towel. She had picked some of the mint that grew around the back porch, crushed it between her fingers, and mixed it with a little sugar in the cup of ice chips, so that both the chips and the room smelled of mint. After the birth she would add bourbon and a little water to the drink, and it would help her mother to sleep.

The child, the blossoming, came quickly and quietly. The smell of blood, sweat, and mint filled the room. The wind began to pick up. Victoria registered that it was hurricane season.

"Go tell your papa," she said to Delphine.

Delphine paused only a moment before she ran out through the hall, to the kitchen where red beans had been soaking all day, to the living room, the gallery, and out into the fields where her father was working. It was early evening. Black flies buzzed around pieces of half-ripe fallen fruit that birds or squirrels had partly eaten. Delphine loved the smell of sweet, ripe oranges, but these were rotting and smelled sour.

She found her father picking up tools, clearly preparing to come in for dinner. He turned; she gulped and came out with the news, quick as her mother had given birth. She wanted to run back to her mother's side, but she stood rooted there, as if in a nightmare. Later she would say it was as if the earth had come up around her and held her there.

When Delphine told her father that the child was a girl, he cursed. She swears lightning crossed the sky at that moment, revealing the clouds moving toward them. Alfred was French, so he cursed in French, and Delphine understood him. He cursed his wife's womb. He cursed the earth he was standing on. Finally, he cursed God. He would never walk into a church again.

I don't know which curse was his biggest mistake, perhaps cursing the land, but as he cursed he reached for his shotgun, which he always brought with him. He slammed the butt of the gun down on the ground, which was wet from previous days of rain. It slipped and the gun went off. The rain *began to come down hard. Delphine would say it seemed as if the sky were sobbing, and she looked up at it as if it could tell her something. When she looked down again rain and blood were mixing in the hole that had once been her father's left eye.*

She looks up at me and smiles weakly. *That's why our family has such bad luck,* she says.

Soon she is asleep, breathing easily. I let go of her hand and sink back into the chair next to her bed, a little tired at the weight the telling and the hearing of that story always seem to place on me. As a believer in the power of words I worry sometimes that Alfred's curse has settled itself into our family, might somehow be the thing we can never shake off, some inheritance another might explain as genes. I think my mother, raised by a superstitious mother herself, must have unspoken worries as well, which is maybe why she tells this story so much.

I have two photographs of my great-great-grandfather, who lived to be ninety-seven years old, one a group photograph with his wife and nine children, one of whom is a boy, and another with just Victoria, for their fifty-year wedding anniversary. Both are full-face shots. His missing eye appears as a heart-shaped bruise in both photographs, a richly colored emptiness that is his legacy to us.

Trying to Sing

Behold, God is born!
He is bright light!
He is pitch dark and cold!
—Dylan Thomas, "God Is Born"

Winter-storm warnings in Iowa. It's a couple of weeks before
Christmas, and snow has been falling almost without a break
for several days. The windchill makes it feel like forty below outside. I
look out of my study at the thick cover of snow that brightens the world
as far as I can see. Not only does snow change the color of the land, but
it also changes the feel of it. With all the corn and soybeans harvested,
the Iowa landscape for the past few months has seemed even flatter than
usual, more tired and used up. Now, with almost two feet of snow, some
of it mounded into soft hills by the wind, the land seems fatter, softer.
I'm relieved we're having this heavy snow, even though the weather is so
bad the schools are all closed; the snowplows can't keep up with the

snow, and it's dangerous to drive even to the neighborhood store. I'm happy because it's as if nature has cleared its throat and stated definitively, *It's winter.* Never was there such clarity about winter in Louisiana. Winter there isn't much different from fall. Air conditioners continue to hum, the grass turns brown, leaves fall off trees, and it almost never snows. We understood snow as we understood God: it was something you were supposed to believe in even though you never saw or touched it.

And like all things you can never have, or are difficult for you to get, we wanted it, especially around this time of year, and especially when we were children. In this I don't think we were alone: most southerners would happily suffer through winter storms if only to have a frosting of brilliant white masking the brown mush that dominates Louisiana winters. In the Midwest, the killing freezes and cover of snow that usually follow provide a new beginning. The slate has been wiped clean, everything is forgiven, and one gets to start all over again. The landscape of the Deep South doesn't allow for that because winters are so mild that nothing—not the insects, the rodents, the noxious weeds—ever gets totally wiped out. We can never utterly begin again. As if there's too much history, the southern landscape filled with the weight of too much knowledge that can never be scraped away or hidden under ice and snow.

It's dusk, and almost every house in my neighborhood is lit up with Christmas lights. My boyfriend, Paul, who is from England, finds the multicolored lights, giant lighted trees, plastic Santas and reindeers that decorate my neighbors' homes tasteless and garish. On some level I agree. But the decorations and snow also awaken a kind of hope: I can feel knots in my body loosen around the grief and joy I associate with this time of year, one of two seasons—the other was Mardi Gras—when my family seemed happy.

Perhaps my family took Christmas so seriously because we knew Mardi Gras was just around the corner. Hardly were the Christmas trees undressed and tossed into yards when the first King-cake parties would begin. The first week of January marks the beginning of the Mardi Gras season, which is, for us, the season of deception, wit, and irony.

Trying to Sing

Christmas, though it involved pageantry and costuming as well, was the season of earnestness.

Oddly enough, the two seasons were more tightly connected historically, and indeed at some time may have been part of the same festival. Christmas has been linked to the Roman feast of Saturnalia, which was a day when everything was opposite: children dressed as kings, slaves as masters, etc. The homes and public places were decorated with some of the items we now associate with Christmas: holly, ivy, evergreen, candles, and torches. Mummers also ran about in the streets. The people chose a Lord of Misrule who presided over the "Feast of the Fools." The playfulness of this celebration is not unlike that of the Mardi Gras season, which not only closely follows Christmas, but also overlaps it. The magi who were said to follow the star to pay homage to the infant Jesus are the kings honored in the Mardi Gras tradition of the King cake. January 6, also known as "Little Christmas" or the Feast of the Epiphany, is the day that officially begins the Mardi Gras season. Throughout the Middle Ages January 5 was the final day of Christmas, which came to be known as Twelfth Night.

I stare through the window at the house across the street. A lighted, life-size plastic choirboy stands in front of it, his red robes stark against the snow, his mouth open in frozen song. Something about him makes me shiver. He looks very much like one of the three plastic choirboys my father used to set out in front of our house every Christmas: the red flaring robe, that singing O of a mouth, and dark round eyes raised to the heavens. He is the picture of earnestness.

I was seventeen when my father last displayed the plastic choirboys. The year was 1971: a warmish day in early December, and on our browning front lawn a small mountain of lights and cords. Next to these a life-size plastic Santa lies on its side. The plastic choirboys are set upright but without their heads, which come off so you can put lights inside the bodies. My father replaces the lights inside each of the three bodies, then settles the heads on top of two of them. He looks through the pile of lights and wires, but cannot find the third head. He curses softly, then lights a cigarette and stands smoking and thinking for a few minutes.

After he finishes the cigarette, he sets the two boys with heads in the middle of the lawn, and then, almost as an afterthought, puts the third one out too.

That Christmas our house and the mimosa tree and hydrangea bushes in front would be outlined as usual with lots of lights, and would become, as usual, a backdrop for the Santa and the three choirboys, except that this year the middle one will be headless. Maybe my father hoped to find the head somewhere in the attic and never got around to looking for it. Maybe he was being ironic. In any event it had a chilling effect: the rest of the house decorated in all seriousness and that headless choirboy in the midst of it all like some macabre, cutting criticism of the whole thing.

This would also be the last year my father would put up Christmas lights; the last year things would seem relatively quiet in the family, although it was a kind of uncomfortable quiet. My father is drinking heavily, but no one has yet begun to call him an alcoholic. My brother François is thirteen, and though he has always been a difficult child, he hasn't yet been expelled or arrested, and hasn't yet started doing drugs. Certainly, there are signs of trouble with both my brother and my father, but none of us would have predicted then the paths their lives would ultimately take. My younger sister Aimeé is fifteen and pregnant that Christmas, though we don't know it yet. She will drop out of school early the next year to marry and have her child, a boy, my godchild, who would be killed by a drunk driver a dark New Year's Eve night years later. The two youngest siblings, Jules and Marie, are seven and three, respectively, their own troubles far in the future. I have just graduated from high school and will be leaving home and starting college at Southeastern Louisiana University in January. I am engaged to be married to my high school sweetheart, Ricky, who is in his first year at the Annapolis Naval Academy.

My maternal grandfather, whom we called Paw-Paw, is very sick this year. He has stomach cancer, and Christmas Eve 1971 will be the last time I will see him alive. But I am infected with the hopefulness of the season, naive in all ways about death, and believe he will recover.

Trying to Sing

I am happy. Except for my grandfather's illness, everything seems possible, as untarnished and bright as Louisiana in December can manage. That Christmas Eve I work until seven at Woolco, the department store in Kenner where I have a part-time job. It is just cool enough to wear a jacket, although it will warm up later in the evening. Ricky, who is home on Christmas break from Annapolis, picks me up from work. He has agreed, with much prodding on my part, to wear his dress uniform that night to my family's annual Christmas Eve party. I know Paw-Paw, who had been in the Navy, will be there. My father had also been in the Navy as a young man, and I tell Ricky they will both be proud to see my fiancé in his white midshipman's uniform.

Ricky and I will break up the next month, and he will resign from the Naval Academy, which he hates, before the end of the year, but no matter. We believe, at least for this night, that we'll be together forever.

That week my family's small house has been transformed as Mother went into her annual cleaning frenzy, sweeping and dusting where no sweeping or dusting had occurred all year, and clearing off cluttered countertops whose surfaces we hadn't seen since the previous Christmas. She had even gotten on her hands and knees and scrubbed the floors. She had to use a butter knife to get at the flat hardened gum—like hard dark nipples—that turned up wherever she scrubbed. The house, which the week before had been cluttered and overstuffed, suddenly revealed itself to be clean, with space somehow cleared for a tree and crèche.

I never fully understood where all the clutter went, although I knew a lot of it went into my parents' bedroom, which became something of a junk room during the holiday season. The house had the feeling, in the days leading up to Christmas, of having sucked in its breath for a few days; you knew that soon the breath would be let out and the fat stomach of the house would make itself known again.

Christmas music filled the house the entire month of December, mostly because of my mother, who loved this time of year and had a large collection of seasonal music. The record player was stacked with LPs waiting to be dropped and played: Robert Goulet, Mario Lanza, Frank Sinatra, Johnny Mathis, and Bing Crosby, as well as Handel's *Mes-*

siah and Eydie Gorme y Los Panchos and their *Blanca Navidad* album, which my mother played over and over, though all the lyrics were in Spanish and none of us spoke a word.

Our finest piece of furniture was the spinet piano my parents struggled for years to purchase. The children all eventually took piano lessons, and most everyone else in the family could play by ear. François, who actually had a good ear for music, had a horrendous experience with the man the rest of us took lessons from for eight years, Mr. Harry, our next-door neighbor, who was not particularly gifted as a teacher. I was dutiful and dull; I practiced and did everything he asked of me, so we got along fine. But François challenged him every step of the way, and refused to practice. He couldn't be bothered with counting measures or with correct fingering, and saw no need to learn how to sight-read when he could pick out any melody by ear. His weekly lesson soon became a shouting session, and eventually my mother stepped in, mercifully, and canceled the lessons.

Every Christmas Eve those of us who were currently taking piano lessons with Mr. Harry would take part in an informal piano recital where we played a piece we'd been practicing for several months. In 1971 I would play the largo from Chopin's *Fantasie Impromptu* and Aimeé would play something from Debussy. Marie and Jules were still too young for lessons, and François had already stopped taking lessons. He still played piano, but only picked out things by ear that he liked. Rarely would he play in front of anyone.

My father and Maw-Maw also played by ear and would play some popular songs and Christmas carols as well. Eventually, we'd all sing carols around the piano, and sometimes we'd go caroling in the neighborhood later. I was always the instigator of these trips because I loved to sing. During all four years of high school I belonged to both the high school chorus and our church choir, though my voice was not a strong one and I couldn't, as a soprano, always hold the melody if I were placed right next to someone singing alto or second soprano.

Still, if anyone had asked me what I wanted to be when I grew up, I would've said *a singer*. I remember many summer evenings swinging in our backyard, singing my heart out as I swung, mostly popular songs from the radio and musicals I'd watched with my mother. I had the idea that maybe someone would pass by, someone would recognize what a good voice I had, raw, yes, but also pure and strong. When I sang as a child it felt like a string vibrating through my body, from mouth and tongue to the tips of my toes, a string to which all other sounds were tuned. I lost the exuberant faith of that swinging child after I became an adult, and with it the ability to feel the physical excitement she felt when she sang.

This Christmas my mother was a little more subdued than usual, because she understood, certainly more clearly than any of the children, that her father was dying. She had a complicated relationship with my Paw-Paw, a loud, gruff man she loved, but who had not, she thought, treated her mother right. He was German, square-jawed and blue-eyed, and she had inherited both his jaw and his eyes. He loved to cook, and he loved poetry—as did she. He also loved to argue with his wife's mother, who was French, about why the Germans were better than the French. My mother thought he was intelligent, and liked to tell the story that, when he was in high school, he had pointed out to one of his teachers that their mathematics textbook had a mistake in it. My great-grandfather pulled him out of school when he was fifteen, though, to help with the family business, and he never returned to graduate. He and his father eventually parted ways, and Paw-Paw spent most of his life working as a painter for a hospital in New Orleans, a job that offered no benefits, a job for which he was clearly overqualified, and a job that left him bitter and in the bars most nights. My grandparents remained poor all of their lives, and were never able to buy a house of their own. They rented half of a shotgun house—a house where the rooms were arranged one after the other such that if you shot a gun through the first room the bullet would pass through all the rooms. They lived there, in an old neighborhood in east New Orleans, for almost half a century.

They made the ten-mile trip from New Orleans to Kenner every other Sunday, though, in their ancient car, to visit. Paw-Paw always brought a nickel box of Crackerjacks for each of the kids, and gave us full-bodied hugs and spirited kisses. I don't remember ever feeling his face against mine for a kiss when it wasn't covered with white stubble. He loved to eat and drink beer, as his ample belly betrayed.

My mother would not tell me until years later the details of my Paw-Paw's betrayals of Maw-Maw. All I know this Christmas is how glad I will be to see him again, as I haven't seen him for several months. He has been too ill to travel for the past three months, and I take it as a good sign that they are able to make the trip from New Orleans to Kenner for the party. Even though I'm older now, graduating from high school, I still look forward to watching him hand out Crackerjacks. I still crave the crisp, rich peanuts and sticky caramel popcorn, the sweetness that would catch itself in my teeth for hours.

In some ways Paw-Paw reminded me of Scrooge. Flinty, inscrutable, but somewhere in him a generosity ready enough to show itself to children, but needing the right coaxing around adults. I had been thinking of him the night before when we gathered, mother, father, and the five children, around the hi-fi to listen to Basil Rathbone as Scrooge in *A Christmas Carol.* My mother turned all the lights in the house off and lit some candles. We each had a mug of eggnog with freshly grated nutmeg sprinkled on top. My father lay in his easy chair, my mother sat on the sofa with Marie in her lap and Jules sitting closely next to her. Aimeé, François, and I lay on the newly cleaned floor. I listened to the voices and sounds and music and stared at the small red light that indicated the record player was on, the light that looked like my grandfather's nose when he'd been drinking. The melancholy clanging of Marley's chains sounded deep in my body, a metaphoric ringing the literal movie versions could never manage. I wondered what chains Paw-Paw might be dragging around. I wondered if whatever it was that made my mother sad about him could be changed. Maybe, I thought, he could be redeemed, pulled back from his sickness, which was surely a punishment for something he'd done in his life.

Before I could read myself, my mother would read *A Christmas Carol* to me, and later she gave me illustrated editions of the story and took me to see its film versions whenever they came out. Christmas after

Christmas, this tale entered me, and with it the belief that characters change—for better or ill. If I could not effect transformation in my own life or those of my family members, I would continue to believe that stories might change and inspire us for a time.

By the time Ricky and I arrive at my family's house this Christmas Eve, he in his white Naval Academy dress uniform and I waving around a small diamond engagement ring, most everyone else has already arrived. In the living room are my aunt Alta, and my uncle Emile, as well as my paternal grandparents, who are deaf-mutes. The only people who can communicate with them effectively are my father and Aunt Alta, my grandfather's sister. Though my grandparents can't speak, it doesn't mean they don't like to have a good time. They both love to eat, and they both like to drink a lot on occasion. My grandmother can perceive some low sounds, and claps along to music if there is a deep bass line whose vibrations she can feel. Sometimes she makes a low moaning that sounds like singing. She is clapping and trying to sing when we walk in. She looks happy, slightly drunk, pleased with her one syllable *Ahhh*. Albin, my grandfather, is sitting next to her, bending over to dip a potato chip into the garlic dip, for which he has an unholy love. We all love my mother's dip, made with lots of garlic, sour cream, and cream cheese, dyed green or red. The house will smell of garlic for days after Christmas day. Tomorrow morning it will be in all of our breaths, like a secret we have all shared.

Frank Sinatra, singing "Jingle Bells," wafts from the hi-fi in the back of the house. All along one side of the living room is my mother's crèche, set out on a long table covered with fake snow and pine branches from the Christmas tree. The lights are dimmed, and the Christmas tree, against the back wall, welcomes us with blinking lights of red and blue and green and gold.

The house smells warm and full, a complex polyphony of scents— pine and whiskey, tomato sauce and coconut. Underneath, like a chorus of full, deep bass notes, the everyday odor of the house—the smell of books and the smell of my mother's perfume, my father's cigarettes. The tree has a pile of presents underneath it. Sometime during the night these presents will all get opened, then, much later, after we are in bed, my mother, with the help of my father, will put the presents from Santa under the tree. My mother has a Christmas Club account where she saves five dollars a week to have money to buy presents, and my father also usually takes on an extra job at this time of year to help pay for presents. No matter how poor we are, there are always lots of presents under the tree Christmas morning.

My father, dressed in a paisley silk shirt, jumps up when Ricky and I arrive, and walks over to give me a hug. He smells of garlic and scotch, Old Spice and smoke. He makes a joke about Ricky's uniform and asks what he wants to drink.

"I'll have a hammer if y'all have it this year," Ricky says.

"How about you, Sherry, what do you want, sweetie?" Even though I'm not old enough to legally drink, all the children are allowed to drink on Christmas Eve.

"I'll have a hammer too, Daddy, thanks."

A "hammer" is a potent drink my mother always concocts gallons of for Christmas Eve. It's a sort of heavy-duty piña colada, made with all the white liquors, pineapple juice, and coconut cream. Usually the younger crowd, who hadn't yet developed a sophisticated taste for liquor, favored this mix. My father serves us our hammers in large plastic cups, and Ricky and I wander to the back of the living room to look at the tree.

My favorite ornaments on the tree are the plastic clear ones that look like round houses but have small blades inside. When you place them over the lights the heat from the light rises and makes the blades turn, causing the tree to seem alive, casting small, quick shadows about so that it looks as if large insects, or small birds or fairies, are darting about, although all you can see is the movement of their shadows before they disappear.

You can hardly see any of the ornaments on the tree this year, though, because of the icicles, which cover it from top to bottom. Mother always says it's the icicles that make the tree. She would caution, when we helped decorate, that we should add one icicle at a time, and not throw them on in clumps. She would show us, yet again, how to carefully drape them. Eventually, we would tire of this careful draping, though, especially my brothers, who would wind up throwing them on in clumps with great glee. She'd redo our handiwork after we went to bed. Mother saved icicles from year to year, painstakingly removing each one from the tree and laying it flat in the icicle box—hundreds and hundreds of them. Often they were crinkled and creased from several years of use. Long after this Christmas the memory of those recycled icicles would be a painful reminder of how poor we were. When I become an adult I will never be able to bring myself to buy tinsel, though it costs less than a dollar a box.

"I'm hungry." Ricky nudges me, and we turn from the tree and walk toward the kitchen where people are sitting around the kitchen table, and where the serious food is located. My mother always makes the same dishes for Christmas, and this is comforting in the same way the familiar narratives of the season are. Ricky grabs a couple of crustless ham sandwiches from a platter on a small table near the door and wolfs them down. I helped my mother make the meatballs that are now simmering in a spicy tomato sauce on an electric skillet. I walk over to the meatballs and jab one with a toothpick. It always took a long time to get the meatballs just the way my mother wanted them. She had the magical ability to roll them just right, all the same size. Mine were always coming out too big or too small, or somehow lopsided, and I'd have to start over. The meatballs are slightly sweet with barbecue sauce, and spicy with Tabasco sauce. The sweet and the hot are a lovely combination in my mouth, a combination that always reminds me of my family at this time of year.

My mother is standing up against the counter holding a glass of wine, and Maw-Maw is sitting at the kitchen table, drinking a glass of beer. A beautiful dark-haired woman with high cheekbones and olive complexion, she does not look like a typical grandmother. Raising four children with a difficult husband during the depression has not visibly taken its toll on her, at least not in her physical countenance.

"Hello, dawlin'," she says. "How ya doin'?" and gives me a beery kiss. Maw-Maw has lived deep in the heart of New Orleans all her life and has a thick New Orleans accent, as does most everyone in my family, although Maw-Maw's and Paw-Paw's accents are the heaviest. To an untrained ear this accent, primarily associated with downtown New Orleans, sounds a bit like a New York City or Hoboken, New Jersey, accent, except that northerners don't, of course, use the expression *y'all*, which always gives a New Orleanian away, and which we sometimes use not only as a pronoun but as an adjective: "Y'all got y'all books?"

I would come to love this accent in my middle age, and would come to think of its slow sloppiness that connects every syllable to every other syllable as like the water that dominates the landscape, slow and sloppy and muddy and lovely. But it embarrassed me as a young adult, and I eventually tried to lose it. I thought I *had* lost it after I moved to Texas in my twenties. But even after twelve years in another state I'd still fall back into it as though falling into the gutter whenever I visited home, or even on the phone, whenever my mother called, forgetting I was a college graduate, forgetting I was an English major, saying things like *Wheah ya at sweethawt?* or *Dat doan mean nuttn, ya awta seen da way she pawks dat caw*, the sounds I was fed like milk as a child, the *aw* sound predominating as if it was just too much work to pronounce the *r*. I tried hard to get rid of it, to make my voice sound as if I had nothing to do with the black smell of the lake, nothing to do with my mother's cooking, nothing to do with my father's breath, my brother's track marks.

That Christmas Eve, though, I have never been outside of Louisiana, and I can't really hear the accent; it is just the way we all talk, and as linguistically comfortable as an old nightshirt. My mother is the only one in the family at this point who can choose to speak without a pronounced accent if she wants to, though my father would always say she was "putting on airs" when she spoke in unaccented, grammatically correct sentences. Today, when I return home, I cannot imagine speaking to any of my brothers and sisters in unaccented, grammatically correct sentences. If, because of so many years of being an English teacher and living away from Louisiana, I happen to fall into standard English when speaking to my family, the air becomes immediately and almost unbearably tense; it feels as if I have switched to an almost foreign language, a language in which it will be impossible to say anything meaningful.

Trying to Sing

Jules and Marie are playing on the floor with toys they'd received earlier in the evening from some relative or another. Mr. Harry, and his wife, Lucille, are also in the kitchen. Mr. Harry gives us lessons for free in exchange for my mother letting him play the piano whenever he wants. She always gives him an extra-special gift for Christmas to repay him for the lessons.

I say hello to everyone, then attack the artichoke balls, which are my favorite, and which I also helped make the day before. We'd mashed up artichoke hearts in a big bowl, added lemon juice, olive oil and lots of garlic, Italian bread crumbs and Parmesan cheese, then rolled the mixture into small balls. The balls are soft and squishy in your mouth, and when you bite into them you're likely to bite into bits of garlic. The artichoke balls contributed significantly to the family's collective garlic breath that would infect the church that night when we sang at midnight mass, and that would not begin to dissipate until the day after Christmas.

Maw-Maw pops an artichoke ball into her mouth too, and between chews notes how fine Ricky's uniform is and how beautiful my engagement ring is.

"Where's Paw-Paw?" I ask.

Maw-Maw swallows, sips her beer, and looks at my mother. My mother, in turn, looks at her hands. "He's in the back bedroom." She means my parents' bedroom.

"Oh, is he okay?"

"Well, he's tired, and can't really get up, but I'll tell him you're here, and y'all can go back and say hello." My mother steps carefully over my sister and brother and the trucks and dolls on the kitchen floor and makes her way down the hall to her bedroom.

Mr. Harry has started a conversation with Ricky. He is speaking much louder than he usually does, which means he too has had a lot to drink. I sip the sweet hammer drink, which reminds me we made some sweet things yesterday too. I search the counters for the stuffed dates. We used pitted dates and stuffed them with marshmallows and topped them with half a pecan, then we rolled the whole thing in granulated sugar.

I pop one into my mouth, the rich date flavor and pecan and sugar filling my mouth all sticky and even more complicated than the Crackerjacks. Robert Goulet sings, *Fall on your knees, oh hear the angel voices,* and Mother enters the kitchen again, the scent of her perfume, Chanel Number 5, enveloping me, so sweet I wish I could taste it. Chanel Number 5 cookies. Someone should invent them—I would eat them. My mother looks pretty, her blond hair curled and pulled back off her face with an ornate barrette, but her face is flushed.

"He knows you're here. You can go see him. Don't stay too long, though." She bends to pick up Marie, who has started crying. I look at Ricky. "Ready?" I say.

"Ready."

I fluff my hair, grab Ricky's hand, and lead him into the hall, underneath the entrance to the attic, and past my own bedroom to my parents' bedroom. Only the lamp on the night table is lit. The room is filled with the detritus that has been removed from the rest of the house to make more space for the party. The gifts from Santa are also stuffed into this room, in the closet and underneath the bed. Christmas boxes and ribbon and paper are piled on the floor, as this is also the room where gifts got wrapped. This is the room, in fact, where many important things happened. It is the room where my youngest brother and sister were conceived, but it is also the room where my mother sat Aimeé and me on her bed and explained about menstruation. It is the room where, many years ago, my mother sat me down on the bed and explained that no, Sheryl, there actually isn't really a Santa Claus, not a man, anyway, but a spirit, a spirit you could still believe in. It is also the room to which my parents retreated when they talked about the possibility of divorcing. It is the room where my mother would lie in bed for hours at a time and read books into the small hours of the morning, my father not home yet. And now it is the room where I will speak to my grandfather for the last time.

A pathway leads from the entrance between my mother's bureau, cluttered with jewelry and makeup, to the bed where Paw-Paw lies, breathing heavily. Three months I had known about the cancer, but nothing could have prepared me for this, for the way the body looks when it has given up, skin crying out in retreat, eyes flagged in surrender, belly gone flat and valleyed. I fall silent for a moment.

The music from the front room pauses, as if on cue, as another LP drops down. Ricky shifts nervously next to me, then Bing Crosby's voice singing "White Christmas" begins to fill the house. Paw-Paw likes this song, and would always talk about how one Christmas, mark his words, it would snow.

I have never been around any kind of dying before. I've only read about it in books. But it's not his conspicuous dying that causes me to recoil; it's not knowing how to kiss the face shaved so clean, and it's the strangeness of his sober lips, robbed of the yeasty breath I recognize as his. Boyfriend planted like a hedge at my side, I finally open my mouth, chatter about our engagement, and hold my hand out to show him the ring. His eyes are bright-blue pools of agony. Sunken into the bed, he looks at the ring, then at Ricky. He gathers himself up, voice sudden, and speaks, looking right at Ricky: *You take good care of her, son.* Ricky doesn't respond, but smiles weakly and squeezes my hand. Then, becoming something like the man I thought I knew, so that it seems as if belly rolls over belt again, whiskers grow again, Paw-Paw pulls himself up and charges: *Promise me, boy.* He falls back onto the bed.

Ricky gulps out the promise like a belch.

These days when I think of my grandfather I like to think of him extracting that promise, becoming himself one last time. I hold on to the idea of it like some treasure or inheritance. Ricky and I left that dark room and went into another, drinking our way from room to room until it was sufficiently late and we were sufficiently drunk enough to attend midnight mass with my mother and father, brothers and sisters. This was the only time of the year my father went to church, and the only time we all stood together and sang hymns to celebrate Christ's birth.

Afterward, Ricky kisses me in the car, and holds me for a time, staring at the lights on the house, and at the lighted Santa and choirboys in front of it.

"What happened to the head of that one choirboy?" he asks, twisting the ring on my finger.

"Someone must have stolen it," I say. I press his hand and close my eyes.

When I walk into the house a half hour later there's no music on the hi-fi, but I can hear someone playing "Silver Bells" softly, on the piano. I tiptoe into the living room. François, who clearly thinks he is alone, is sitting at the piano, pecking the notes out, staring at the keys as if they hold some secret to his life. My mother is standing in the darkened hallway, listening, though I'm sure he doesn't know she is there. When the lights from the tree flash on I can see that her lips are pressed together. Tears, reflected in the light like tiny glass ornaments, fill her eyes.

We are sometimes given moments—I do not know if we are blessed or cursed with these moments—where we can see the future with stark clarity. I do not mean epiphanies, for those are often the result of much thinking and unconscious work. I mean something more like a gift. You are given the gift of sight for a moment. I think my mother, early this Christmas morning, was experiencing such a gift. She could see something of her son's future from that hallway, something clear, something irrevocable, something I could not see. I tiptoe past them both and go to bed, falling asleep almost immediately.

The snow continues to fall outside in large wet, fluffy flakes, the kind we used to draw as kids, the kind that feel like cold, sloppy kisses when they land on your cheek. I am forty-six now, and have lived in the Midwest for seven years. During that time, for several Christmases, I have gotten what I so wanted as a child: snow. My sister Aimeé also has snow. She lives in Nebraska now, where they see even more snowfall than we do in Iowa. We both miss Louisiana, but we've both made lives away from it, both in places with killing freezes and winter-storm warnings, and it seems unlikely either of us will return to Louisiana to live, though we both visit frequently. My youngest brother and sister, who are both now married with children of their own, still live in Louisiana, and often speak wistfully, when I call, of hoping for snow. This year my mother dubbed off a tape of the Basil Rathbone *A*

Christmas Carol for me. The record had become scratched and warped with so many years of playing, and the tape had recorded all the hisses and pops of the old album. I put it on the cassette player and watch the snow outside my window as I listen. I think I can hear the small seasonal joy of our family through the pops and hisses, can almost see the ghosts of all those who are no longer here. It's not Marley I hear when the chains sound, but my brother, my father, my grandfather. And when the carols come in at the end of the tape, after Scrooge's transformation, it's all of us together again, singing at midnight mass, all of us alive, our imperfect, passionate, drunk voices ringing in the snowless night.

Controlling François

One who knows the Mississippi will promptly aver—not
aloud but to himself—that ten thousand River Commissions,
with the mines of the world at their back, cannot tame that
lawless stream, cannot curb or confine it, cannot say to it, "Go
here" or "Go there" and make it obey; cannot save a shore
which it has sentenced, cannot bar its path with an obstruc-
tion which it will not tear down.
—Mark Twain, *Life on the Mississippi*

"That boy is like a cancer in your head," my father said to my
mother, pushing himself up from the kitchen table.

He was talking about my brother François, on the verge of being
expelled from St. Jerome Catholic School where he was in eighth grade.
François had been exiled to his bedroom, punished for his latest misbehavior: fighting on the school grounds. My mother had served him a
bowl of gumbo in his room before she called everyone else to the table.

I was relieved he wasn't sitting with us. At seventeen I was sensitive about my looks, and not a dinner would go by without François calling me "pimple face" or "fatty." His favorite taunt for our younger brother, Jules, was "mountain nose," which usually brought on much yelling, sometimes tears, and a mutual pummeling.

My father sat down again, reached for the filé, and sprinkled some into his gumbo.

"We have to do something; it can't go on like this." Mother wiped at her eyes with the corner of a dishtowel. "I can't not think about him. I can't leave him alone because he gets into too much trouble. And now the nuns are giving him four demerits for every infraction, instead of just one. They want him expelled. It's not very . . . ," she pressed her lips together, "charitable."

"Let them expel him then." My father spoke with a mouth full of French bread that he'd sopped in his gumbo. "He can go to public school. Roosevelt isn't a bad school. Not everyone has to go to Catholic school."

My mother glared at him.

"He needs to go to a psycho ward," my sister Aimeé said. "He's crazy."

Aimeé had had a run-in with François that weekend. They had been arguing about something in the backyard, and a number of the boys from the neighborhood had gathered to watch the fight. At one point François grabbed at Aimeé and ripped open the army shirt she was wearing, exposing her just-developing breasts to the boys. She was so angry at him—she told me years later it was an embarrassment of such magnitude she would never forget it—that she charged at him, chasing him into the house and the kitchen. She grabbed a knife and had him over the sink, threatening to kill him, when my mother walked in and stopped her.

"He's not crazy," my mother said. She pinched off a sprig of mint from the bowl in the center of the table and dropped it into her iced-tea glass. "Just troubled. He should have been an only child." She glared at my father again. "Couldn't you have gone to more of his games?" At this point we all looked at my father, who looked, in return, deep into his gumbo.

Mother was referring to the football games of the Green Lawn Terrace football team, the neighborhood team. François had played on the defensive line for them the past two years. It had been a troubled participation, though. He was always getting into fights and causing the team to accumulate penalties that sometimes cost them their games. During the last game we had had to listen to the Maloneys, the neighbors my mother called white trash, yelling, "Take St. Germain out of there!" as François racked up penalties for the team. The coach kept him in the game, though, because he was such a good player that he sometimes made up for the penalties. My father almost never went to these games, but my mother attended them all, and sometimes I went, though mostly to check out the older boys in the stands. I rarely paid much attention to the game except when I heard my brother's name mentioned.

He would eventually make it to the "All Stars" team for Kenner in later years, his fiercely muscled, stout, and angry body proving a tough match for all competitors. But his football days were numbered. Just a few weeks earlier his coach, a former semipro who pushed the boys, especially François, hard, had exploded. He had been dealing with François's lip for two years by giving him extra pushups and laps to run. It was the end of a game they had lost, and we were waiting on the sidelines for François, who was refusing to do laps. This time the coach had had enough.

"You wanna hit me?"

François looked at the trees behind the coach and did not reply.

"Hey, you, I said you wanna hit me?"

François folded his arms and continued to stare at the trees.

"Come on, you wanna hit me, you know it, so go ahead, hit me. Think you can hit me, big man? Well go ahead. Just try. Hit me. Hit me."

I can only guess what was going through François's head at the time. Maybe he was thinking about all those extra pushups and laps. Maybe he was thinking of all the times my father had come home from work, his first words "Go to your room." This usually meant my mother had called him at work to tell him of some trouble François had gotten into that day. Often it would be fighting, sometimes stealing, and when he got

Controlling François

59

older, drugs. My father would follow him into his room, pulling off the belt from his National Guard uniform. Then would come sounds of shouting and the thwap of the belt hitting bare flesh, and, before François got older, crying. Sometimes these beatings took place in the entrance hall to the house. François would refuse to go to his room, and my father would grab him right there in the hall. My father would not stop until François cried. When he refused to cry, my father resorted to taking François's head between his hands and hitting it on the door to the hallway. Next would come a horrible knocking punctuated by my father shouting, "You're no good, no goddamn good." Sometimes what with the sound being muffled because I had my bedroom door closed, it sounded like he was saying, *not God, not goddamn God.* The knocking would continue, François's head like an egg that wouldn't crack. I prayed for him to cry.

Sometimes, instead of crying, François would have an asthma attack in the midst of these beatings, which usually meant my mother would intervene and my father would stop. When he was very young, the attacks meant a trip to the hospital where the doctor would give François a shot of adrenaline and tell my mother to try to keep him still, which was nearly impossible.

The beatings rarely accomplished what they were meant to accomplish. Sometimes François was "good" for a few days afterward, but this spell of goodness rarely lasted more than a week. Sometimes he ran away the night after a beating. Eventually, my mother stopped reporting François's misbehavior to my father altogether.

François, nevertheless, found a surrogate authority figure to confront: he punched the coach and broke his nose. That was the end of his promising football career.

Later that night, after the dinner discussion about François, I was parked with my boyfriend a block from our house. We were kissing. Without warning a face smashed up against the fogged-up window on the passenger side of Ricky's car. It seemed as if some bodiless head had been bowled across the lawn and into us, and I screamed. The face was horribly distorted. Slowly, the face unpeeled itself from the glass, and the smashed nose and cheeks, mouth, and eyes began to take on a recognizable shape. It was François. He laughed and said he was going to tell on me.

In several of the photographs I have of François as an older boy he's making some kind of face, pulling his mouth apart, sticking his tongue out, putting his fingers in his nose, or turning his head upside down and peeking between his legs. If the photo was supposed to be of someone else, he'd often insert himself into it. In one photo of Ricky and me dressed for Sunday mass, arms around each other, smiling seriously into the camera, François is caught in a midair jump behind us, his mouth open in a mock scream. More than the proverbial thorn in one's side, he was a tireless clown whose antics, usually some sort of distortion of our daily activities, made us feel the absurdity of our own actions. He paid particular attention to me, and though I felt tortured by him as a young girl—it seemed I could never escape his gaze—when I grew older I came to understand his attention as a kind of misplaced affection, maybe even a kind of attraction.

After transferring to Roosevelt High in ninth grade François got in with a bad crowd, most notably one Kenny Pequet, whom my mother blames for almost everything that happened to him later in his life. Kenny is currently serving time in the Louisiana State Penitentiary in Angola for numerous offenses, among them stealing a gallon of morphine from a pharmacy. A newspaper article in the *New Orleans Times-Picayune* about his most recent arrest showed him, thin and wild-haired, biting the arm of the arresting police officer. The article quoted Kenny as yelling, "I have AIDS and now you're going to have it!" before attacking the officer, with whom he fought viciously. It took three patrolmen to subdue him.

Kenny and François got in a lot of trouble together during their teenage years, but Kenny's father was a Jefferson Parish cop and managed to keep his son out of prison, at least when he was young. One of François's teachers from Roosevelt warned my mother about Kenny during a conference: "Kenny Pequet is a stick of dynamite ready to explode," he told her. "Keep your son away from him."

Controlling François

By that time, though, nothing Mother did had any effect on François. At one point she wrote him a letter saying that she thought he had chosen the wrong path, that she would love and take care of him if only he would give up Kenny, if only he would please choose her over Kenny. François never responded to the letter, and later she told me she imagined he'd had a good laugh with Kenny over it.

My brother was sixteen when my mother let him drop out of school. "He only gets in fights," she said. "It's no use." At seventeen he left home. One night, several months later, when my mother was home alone, he knocked on the door, loaded out of his mind. She fed him some gumbo, her panacea for everything, and tried to get him to stay for a while. He ate the gumbo, but told her he couldn't stay. He hugged her and said, "I love you." Before she could reply, he continued, "But I don't know you."

Kenny and François were arrested not long after François turned eighteen for possession of drugs and for breaking and entering. Kenny got off; François spent a year in Angola.

Angola is the largest correctional facility in the South. It comprises eighteen thousand acres and is home to some of the more violent criminals in the state. The vast majority of those serving time will never leave. In the 1970s prison murders often exceeded forty a year, more than natural deaths. The facility is nestled in a bend of the Mississippi a few hours northwest of New Orleans. It is surrounded on three sides by the Mississippi and on one side by swamp. I visited François there once with my parents, but was so numb to the whole idea of his incarceration that I would remember nothing about the drive there or its location.

I did register shock, though, over my brother's appearance. Normally ruddy-cheeked with an olive complexion, he turned sickly pale in prison, shaved off the thick mustache he'd worn for many years, and lost so much weight I hardly recognized him. He was clearly miserable, chagrined, and scared, but he managed to joke when we visited about there being no gumbo or good food "like Mother's" as the reason for his weight loss.

He wrote letters detailing the threats he received from other inmates and how afraid he was for his life—articulate letters of his fears and regrets. I was moved by how well he could write, surprised, too, given how poorly he had done in school. His sentences, though, were strong and muscular, his paragraphs clear and uncluttered.

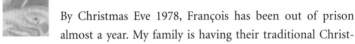 By Christmas Eve 1978, François has been out of prison almost a year. My family is having their traditional Christmas Eve party. It is late, and everyone is feeling pretty happy. François has recently arrived with some friends, neighborhood thugs. He has on a black silk shirt with the top two buttons undone, showing off his muscled chest. A slim gold chain hangs around his neck. Black pants just tight enough to show off his ass. Everything nicely ironed. His dark hair combed into a side part, hiding the cowlick he was plagued with as a boy. His dark eyes sparkle. He has a mustache, which he's grown back since prison, and which he strokes when he's feeling pensive. He's filled out and his color is good. He is the kind of man who knows he is handsome and is proud of it.

My brother and I look alike except that I am not as good looking a woman as he is a man. When I look at him I see a darker, angrier version of myself. It's not just that we're both dark and have eyes and mouths that are similar, not even that we have twin scars under our left eyes from childhood accidents. There's something about our spirits that rhymes, and it's that inner rhyming that shows through on the surface, the way it does with long-married couples. This is odd, because on some level we are deeply opposite. I went to college and he went to prison. But things could have easily been reversed, and I will never know what force moved me in one direction and him in another.

He hands me a large card and a huge stuffed lion wrapped with a large yellow bow. I am a Leo, and the lion is meant to symbolize my zodiac sign.

"Merry Christmas, sis," he says. He likes to give elaborate gifts, even when he can't afford them, and I know this lion, about four feet long and three feet wide, is expensive for him. The card is elaborate, embossed, the kind with inner and outer sleeves and a sentimental message. He's

Controlling François

scribbled on the left-hand side, "Thanks for being there when I needed you. Love, your brother, François." I give him a hug.

"Play the guitar, Sherry, can you? Play that song, you know the one, that needle song?" He sniffs and looks around at his friends. He is proud that I know how to play the guitar, and I'm just tipsy enough to not care who is around. I've learned a few Joni Mitchell songs and one Neil Young song, the one François wants to hear, "The Needle and the Damage Done." I place my fingers in the D-chord position and begin the plucking that starts the song. I'm not very good at singing or playing, but we're all drinking and there's noise from the living room, Christmas songs, our Maw-Maw playing the piano, warm sounds of people laughing and talking, enough to offset the wavering and unsure quality of my voice. François sings along. It is a song about loving a friend who loves the needle, a song that suggests that love of the needle is somewhere in all of us. I know why he likes this song, and I know why I went to the trouble to learn it. It is a secret we share.

 I experienced my teenage years and young adulthood in Louisiana as a time of intense wanting. It was the early seventies, and I wanted to feel everything, deep in the marrow of my bones. The culture of the sixties and early seventies was part of this, some of it was surely typical of my age, but the curious intensity of that desire to feel is still a mystery to me. If you had asked me then I might not have been able to articulate it, but I know I wanted some joyful, unrestrained, untamed thing, something to stomp on coffins, flip a finger at Death, howl in the wind, frighten children—and me—with its wild heart. I imagine it now as the urgency and longing the Mississippi might feel, if bodies of water were sentient, making its way to the Gulf of Mexico. Throughout those early years my body ached with that want, felt swollen with it. When I looked at the river, it seemed to know something about what I desired. The Mississippi ran without stopping, not quickly but powerfully, as if drawn by its own nature to some inevitable end. Drugs were the synthetic means I found to satisfy that end.

It's the summer of 1978, and I'm a senior English major at Southeastern Louisiana University in Hammond. I'm taking an independent study course in poetry writing, which will become my genre of choice for many years. I'm working as a bartender at a college bar at night to supplement the grants and loans I've taken out to pay my tuition. And I have been shooting up cocaine for the past couple of months with a man I met at the beginning of the summer at the bar where I work. Frank slithered into Gef's one night, a tall, thin weed of a man with dark hair and mustache. He was not a handsome man, but he was persistent. He played guitar and liked music. As he drank and we talked I found him knowledgeable about Latin, jazz, and New Orleans music—he claimed to have played percussion with the Neville Brothers. He also liked Joni Mitchell and offered to teach me one of the tunings for a song of hers.

Within the first week of our sleeping together he had turned me on to coke. I had snorted coke before—so had lots of my friends at Southeastern. Hammond is situated on swampy land between Baton Rouge and New Orleans, and drug traffic between those two cities tends to mire there. There were drugs aplenty to be had for the asking. Not long after meeting Frank I learned that not only did he buy lots of coke, but he also sold it; that was, in fact, how he made his living.

I can still recall the orgasmic pleasure cocaine gave me. It was the engulfing I had always desired, the flooding of the untamed into my blood. With a lover it was also a deeply sexual experience, for shooting up is infused with sexuality, both literal and figurative: you hold your arm out, trusting and bare, the vein pushed up blue, throbbing and wanting to be pierced, hand in a fist, then your partner enters the vein with the needle, easily, slowly, then he pulls back until you see blood, then he holds the needle still, and slowly shoots the sweetness into you. Then you let your fist out and you're coming in your fingers, your hands, your earlobes, heart, thighs, tongue, eyes, and brain are coming, thick and brilliant as the last thin match against some piercing cold.

The only person I could really talk to about my new experience was François. I knew he would understand, and I knew he wouldn't judge me. When he learned that I was dating a man who sold cocaine he became excited.

"Can you get some for me? And for a friend?" he asked.

I considered. Clearly, this wasn't a good idea. But I was lost in my own search for pleasure, and more interested in forming a friendship with my brother than guiding him toward a better life. Sometimes, now, I believe I wanted more than a friendship with him, and he with me. If we would never act on the attraction we had for one another, which I understood then as a kind of excitement and tension I felt whenever he was near, there might be a more sanctioned though potentially more destructive bonding that could take its place: we would share drugs, needles.

I am trying to tell the truth of what happened between us, but providing my brother with drugs—although it was only once—is something I can barely stand to admit to, even now. My mother, whom I eventually told about this incident, would say to me, "You were someone he looked up to, Sheryl. When you did it with him it was like you were affirming it, authorizing it."

At the time I lived in a large, falling-down house near the university with four other students. On the day of the drug buy François drove to my place in Hammond to get the coke. Frank met us there. We were on the verge of breaking up, so there was tension between us. He was bored with me, and I knew he was looking around for someone else.

François arrived with his "friend," a pasty-faced, thin woman who looked to be in her early twenties. She called my brother baby. When she rolled up her sleeves she had so many track marks my brother couldn't find a place to enter her with the needle. She lay down on my bed and told him to try the veins by her ankle. He found one there that worked and entered her with a jerk. Frank shot me up, too, but instead of joy I felt pain. Pain to see this ruined woman, pain to watch my brother stick the needle into his own veins and hear the quick intake of his breath that signaled his own small, pitiful joy, pain to be involved with Frank who only wanted to make a sale.

That was the last time I ever shot up. It ended as abruptly as it had begun. I remember examining my left arm the next morning, dots of bruises like purple stars nested in the crook of it. I fingered the bruises and knew I had it in me to follow my desires until I had no veins left to assault. There would be no middle ground for me. I would continue like this until I died, or I would stop, and live. I chose the latter.

In 1979 I moved to Dallas to attend graduate school. François had been out of prison two years, was holding down a job at an auto parts store, and was engaged to be married. He seemed chastened by his prison experience, although he wouldn't talk about it, and we had hope for his future. In the back of my mind I kept thinking, though, of my father's beatings, and how they reformed him, when they did, only for a short period of time. Prison represented both a physical and an emotional beating, and I wondered how long its effects might last.

In the summer of 1981 François married Laureen, his high school sweetheart, and I flew down for the wedding. I had never seen him so happy. Laureen, just eighteen, had lived three doors down from us and had always loved my brother, even though she'd seen the worst of him. Throughout his betrayals with other women (including her cousin), drugs, and even through the year he was in jail she loved and waited for him. She loved him with a love most of us rarely experience. I hoped that marriage with her might solidify the new path he seemed to be on.

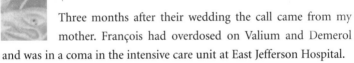 Three months after their wedding the call came from my mother. François had overdosed on Valium and Demerol and was in a coma in the intensive care unit at East Jefferson Hospital.

It was October, which I came to associate with dying when, a few years later in that month, my father would also die. In an ironic twist they would both succumb, ultimately, to liver failure, unable, finally, to filter the impurities in their blood. Years later, in yet another twist, I would discover that my own liver was damaged by hepatitis C, which I may have contracted during that summer of drug use. I will carry for the rest of my life that damaged liver and the knowledge it represents: a strange intimacy with my brother and father and the inherited inability of our bodies to purify the poisons we put into them.

My mother had sounded confused on the phone, not sure of the details, presenting them to me almost as if they were questions. They had found liquid Valium and Demerol in his apartment, she'd said, that he was apparently planning to sell, but that he'd also been taking, possibly shooting up. The doctors said the effect of Valium is cumulative, that he had probably been taking it for quite a while, and that his liver just hadn't been able to process it.

He and Laureen had been getting ready to go out to dinner with Laureen's parents. Laureen had gone into the bathroom to take a shower. When she emerged she found him slumped on their bed, not breathing, brown liquid frothing out of his mouth. She called 911, and tried to give him mouth-to-mouth resuscitation. Then she called my mother.

When my mother arrived at their apartment François was being loaded into the ambulance. "His stomach was bare," she said. "They'd ripped off his shirt trying to get his heart going."

Because he was young—twenty-three—and because patients often come out of Valium-induced comas, the paramedics resuscitated him, even though he'd been without oxygen long enough to suggest that had he lived, he would have been little more than a vegetable.

"They say he has a strong heart," my mother had said.

When the call was over, I knew I had to move fast. I started going through the perfunctory motions that seem programed into all of us, those ready responses to sudden tragedy that get us on our feet, moving however unconsciously: I told my professors I'd be gone for I didn't know how long, borrowed some money from my major professor for the flight home, and boarded a plane to New Orleans that afternoon.

When I settle into the seat of that plane, awareness of what has happened returns. The waste of my brother's life stretches before me like scenes from a Civil War film—the unending fields of dead young men, bloody and dismembered from fighting. I try to remember the last time I'd spoken to him. It had been a few weeks earlier. He had called to find out how to make a banana banshee, a drink Laureen liked. He seemed to be doing okay, at least for him. He'd gotten in a couple of accidents and had had his driver's license taken away, but he was getting rides to work, no problem. He liked being married, he said. He sounded straight.

But my brother has never been one to speak openly of whatever demons lived inside of him, choosing instead to keep everything inside. Ever the tight-lipped boy with the red eyes who, after a certain age, would not cry, no matter how much my father hit him.

I close my eyes. His eyes. Large, almond-shaped, deep, swamp-brown. They are like my eyes, my father's eyes.

Think of something good, I tell myself.

He is five and I am nine. We are lying on the neutral ground in front of our house. I am watching him. I am showing him the fairy flowers that are so delicate and have gold-tipped ends like little globules of gold semen. We tie together the stems of clover flowers to make necklaces. We look for four-leaf clovers. He laughs when I tickle his stomach.

I sink back in the seat. The night before the overdose he had called my mother. And he'd called Aimeé. He'd told them he was calling everyone in the family to say he loved them, that he was sorry he had messed up so much. Maybe he had tried to call me, but I hadn't been in most of the night. Mother said his voice had been slurred. He had just lost his job a few days earlier. Laureen's birthday was the next week. He knew her father was going to get her something big, he told my mother, and he didn't think he would be able to compete with the father's present. Laureen's father was a large presence in her life, and their family a tight-knit, supportive group.

"I told him he didn't have to compete with her father. I told him—I tried to console him," my mother had said. "He . . . he," she stammered, "he said *I love you* as we were hanging up, but I was already hanging up the phone when he said it and I just kept hanging it up. I didn't say it back," she said, her voice thick with grief.

Aimeé was also flying down from Nebraska where she now lived on a farm with her husband and four children. I had called her after talking to my mother. She and François had not been close, but he had lived with her for a few months, right after he got out of prison. They had parted badly because she found out he was stealing her children's pare-goric, which she said he was shooting up.

Controlling François

My mind drifts, the hum of the airplane engine providing a thick sound cushion for my thoughts. The plane begins its descent into New Orleans International Airport. We are flying over Lake Pontchartrain. I look out of the window at the gray water and wait for the land to appear.

Jules, who is seventeen and has had his driver's license for about a year, picks me up at the airport. Unlike François, Jules managed to graduate from high school and currently has a job working at Louisiana Purchase, a popular restaurant that serves New Orleans food. Jules has always been a quiet one, and I can hardly get him to say more than one or two sentences the whole way to the hospital.

"He's in intensive care," he says. A useless piece of information, I already know this. "You can only see him once an hour for ten minutes at a time," he continues.

"I'm his fucking sister," I say, "and I'll fucking see him when I fucking please." Jules looks at me, worried. He's never heard me talk like this. I'm sure he'd like for me to play my right role in the family. I'm supposed to be the responsible one, the one who went to college. He looks away and studies the road. When we reach East Jefferson, he mutters, "This is fucked, really fucked."

The hospital waiting room smells of my mother's perfume, Chanel Number 5. My mother, whom I expect to look bedraggled and hopeless, looks strangely serene and beautiful. I had forgotten she'd lost a lot of weight in the past few months, more than fifty pounds. She looks years younger, is dressed in a white skirt and red blouse, her blond hair pulled up off her shoulders, in curls, red lipstick. I do not like this. I want her to play her right role as well: unhappy mother. My father is at work. Aimeé is there, and Laureen, with her family. Laureen's face looks like a swollen water balloon.

A few minutes after I arrive I'm allowed to enter the room where François lies, hooked up to more machines than I knew could possibly be hooked up to a person, looking, for all that medical paraphernalia, dead. He is naked, his lower body covered with a thin sheet, a towel next to his head. His skin is yellow, as are his eyes when I pull back his eyelids. A sickly, baby-vomit yellow. There are tubes going into every orifice in his body. He cannot breathe or piss or shit on his own. He has some tape on his foot that tells what the temperature of his body is. His body reveals nothing of the vital, angry, vain young man who was my brother. He would not have liked this; he always liked to look nice, to wear good clothes, expensive clothes, clothes that fit well.

I touch his forehead, his hair, his strong arms, his legs. He is cold. It is an odd, icy cold; I do not think I have ever felt this kind of cold on a skin before. Cold or no, yellow skin or no, his body is still beautiful, even in his not-being-there-ness. He has the body of a superhero, which is what he wanted to be when he was little. I remember that he used to like Batman. My mother had made him a cape out of a towel and a safety pin when he was little, and he used to run through the house, his fat legs pumping, yelling, Na na na na Na na na na Batman! He was Batman several years in a row for Mardi Gras. But there is nothing here, no spirit, no spark in the eyes, only a husk. I whisper something in his ear, feel empty and stupid, and walk out of the room.

My mother is talking to Laureen in the waiting room.

"It all started with his kindergarten teacher," my mother is saying. She is wringing her hands, pacing back and forth. "There were too many children in that class, I can show you a photograph, there were at least thirty. I'll show you."

Laureen, eyes like burning red coals, looks up at her, not comprehending.

"She had a nervous breakdown, you know, that teacher. Because of the kids."

I sit down in the waiting room with the rest of them.

"Has Daddy been here?"

"He's been here once, stayed in a minute, came out shouting, 'I can't take this,'" Aimeé says. "He's occupying himself by making funeral arrangements. Really positive thinking, huh? Jules has only been in once, too. He can't take it either. He left while you were in there. Says he's going to see a movie tonight, *Halloween*, I think."

"Let's go have some lunch," she says. "You must be hungry."

I realize that I am hungry, but I don't feel like eating. I walk down with her to the hospital cafeteria, get a ham sandwich, and some iced tea. Aimeé gets a shrimp po'boy and a Pepsi.

We eat in silence for a while. Aimeé pushes her plate away, after having eaten only half the sandwich, and lights a cigarette.

"I was trying to think of something good," she says.

I am playing with my sandwich, pushing it around the plate.

"As in?" I say.

"As in how he sort of protected me from Timmy when he lived with us. Said if Timmy ever hurt me he'd kill him."

I nod. Timmy was her crazy second husband who used to lock her in closets because, he told the kids, "Your mom is too ugly to be seen."

"And he helped put up the kids' toys one Christmas Eve. Stayed up all night helping me do it."

I look out the window. It's hot, the sun burning stupidly, brightly. "He wrote sweet letters and cards from prison," I offer.

Now it is Aimeé's turn to stare out the window. Everything is green and lush. She finishes her cigarette. "It's so beautiful here," she says. "I miss it. Remember that red convertible he had when he was living with me? The body of the car was mint, but it didn't have a top."

I nod.

"He used to park it in the garage while he was having the top made for it, so it wouldn't get wet when it rained. But I remember one time," she stops and purses her lips, trying to stifle a laugh, "one time he took it out and there was a thunderstorm. I was sitting on the porch with the kids when he drove up, all dressed up, soaking wet, some wet woman with him too, the rain just pouring, pouring into the car, and him with those windshield wipers on. It was the funniest thing I'd ever seen, those windshield wipers going full blast and no top to the car, the rain flooding it—" she explodes into giggles.

I let out a laugh, and we both collapse into hilarity.

Aimeé wipes her eyes after a few moments. "Do you think he meant to do it?"

That night we return to my mother's house. My sister and I share the sofa bed in the living room. Aimeé and I lie together in the bed with just a lamp on looking at some of the photograph albums my mother has gotten out. Here's François as a fat baby. "Just an average one," Mother had said, "not like you, you were into everything. He was good until Jules was born."

A photo of him at two shows him dressed for Mardi Gras in a clown suit my mother had made, a big red ruffle almost hiding his face. Another Mardi Gras picture shows him dressed as a cowboy. "He loved cowboy shirts and clothes," Aimeé said. "Even when it wasn't Mardi Gras he used to like to wear them. Remember how he liked that show, what was it, the one with the tall guy and the rifle?"

"The Rifleman," I say. Mother once asked him, when he was little, what he would do if someone did to him some of the bad things he had been doing. "I'd shoot 'em," he said. "I'd just shoot 'em."

I wake in the middle of the night, throat aching, eyes burning. I can hardly breathe. Allergies. I reach for the medication in my purse at the side of the bed. My father smokes and so does Aimeé, and the whole house smells like smoke; it's everywhere like a stain. François's yellow face, his spiritless eyes, swim into my mind. It is this version of his face that I will remember and that will haunt me in dreams for years to come.

Aimeé snores softly. I get up out of bed and walk to the kitchen for some water. A roach scurries into a corner when I turn the light on. I fill a glass with water, turn out the light, and walk through the hall that leads from my mother's library to the front room where my sister is asleep. I flip on the hall light to look at the photos on the wall in the hall. There are about fifty of them. All of us are there, my mother and my father when they were much younger, high school graduation photos, school photos for the younger kids and grandkids. No graduation photo for François, but his wedding pictures are here, just a few months old. A picture of him as a kid with Santa Claus.

My parents never knew what to get François for Christmas. He didn't like typical boy things, like trucks and cars. If he wanted something, it was always some outrageous thing they couldn't afford. When he was thirteen, my mother asked him all year what he wanted for Christmas. At first he said he wanted a motorcycle, and when they nixed

Controlling François

that idea, reminding him he wasn't old enough to drive nor did they have the money for it, he said he'd have nothing.

"You have to want something," Mother would say.

"No," he would say, "nothing."

"Nothing?"

"Nothing."

That year she wrapped dollar bills up in many tiny boxes and put them under the tree.

A few years later, when he was sixteen, my father finally took out a loan and bought him the motorcycle he'd continued to ask for every Christmas. François didn't take care of the bike, though, and it was stolen a few months later.

Here's my father with his bowling ball. When François was little he wanted to be a bowler like my father, who has dozens of bowling trophies stuffed in the closet at the end of the hall, and who used to take us with him to his bowling tournaments. When he was five François had his own bowling shirt like my father's, a set of ten plastic bowling pins and a plastic bowling ball. He and my mother used to set up the pins in this hall and pretend it was a bowling lane.

This hall is also the hall where my father sometimes beat my brother. It's this door, the door to the hall closet against which my father would beat François's head. The light from the lamp reflects off the photographs making them seem like strange, colored candles. The air in the hall feels heavy, thick, a breath. This hall is the throat of the house. *Welcome to the St. Germains'.*

We go on for a few days in a ritual of sorts. We get up, have breakfast, then the women go to the hospital and the men go to work. We stay all day at the hospital, visiting the nonspeaking, still thing that is supposed to be my brother at our allotted ten-minute intervals each hour.

Every night after we get home I take a walk down to the lake. It is a little chilly, and tonight I wear a light black coat I got at the Salvation

Army. I walk with my hands clenched, indeed my whole body feels clenched. I keep my hands punched into the pockets of the coat, both of which will have fist-size holes in them when I return to Texas. I walk and mumble. I walk and curse. I cannot say *fuck* enough, though I do not say it loudly, and there is no one else on the neutral grounds to hear me.

I am even angrier tonight because the family priest came by the hospital this evening. I asked him where my brother's soul was, and he said the church didn't know where the souls of the brain-dead went. I am angry because I think that it should know. Priests should know these things, I think. I will turn away from the church after my brother dies.

The doctor said this evening that he didn't know how long François would stay like this. A week, a few days. A year. I can't stand it anymore, so I do what I always do: I leave. I go back to Dallas the next day to try to finish up the semester. I throw myself into writing a paper about Jean Genet, who also spent time in prison. I pretend I'm writing the paper for François. It is better for me to be in Dallas. The air there is dryer, the buildings new, cold, glassy, and shiny, the land dried up, stripped of any emotional content.

François dies a week after I leave. My parents decide to take him off life support, and his heart stops soon afterward.

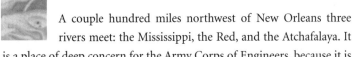 A couple hundred miles northwest of New Orleans three rivers meet: the Mississippi, the Red, and the Atchafalaya. It is a place of deep concern for the Army Corps of Engineers, because it is at this precise place that the Mississippi has wanted, for about fifty years, to give up its current route and flow wholeheartedly into the Atchafalaya. The Mississippi's "natural" desire is to roam about in search of the shortest and steepest route to the Gulf; it has jumped its banks and changed its route, sometimes violently, several times over the millennia. Some geologists think it is an act of hubris to believe—as the corps does—that we can keep the Mississippi from changing its course again.

Over the years as more and more silt has raised the bed of the current channel and built more land near its mouth, the main route has become less steep and the route to the Gulf much longer. If, at that critical bend where the Red, the Atchafalaya, and the Mississippi meet, we were to allow the Mississippi to have its way, it would reach the Gulf much quicker, as the Atchafalaya route is less than half the distance to the Gulf than the current route. But the Atchafalaya route would bypass New Orleans and Baton Rouge altogether, in effect destroying the economy of both cities to such a degree that neither one would likely be able to survive such a catastrophe. This is one reason the corps built what they call the "Old River Control Structure" where the rivers meet. A prison of sorts, only for water, not for men, the purpose of the structure is to keep the Mississippi in its current path. An auxiliary structure was built to assist the primary structure when a flood in the early seventies damaged it so severely it could not be fully repaired. Both structures, via a series of powerful gates, control the amount of water allowed to flow from the Mississippi into the Atchafalaya.

Ten years after my brother's death I am driving around Louisiana looking for the Old River Control Structure. I have read John McPhee's wonderful essay "Atchafalaya" about the history and the complex environmental issues surrounding the structure, and I want to see it, and the place where the rivers come together, for myself. I've set out without a good map, however, and gotten lost on the back roads. After about thirty minutes of driving around futilely, I come across a small building that looks like the entrance to some larger public building. I feel that I'm very close to my destination, and can even see the Mississippi off to my left. I drive up to the building. A guard appears.

He informs me that the building ahead of me is not what I'm looking for, but rather the Louisiana State Penitentiary: Angola. The Old River Control Structure, he says, is just across the river, only a few minutes. He gives me directions and bids me good luck.

So it is that a search for a structure built to control water leads me to one built to contain men, one that once contained my brother. I find it ironic that the two, the largest prison in the South and the largest engineering structure built to control water in the South, are located so close to each other.

The Old River Control Structure is just a few miles upstream from the prison. When I finally make it there my mind is on my brother. I stare into the waters of the Mississippi, then the waters of the Atchafalaya, then the Old River Control Structure built to keep them separate and can think of nothing but François. The control exercised by my father, the school, the prison, and even my mother's love had not been enough to keep him from the path he finally took, and I wonder if it will be the same for the Mississippi.

Perhaps, I think, looking into the calm, flat waters, we are not unlike the Atchafalaya and the Mississippi, my brother and I, born of the same waters, possessing the same desires, making our way to the same end through different routes, mine longer, more meandering and slow, my brother's much more quick and direct.

I leave about an hour later, disappointed that the waters are so placid, almost beaten, or so it seems to me. This is not the churning wound I had thought it would be, and I'm not interested enough in engineering to stay and admire the structure. I drive home to Lafayette, and after arriving I go up to the attic and pull out the stuffed lion François gave me so many years ago. I bring it into my bedroom and set it on my bed. This lion, its fur matted and dusty, and a Christmas card are all I have left of François.

I don't know what to make of my brother's life, I say to the lion.

Its brown plastic eyes, scratched and unforgiving, stare ahead.

I turn out the light and lie down in the dark next to the lion. In the end, I know so little about him. *I don't even know if he meant to take his life or not.* But the lion is not listening. It's just a stuffed animal, an old one at that. It smells like the attic, like dust, like the past.

Sweets and Shiny Things

When I think of my father I think of carnival season, a season
of eating and drinking, dancing and masking, a season he
embraced as intensely and fully as a lost child might embrace a mother.
Carnival was the time of year my father was most at ease; it was as if the
season rhymed with a way of being he found most natural. In a season
when everyone eats and drinks too much, his own eating and drinking
habits didn't seem out of place. It was a time of pretense, joking, and celebration, so his own love for deception and parties made him seem king
of the season.

I'm fifteen, it's Mardi Gras season, and I'm in uptown New
Orleans, on St. Charles Avenue, at a night parade. I'm sitting
on a boy's shoulders for the first time, lifted high and parentless above
the swaggering crowds. I'm gripping the boy's head with my thighs, waving for beads and doubloons. The beads curl over us like coupled snakes,

doubloons ring escape on the streets, and the boy is breathing hard underneath me. Here are the Shriners and the slobbering grumbles of their motorcycles like the first grunts of sex, and the policemen on their beautiful horses with the muscled, shiny flanks, hard as those first hardnesses felt in the first groping darks, and here are the marching bands, the mouths of their tubas and trumpets shining and wet in the warm, humid night, and the dancers and baton twirlers in rhinestones and boots, their dark skin wet underneath their shiny, thick pantyhose, and here are the floats, larger than life, all lit up and moving toward you like your first and last chance.

And here come the flambeaux carriers. Their burning torches, tubes filled with chemicals, produce brilliant, sometimes colored, light. Red-eyed and sweating whiskey, they seem to me the true gods of the night. They lurch and stagger, mambo, and zigzag their way down the street, showing off the fire like words or wounds or just light, pieces of it dropping to the ground like perspiration, torch and carrier so united it seems as if the carriers themselves are sweating fire.

Their shuffling, drunken gaits remind me of my father's gait. As I am becoming a woman, he is sinking deeper into his drinking, and it is now a rare evening or night that he walks into the house on steady legs. When he's drinking, unsteady as his gait might be, there's a lilt and a rhythmic bounce to it that's absent when he's sober, as if the alcohol synchronizes him to some rhythm he can't feel when sober. It's a kind of one-step-forward, two-steps-back rhythm, accompanied by a relaxing and loosening of all the muscles of the body.

Carlos, the boy on whose shoulders I'm sitting, bends down, and I climb off. He's sweating, and needs a break. And I don't need to be on his shoulders to see the flambeaux carriers. Carlos rubs his shoulders and I offer him some cotton candy. He shakes his head no, and I stuff a cloud of the sweet stuff into my mouth.

I love cotton candy. No matter how poor we were, my father always managed to find enough money to buy us some cotton candy at parades when we were younger. Other children were eating these sweets as well, and the sugar rush was enough to account for much of the madness of

Sweets and Shiny Things

the kids the hour before the parade started. We were rushing, we were tripping, we were loaded, stoned, high on sugar.

But once the parade started, the noise of it—the sirens, the drums, the brass bands, the yelling of the crowds when the floats came by—seemed, oddly enough, to calm us down, perhaps because it rhymed with what was going on in our brains and in our blood.

The parade has stopped for a few minutes, and the flambeaux carriers are dancing around for coins, which people throw at them when they make a particularly nice move. Maybe I love those flambeaux carriers because they remind me of my father, and seem to give a pathetic nobility to what he is becoming. Or maybe not. Maybe I love them because even as young as I am I sense that the poems and stories I struggle to write in the dark of my bedroom are like this, drunken epiphanies of light, stuttering moments between the garish floats of Dream and Nightmare. I didn't know it then, but in the daily journals I was keeping, filled with family events and dreams, disappointments, desires, and badly rhymed poems, I was teaching myself how to write. I was growing away from my father, becoming more embarrassed at his public drunkenness, which was manifesting itself more and more. There were times when he arrived home so drunk he could hardly speak. Other times what he said when he did speak was so obscene I couldn't bear to listen. Sometimes he didn't come home from work at all. I wanted to distance myself from him, and at the same time I felt drawn to him. I was retreating more and more into my journals, becoming more and more reflective, something my father had never been. Maybe, then, I'm drawn to the flambeaux carriers because I sense that their job might be like the job I had cut out for myself, to carry this, the burning night of our family, to hold high, for everyone to see, our stumbling, illuminating, street-dancing selves.

It was at these night parades that I first started to understand sexual attraction as a sort of sweetness that was all the more desirable because I couldn't fully experience it. This was something I shared with my father, whose love of women and sex was something he was hardly able to conceal. I noted the easy manner he had with women, how quickly he slipped into calling them baby. And when I accompanied him, as I sometimes did, to his second job as a night manager of Paradise Bowling Lanes, I could see how he always flirted with women, and I could see that women responded to the joking, teasing man he seemed to be. Physically, he had the dark, handsome looks of Dean Martin, whom he resembled in other ways as well. He'd raise his thick eyebrows, tell a joke, take a sip of his scotch and water, which he always had while working at the bowling alley, then laugh, looking straight into the eyes of whichever woman happened to be at the counter. Women always treated him deferentially, and he ate it up as surely as he ate up other sweet things he loved: King cake, doughnuts, and spoonfuls of sweetened condensed milk.

Carlos yells, "They're moving again," and bends over so I can climb back on his shoulders. Another band passes by, and then I see the float I've been waiting for, Float Number 12, round the corner and begin to make its way up St. Charles.

"It's coming. This is the one!" I shout to Carlos. He moves closer to the front of the pressing crowd. The float has a huge laughing face on it about ten feet high and eight feet wide, with arms stretched out over the crowd as if blessing it. The float is outlined in purple, green, and gold lights.

"Get closer!" I tighten my thighs around Carlos's neck as if he's a horse. He inches his way up to the front of the crowd. People to either side of us give us dirty looks, but I don't care.

"Are we on the right side?"

"Yeah, number three on this side."

The tractor pulling the float rumbles by, and the crowd presses forward, yelling, "Throw me something, throw me something, hey, hey, me," to the masked riders on either side of the float. Lifted up by Carlos, I've got my head just at the riders' waist level. They're all dressed in green satin costumes outlined with silver sequins. Their faces are painted white, and white half-face masks hide the upper part of their faces. Bucket-shaped hats with satin cloths down the back and sides cover their

hair and disguise their profiles. They are all throwing beads and doubloons to the crowd, and they all look alike. But I know that number
three, on the left-hand side, is my father.

"Daddy, Daddy, it's Sheryl," I shout, beating my fist on the side of the
float. He doesn't hear me. He's looking to the back of the crowd, throwing a pair of beads to a pretty woman on a ladder.

"Daddy!"

"Mr. François! Hey!" Carlos shouts, pounding on the side of the
float.

He doesn't see us.

"Daddy, it's Sheryl!" Still he's throwing to the back of the crowd. The
float is passing us by. Carlos walks alongside the float, trying to keep up
with it, yelling, "Mr. François! Mr. François! It's Carlos and Sheryl!"

I'm yelling, we're pushing people out of the way, but still the masked
man I think is my father is ignoring us.

"Daddy!" I shriek, with all the energy and breath I have left in me.
The man looks down at me. I still can't tell if it's my father or not, the
disguise is so complete. He lifts a gloved hand up, as if asking us to wait.
He bends down to get something, then rises up and throws a clot of
beads at me, then another, then a huge plastic bag of beads, another,
another, I am dropping them, Carlos is catching whatever I drop. I can
hardly hold any more beads. Carlos is tiring and can't keep up with the
float. The masked man reaches down again, then throws a fistful of doubloons at me, green, gold, and silver. The float pulls away, and in the rain
of shiny doubloons the man—I'm sure now he's my father—blows me a
kiss. Some of the doubloons hit me in the face, some go down my shirt.
Carlos catches some, and I catch a few more. Arms full, we wave awk-
wardly to the disappearing float.

We arrive home later that night with piles of treasure: bags and bags
of beads, plastic toys and cups, and doubloons. That night we caught
almost as many beads as we usually catch the entire day of Mardi Gras,
and I feel rich. I love beads almost as much as I love cotton candy. I pick
up a pile of them and let them run though my hands.

As kids, we'd play with our loot throughout the year. We used the cups to drink out of, but also filled them with dirt and sand and shells. We wore the necklaces, but we also sometimes broke them apart and melted the beads into different shapes that we used to make pins, earrings, toys, or oddly shaped multicolored things that had no real purpose. The melting was what we liked best, watching the beads bubble and fume behind the window of my Easy-Bake Oven. Sometimes we cut up the strings of beads and made them into necklaces or bracelets for our dolls. We drilled holes in the doubloons and made earrings or pins out of them too. Or we put them in one of the plastic pages of the books that housed our doubloon collections. We saved the best necklaces, the strands that looked like shiny colored pearls, to wear as part of our costumes the next year.

Mardi Gras beads of various colors are everywhere during the season, and the long ones are among the most prized possessions. People wear them on their necks, make wigs out of them, make skirts out of them, and decorate their houses, both in and out, with them. Even though a parade goer may have thousands of beads at home, he or she will fight to snatch a pair of beads right out of your hands, or grab them from under your foot. Chris Rose, columnist for the *New Orleans Times-Picayune,* once wrote that he couldn't explain the bead phenomenon that overtakes New Orleans during Mardi Gras. What was all the fuss about? He didn't know, he admitted. In response to the column he received a call from a Destrehan woman: "We do this," she said, "for the same reason the Indians traded Manhattan for a bunch of beads—because we want to be surrounded by shiny things."

 Carnival season in Louisiana begins January 6, the day known to Christians as the Epiphany, and continues until Mardi Gras day, which is always determined by the church calendar. Mardi Gras (literally translated as "Fat Tuesday") is the day before Ash Wednesday, the day Lent begins, when we receive ashes in the form of a cross on our foreheads to remind us of our mortality.

I usually tried to give up sweets during Lent because I loved them so

Sweets and Shiny Things

much. It was something my father and I had in common, this love of sweets. During carnival season we stuffed ourselves, compensating for the forty bitter days of Lent that would follow. By the time I reached thirty, every one of my teeth had been capped from the havoc that sugar had wreaked on them.

Each morning after I was old enough to fix my own breakfast, I'd get up and eat with my father. He'd sit down to his newspaper and a cup of black chicory coffee. Chicory darkens coffee, making it black as the blackest earth, and imparts a strong, earthy taste to it. As if that darkness needed extra-special sweetening, he'd reach over to the porcelain sugar bowl, dip his spoon in it, and bring it to his coffee, again, again, again, and again, five times, five teaspoons of white sugar spooned into the dark fire of his coffee. I remember wondering, as a child, what could have been so bitter that needed so much sweetening.

I'd sit next to him at the kitchen table, eating a bowl of Cheerios with three spoonfuls of sugar in it, and read the back of the cereal box while he read his paper. Sometimes he would fix a cup of coffee for me, a spoon or two of the coffee, lots of sugar, water, and milk. Sugar and caffeine rushing in our blood, eyes bright, my father and I would leave together in the mornings, bouncing out of the door, he to work and me to school.

He kept a can of sweetened condensed milk in the refrigerator, and would dip his spoon into it first thing in the morning, when he came home from work, and sometimes before he went to bed at night. If I was in the kitchen he'd give me a spoonful too, thick, rich, and overflowing with the sweet viscous milk. He stopped often at the doughnut store, too. Some of my fondest memories are sitting next to him eating jelly or cream doughnuts, the powdered sugar and jelly or cream from the inside of the doughnuts decorating both of our faces like a sweet, edible mask.

When I got older I'd watch him drink whiskey, drink after drink after drink, and think of his love of sugar. The liquor must function, I thought, as a kind of liquid sugar, rushing through his blood. I wondered if the liquor, like the sugar, made the world seem, for a few moments, bright and sweet. I remembered the Hans Christian Andersen tale my mother used to read to me, the story of the little matchstick girl, how the girl would light those matches one after another against the cold New Year's Eve night, how they warmed her, helped her hallucinate food and love. I wondered if my father's drinking were like that, each drink a match lit against some omnipresent cold, the nature of which, as a child, I could hardly understand.

My father died ten years ago of complications related to advanced cirrhosis of the liver. It is not a kind of dying I would wish on anyone. Because the liver is such a powerful organ, you can live a fairly normal life with much of it destroyed. Once it reaches a certain point, though, things begin to deteriorate rapidly. My father became, in his fifties, grotesquely ugly. His skin turned a deep orange, his eyes yellowed, and his stomach swelled as if he were expecting. Almost all his teeth fell out. In manner and appearance he became so hideous I would not take Gray, my young son, to see him the year before he died. The last time we'd visited, my father's face—what was fast becoming his death mask—had scared Gray. "Gramps looks like a monster," he said to me in the car as we drove home after that visit.

We do not bear our wounds, psychologist James Hillman writes; we are our wounds. Our vision of the world is shaped by the wounds we have suffered during our tenure here. The wound and the eye, Hillman claims, are one and the same. Nothing could be more emblematic of that insight, I think, than my father.

Last year I had the bad idea to costume as my father for Mardi Gras. His dress uniform from the National Guard, which I'd inherited when he died, had been hanging in my closet for about ten years. I took it out and laid it on my bed. Its drab olive color was offset by the shiny bronze insignia at the shoulders, lapels, and pockets, and the bronze buttons running down the opening of the jacket. I pressed my fingers over the buttons. They were embossed with the U.S. seal. A black plastic name tag was pinned over the right breast pocket, on which his last name appeared in white lettering: ST GERMAIN. Over the right pocket, a plethora of ribbons—yellow, red, blue, and white. Running down the arm of the left sleeve, the gold bars and patch that indicated his rank: command sergeant major. I could see where the inner lining had been repaired, obviously several times. White stitches ran all around the lining, looking unnatural, and making me feel vaguely uneasy. I pulled my hair back to hide its length, darkened and thickened my eyebrows with eyebrow pencil, and put on the jacket. I looked at the result in the mirror, and was horrified to see my father staring back at me. I took off the jacket, put it back in my closet, and shook loose my hair.

The costume suggested too powerfully for me my connection to my father, the knowledge that my own love of drinking could lead me to join him in whatever underworld he now inhabited. But the costume was also boring. The idea, for Mardi Gras, is to dress as something you are not, although it is true that all costumes reveal something about your character. The bridge between who you are in real life and who you choose to disguise yourself as for carnival offers a rich place for reflection about what connections might actually exist between the two. If the costume is too close to who you are in real life, it's just not that interesting to think about. In my case it was also a little scary to think about.

In the early years of their marriage my parents tried to have a sort of harmony in their costuming. One year they dressed as Chinese in matching black silk pajamas; another year they wore wildly colored pajamas and black berets, and carried long cigarette holders. But as their marriage wore on and wore down they gave up trying to match. My father sometimes wore a frightening gorilla mask with the colorful pajamas. My mother did not approve of this mask, as she thought it too scary for the children. Sometimes he dressed as an escaped convict, another costume my mother didn't care for. In later years she dressed as a gypsy, no matter what he wore.

My father's favorite costume, though, was that of a pregnant woman. He would wear one of my mother's brightly colored caftans, strap on a pillow underneath it, wear one of her bras stuffed with socks, and a long blonde wig. He'd paint his face with my mother's makeup. My mother *really* did not like this costume. "If he had ever been pregnant," she would say, "he would never mock it like that." I thought it was a funny costume, though. All the kids did. I think we liked it when he irritated my mother with his getups. It seemed like a fine joke to us. I'm sure it wasn't a role my mother liked, but she always seemed to play straight man to him. Without her serious disapproval, his antics would never have seemed as humorous to us as they were.

My father was very masculine looking; he had thick dark hair on his face and arms and legs, and even his hands were dark and hairy. We used to tease him about his "gorilla" hands. Those hairy hands sticking out from under the long sleeves of my mother's caftan always cracked us up. By midafternoon he would have a dark shadow on his face, and that was funny to us, too, the stubble showing through, penetrating my mother's makeup.

Years later when I visited Alaska and studied Tlingit transformation masks, I would be struck by how they reminded me of my father's disguises. It was important, for example, that we not ever think he was *actually* a woman; his maleness had to show through. With the Tlingit masks, it's a similar thing. You might see a mask of a man turning into a frog or a raven or eagle turning into a man, but it was important that both the animal and the human be present in the mask. The mask symbolized a joining of two utterly different natures, very much like my father's costumes.

My father did not graduate from high school and never studied drama, but he was instinctively dramatic. When he needed to express emotions—a difficult project for him—he turned to drama. On one memorable occasion, the morning after he had loudly accused my mother of having an affair, he expressed his pain by creating a sort of effigy. He brought a blonde wig on its Styrofoam head from their bedroom and laid it on the sofa in our living room. He fluffed the wig's long tresses, and with a black Marks-a-lot he drew eyes, a nose, and a mouth on the head. He bunched up pillows to mimic a body and covered the pillows with an afghan she had crocheted. He laid a bottle of scotch on top of the afghan. We woke in the morning to find this synthetic creature lying on the couch. After we had all, in shocked and confused silence, witnessed the thing, he gathered the whole mess in his arms, brought it out to the backyard, and burned it, the flames leaping high, as vibrant as the brightly colored yarn of my mother's afghan, above the roof of our house.

I'd like to think my father's lies were evidence of dramatic talent as well. He would lie about the time of day, my mother would say, just because he could. It's clear that in order to try to keep some semblance of peace with her, he had to develop the art of deception. He had sexual relationships with several women while he was married to my mother; many nights he would come home late, smelling of strange perfume, and I would sometimes pick up the phone to overhear him speaking in low tones with a woman whose voice I didn't recognize.

Because my father's parents were deaf-mutes the ease of lying to them may have been too seductive for him to resist. As a teenager he didn't have to speak false words with his mouth; rather, his hands could form whatever lies he wanted to tell. He didn't have to worry about his parents examining his eyes to see if he was telling the truth. Their eyes would be focused on the signs he was making with his hands.

When my mother would accuse my father of something or ask him where he had been, he had to be able to invent something plausible. And often, in the beginning, she believed him. He'd been working late. They'd had drill the whole weekend long. He'd had to go help a friend. He'd had a flat tire. I think over the years she came not to believe anything he said, but often chose not to confront him since it rarely led to any change in his behavior.

He sometimes lied to the kids, too, more benign sorts of lies, promising things he knew he could never deliver. It was sweet, though, to think of the possibility of the promises coming true—of going swimming at the Holiday Inn pool that weekend, or of going to Disneyland the coming summer—so we often forgave him that he didn't always make good on his promises. The gift of desire, we learned early on, was often sweeter than delivery of the thing it promised.

Sometimes, though, his lies were not so easily brushed off. In memory I'm very young, five or six. It's night, and I'm lying in bed, trying to sleep. I can hear my mother and her friend Doris laughing and talking in the living room. My father is still at work. They are gossiping about men, and say something silly about my father—I no longer remember what—giggle wildly, then begin to talk about something else. A few minutes later my father arrives home from work, and Doris and my mother go out for a drink. After they leave he comes to my room.

"You still awake, sweetie?" he asks, brushing my hair back with his stubby, hairy fingers. "Go to sleep, it's late."

I ask him if he can keep a secret. He says he can. Then I reveal to him, with great pride, the silly thing I heard my mother and Doris say about him. This will connect us, I think. I know somewhere in my child brain that he will be unhappy with my mother for what she said. But I love my mother too, and I don't want her to be unhappy with me. I ask him to *please please* not tell her what I told him. He promises, crosses his heart, and hopes to die. He tucks me in, kisses me, and leaves the room.

I have always been a light sleeper, and later that night I hear my mother and Doris when they arrive home, laughing and in good spirits. My father has been waiting up.

"Well, ladies," I hear him saying, "hope you enjoyed yourselves." A small pause in which I hear the clinking of ice in a glass. "You'll never guess what Sheryl told me." I lie in my bed, listening, and as he speaks, unraveling all of my great secret, the bond I thought I had with him unravels too, slowly, the way a doctor might unravel a gauze bandage that's been wrapped around some wound that's not quite healed, and my heart becomes, suddenly, something utterly alien. Where before it had just been my heart, doing its job pumping blood, an organ that had never called attention to itself, now I can feel it; it's as if it has grown larger and heavier and is trying to break out of my body. A stone, a lumpy thing, like the clay in our garden, pulses itself through my body.

Sweets and Shiny Things

It's a reaction completely out of scale with the small nature of the betrayal, but this is the first time I've felt this kind of hurt. I pummel my chest with fists to try to dislodge the stone until I fall asleep.

Carnival season of my fourteenth year was a special one because I was getting a "call-out" to the Pegasus ball. My father belonged to the Krewe of Pegasus, which had their parade the Tuesday before Mardi Gras every year and their ball a few weeks earlier. This year my father was a duke in the ball. The invitation meant my first long dress: pink chiffon, empire style, with see-through sleeves and a thin black velvet ribbon running just under my breasts, ending in a long bow in the back.

A great deal of secrecy surrounds the balls. The entire Krewe is masked, which is why it's called a masked ball. The invitees do not mask, but rather wear formal attire. They are not supposed to know who invited them, but of course I knew it was my father. I had known my call-out was coming, and I had longed for this rite of passage. I was becoming a woman.

The Pegasus ball usually takes place in the Municipal Auditorium in downtown New Orleans. You take your seat in a prescribed area because they have to know where to find you when your turn at dancing comes up. The court, which consists of the king, queen, dukes, and maids, is introduced, and then the court dances while the invitees watch. Eventually, someone called a "committeeman" brings you to the dance floor to the one who invited you to the ball.

I'm excited to be so elegantly dressed, my mother's Chanel Number 5 on my neck and wrists; the lights, the music, the colors are all reflected in my flushed cheeks. My mother, who has also been called out this year, is seated next to me. The committeeman, a young man in a tux, approaches. He calls my name with a flourish: "Miss Sheryl St. Germain, please. Follow me." He escorts me to the dance floor, navigating over the gleaming oak floor through what seem like hundreds of laughing couples, to a man wearing a full face mask and a headdress that covers the back part of the head and hides his hair with a short purple satin drape. The costume, which looks like something out of a Shakespeare play, is purple satin, lined with rhinestones. He wears a cape around his neck, also of purple satin, and also lined with rhinestones. He has on white stockings and black boots. Is this man my father?

I can't see anything that would identify him as such. This man, with his nondescript flesh-colored mask, is a little frightening. He has regal bearing, it seems to me, and if there was one thing my father did not have, would never have, it was regal bearing. I begin to doubt that this man could possibly be my father. I turn around to look for the committeeman, but he's gone.

When I turn back to the duke, he bows deeply, then reaches for my hands. His hands are large and hairy, with stubby fingers. The orchestra begins to play. "May I have this dance?" he asks, his voice muffled because of the mask, but clearly my father's voice. I give him my hand, and he leads me out to an open area of the dance floor.

He's a good dancer, and I feel safe in his arms. I have watched him dance with my mother, and he always seemed at ease on the dance floor. I used to watch them jitterbug; he would twirl and throw and catch her with such confidence I used to think he should have been a professional dancer.

We pretend not to recognize each other, and this pretense seems utterly natural to me. I am not costumed, but I might as well be. I've never been in a long dress before, and have never had my long hair pulled up like this, teased and smoothed into a high bun atop my head. I smile at him, remembering him dressed in my mother's caftan, the hairy arms sticking out, and can sense him smiling back at me under the mask.

He pulls me close, laughs, and I can smell his breath, all smoke and sweetness. He smells a little, as he always does, of Scotch, but his step is sure, and if he has been drinking, it has not been much. He twirls me around. The dance hall is lit everywhere with colored lights, and people like us, in costumes and gowns, dance and move in blurs of color and light. I can see, at the perimeter, all the other invitees, dark shapes

Sweets and Shiny Things

watching us. *Watching us.* We are performing. This is a play, a drama. I am mildly aroused to feel so beautiful and grown up and watched.

Without warning my father breaks out of the pretense, shattering my reverie. "You and your mother settled okay up there?" He holds me closer, moving me in a tighter circle for a few bars.

"Yes. She's waiting to dance with you."

"She's next." He relaxes his hold on me, and moves me, surely and easily, across the floor. This, I think, is what it really means to dance. So many of the boys I had danced with were clods, shuffling around, trying to avoid stepping on my toes, letting me take the lead, as if I had any idea what to do, breathing heavily, thinking more about leaning into me than dancing. Dancing with a boy had seemed a little like fighting with my brother. I hadn't realized it could be like this. I can see my father's intense brown eyes, eyes I have inherited, and even his dark eyebrows, which I have also inherited, through the eyeholes in his mask. He is moving me across the perimeter of the floor, where there are fewer people. I can smell his aftershave, Old Spice, wafting over us, familiar and comforting.

"So how's your love life, sweetie?" This is a standard question of his, sometimes the only one he can think to ask me.

"Okay. Carlos is going to meet us Mardi Gras day at Lee Circle."

"Getting serious?" He wheels me around.

"Oh, you know. No, not really."

"Not thinking about marriage, huh?"

"No." A silly thought.

"He's not rich enough, anyway. You need to marry someone like a doctor or a lawyer."

"I don't want to marry a doctor or a lawyer."

"Well," he says, holding me close, "when you do get married, just don't get married for sex." The room swirls with soft green, gold, and purple lights, subdued Mardi Gras colors. Underneath the mask I can see his big front teeth and the dark recesses of his mouth. I flash on seeing him in his easy chair in his boxer shorts, which sometimes fell open at the crotch, the curly hair underneath hiding the thing that had made me.

"François!" my mother would shout at him. "The girls are too old for you to be sitting around like this!"

"Wears off in six months," he continues. He twirls me around again quickly, as if he really doesn't want me to ponder this too much. I think about how he told me once that he used to go to church just to watch my mother, especially the way her breasts moved up and down when she took a breath to sing. I remember my mother telling me how shocked she was when he asked her to marry him, how she'd never thought he was the type to get serious. How he gave her the engagement ring in a paper bag.

"Wish your mother would get off her ass and get a job." He laughs. "Help pay for this."

The dance is almost over; I can tell by the swelling in the music that we're reaching the song's climax. Soon my father will take his arms from around me, and bow. The committeeman will escort me back to my seat, to my mother.

I close my eyes and breathe deeply as if inhaling some sweetness I can't get enough of. I open them and my father is laughing, whirling me faster, but still with steadiness. I trust him utterly. We make our way around the perimeter of the floor one last time. When I remember that dance with him now it's my father's faces that I see, brightly colored masks of his life, the past and present flashing around us as if time had no meaning, as if all that would come to be is already present in those last moments of dancing with him. His face laughing under the duke mask. His painted face lighting up the night on Pegasus Float Number 12. Him dressed as a woman in a blonde wig and pillow stomach. Him offering me raw oysters. Him putting hot sauce on my tongue for lying. Him grim-faced, burning my mother's afghan in our backyard. His face round and orange and bloated with cirrhosis, his face worn and now missing teeth, his face, falling down drunk, the sour smell of him in the hospital, his face, the eyes rolling back, the thick pool of saliva in his mouth. His face, holding me up high at Mardi Gras to catch beads, his gorilla face, his Chinese face, his face drinking, his face drunk, his mouth opening to the spoon of condensed milk, his face lying to my mother, his

Sweets and Shiny Things

face joking, his face reading the newspaper and drinking his sweet coffee, his sweet face whose sweetness came out most fully during Mardi Gras when he could be the opposite of what he was: a womanizer, a drunk, a man who was not a duke but who had to work two jobs to support his family.

His face as he enters my mother for the first time, full of honest desire, sober and so present he can't hold back, so full of it all he explodes, tender and noisy, into her, and I glimmer into being.

Swamp Songs

When I would recreate myself, I seek the darkest wood,
the thickest and most interminable and, to the citizen,
most dismal swamp.
—Henry David Thoreau, "Walking"

The day my sister, her friend, and her car wound up in the
swamp between Destrehan and Kenner, just outside New
Orleans, happened to be Thanksgiving, a potentially dangerous time for
any family, but especially so for this one. Getting us together for a holiday
is like putting way too much pepper in a dish. Where two or more of us
are gathered in celebration's name there's bound to be trouble. Everyone
drinks too much, we've all done drugs, and some of us continue to do
them. Most of us have been in jail at least once for some offense or other.
The fact that our father, our aunt, one brother, and two brothers-in-law
have died in past years of alcohol or drug abuse seems to have no effect on
us; this is New Orleans, after all, the city as famous for its drinking as it is

for its location near the mouth of the Mississippi. This is a city where as early as 1841 the populace was spending more than three million dollars a year on alcohol and where, for thirty years, by order of the Louisiana legislature, every prisoner in the local jail received four ounces of whiskey every day. This is a city where the most important product of sugar cane was the rum (called "tafia") extracted from it. This is a city that took as its motto a version of *in vino veritas*: "tafia always tells the truth." This is a city that thumbed its nose at Prohibition; even my Maw-Maw sold homemade wine, which she kept hidden underneath her children's beds. This is a state that currently ranks fourth in the nation in the number of alcohol-related fatalities, though it is twenty-first in population.

Liquor was always around when I was growing up; every occasion was an occasion to drink—births, birthdays, baptisms, first communions, confirmations, not to mention holidays. Even our pet parakeet used to drink, perching on the edge of wine and champagne glasses, gurgling the stuff down.

Along with a proclivity for drinking, everyone in my family also speaks too loudly and is fond of using such expressions as "I'm gonna kill him," or "I could'a killed him," or "He's dead" (meaning: "I will kill him now for sure"). No one usually kills anyone, though the family is not known for its peaceful disposition, but this sort of talk has become more disconcerting to me when I return home to visit from the Midwest. Midwesterners don't drink, eat, swear, talk, or in any way act like these people to whom I'm related.

The swamp's near fatal embrace of my sister is really only the latest of a series of tragic familial interactions with water and the watery lands that make up this area. My great-uncle drowned in the Mississippi under "suspicious" circumstances, according to my mother, who hints that he was drinking, and the orange plantation our ancestors worked for hundreds of years on the banks of the Mississippi was destroyed when the river jumped its banks and reclaimed the land after a hurricane. Our current family home, three blocks from Lake Pontchartrain and about a mile from the Mississippi, has been rebuilt more than once due to floods and hurricanes. I can still see clearly in my mind the transformation of streets to rivers, of yards to swamps, those images as fresh as the drunken face of my father; the waters as seductive as the feeling of alcohol and cocaine running in my veins or the mornings when I woke with no memory of the night; the faces, the bodies, the swamped yards, the destroyed houses, the flooded streets, mixed in my mind like ingredients for an enormous gumbo.

I am not there when my sister and her friend drive into the swamp, as I've learned to stay as far away as possible from home on holidays. I get the story when I call to wish my mother happy Thanksgiving. The worst Thanksgiving I've ever had, she says. She's never cooking again for Thanksgiving, she says. Of course, she will cook again, but she wants to stress how deeply she's been affected by the events of this Thanksgiving, and the worst outcome, in her mind, is that she will not cook anymore. In a place where food and pride in cooking are so important, this is akin to saying, "I won't be breathing anymore."

My mother is a Creole, descendent of French and Spanish immigrants who came to Louisiana in the eighteenth century, immigrants who now make up a large part of the culture in south Louisiana. *Creole* comes from the Spanish *crillo*, "child born in the colonies," and thus native-born people of Spanish and French descent would be considered Creoles here. Food, and particularly local cuisine, is so important to Creoles that it's said as soon as they enter heaven they wave hello to Saint Peter and ask, "Comment ça va, Monsieur? Where's the pot of jambalaya?" If Saint Peter says there's no jambalaya they will rub their chins and inquire about the food customs in the other place. Many New Orleanians would, in fact, rather be in hell than eat bad food. Indeed, what better way to understand south Louisiana than as a kind of Dantean underworld where we fill ourselves to bursting with those very vices that tortured us when we lived aboveground: food and drink?

Occupying the absolute bottom of our country, most of our land at or below sea level, we are, some would argue, the asshole of the country, the place through which the shit and fertilizer and soil of most of the country drains and is evacuated into the Gulf. What else could we be but that "other place" where the Creole might find that pot of jambalaya? Or maybe a bowl of gumbo?

Cajuns, unlike Creoles, are descendants of French Canadians who were expelled from Nova Scotia by the British and who landed, many of them, in rural southwest Louisiana, now called Acadiana. There's much intermarriage between Cajuns and Creoles—cross-cultural unions like my parents' are common—but Cajun culture and cuisine developed usually in more rural areas. Creole food is more influenced by the sauces of France and Italy; Cajun food is a heartier, spicier food that makes more use of fresh game. Both were also influenced greatly by African and Caribbean spices and cooking styles.

The food that has come to dominate both Creole and Cajun cuisine is a food that gets its main ingredients from the waters around here. Seafood gumbo, for example, contains crabs, shrimp, and oysters, all of which spend at least some of their life cycle in freshwater swamps or estuaries. One could, in fact, understand gumbo as sort of a culinary version of the swamp. First you make a roux by mixing flour and oil together, then cooking it over a low fire until it is as thick and brown as swamp water. The roux is what will bind everything together. Then you add onions, green peppers, garlic, tomatoes, okra, crabs, shrimp, oysters, water—and sometimes sausage or chicken or duck. It's a complex dish, just as the life in the swamp is complex and diverse—cypress and tupelo draped with Spanish moss, ladies' tresses orchid, swamp-lily, pickerel weed, iris and elephant ear, canna, alligator, snake, frog, bass, sac-a-lait, catfish, crawfish. When I eat gumbo, all that richness of life from the land comes alive in my mouth, the roux-thick broth blessing it all, and it tastes like a rich, peppery swamp.

The word *gumbo* is said to come from the African *gombo*, which means "okra," the vegetable that grows well in Louisiana and is used to thicken seafood gumbo. *Gumbo* is also used to refer to a kind of fine silty soil common in these parts that makes an unusually sticky mud when it's wet, and a patois spoken by some blacks and Creoles in Louisiana and the French West Indies. The connection the three uses of the word suggest between soil, food, and language is real: our food is our land is our language. What we eat is where we live and what we speak. We speak the way we do because of where we live and what we eat.

A holy trinity of gumbo: place and food—and the breath that they both shape into words.

And it was gumbo that was being cooked that Thanksgiving morning. It is a family tradition to eat a bowl of gumbo on Thanksgiving before eating the turkey, which is accompanied by oyster dressing, bourbon candied yams, thick, cheesy macaroni, and warm French bread. We all love gumbo, and my mother is proud of hers. This year, though, my younger brother Jules, in a spirit of goodwill, volunteers to make the gumbo for Thanksgiving, an offer that backfires because my mother doesn't approve of the way he's making it. He didn't let the roux cook long enough, she tells me on the phone, as upset at this violation as if someone had been murdered. He kept running into the living room to watch the football game, she says. He was on his sixth beer by noon; he was drinking too much to pay attention, she says.

I sympathize with her; if your roux isn't right, the gumbo just tastes like soup, and nothing ever comes together to make that gumbo flavor. Good gumbo consistency is hard to describe, but you know it when you see it; it's something like a mix between a stew and a soup, and it's the roux that is responsible for both that consistency and the nutty, sweet flavor it imparts to the gumbo. If you don't cook it enough you taste the raw flour; if you make too dark a roux the flavor might overpower the gumbo; too light and the gumbo might overpower the roux. Each gumbo is different, and you decide what kind of roux you want, light or dark, depending on the kind of flavor you want the roux to impart to the gumbo, and the ingredients you have on hand.

It's tricky enough getting the roux right when you're stone-cold sober; Jules, who was slightly crocked, didn't stand a chance. But the situation was tense before the problem with the gumbo: not only were both my brother and my sister over, but their five very active children were also with them. And neither my sister nor my brother has good parenting skills. Marie, my sister, is twenty-seven. She finished high school, got pregnant, and married a sweet but wild man who turned out to have a problem with crack cocaine. Marie tried everything from cutting her wrists to feeding him dog food (she mixed it up like tuna salad and gave it to him for lunch) to get him to stop doing crack, but he wouldn't. She left him, finally, taking their two small children with her, and he was dead two weeks later, stabbed in the neck during a drug deal gone bad somewhere on Airline Highway. Since then Marie has had a string of boyfriends and a string of jobs, from serving up food in the school cafeteria to modeling lingerie in Bourbon Street bars. Dark-haired and sexy, Marie has what my mother calls bedroom eyes, inviting, knowing, and naive all at once.

My brother, at thirty-one, is struggling to learn how to parent after having spent much of his adult life drinking, selling drugs, and partying. He's there with his three children, one of whom is symbolically disturbing to my mother. This is David, the two-year-old boy whose mother, Velvet, is also there. Velvet claims that Jules is David's father. Jules acknowledges paternity, but my mother and some other members of the family have their doubts. Velvet, they claim, had long tried to seduce Jules away from his wife, and would've said or done anything to get him in her clutches.

Jules *was* sleeping with Velvet while he was married, and she *did* come to be pregnant while they were sleeping together; that much is clear. At the time Velvet was his wife Kathy's best friend. Kathy decided she wanted another child after seeing Velvet pregnant; Jules obliged her, so Kathy and Velvet were both pregnant by my brother at the same time, and would go on long walks together during their respective pregnancies. Their children were born within two months of each other. Kathy eventually found out about Velvet, burned Jules's clothes in a ritual bonfire, and threw him out. Since then Velvet and Jules have been living together, although they fight constantly.

Velvet, a stunningly beautiful woman who strikes most older men as a reincarnation of Marilyn Monroe, entered the Miss New Orleans beauty contest last year, and possibly might have won it hands down, but was disqualified when, during an interview, she revealed that she was a single mother. She and my brother, who is a bodybuilder and a mechanic, make a striking couple. He takes after my father, and is Cajun-looking in a traditional way: dark-skinned, thick-eyebrowed, and even more thickly mustached, he looks like a cross between a gangster and a swamp fisherman. He presents a stark contrast to Velvet, who is blond, sexy, and round.

I am always the black sheep at these family gatherings where most of the women wear tight, flashy clothes, gold chains and earrings, elaborate hairdos, and painted fingernails. The last time I attended one of them my sister said to me as kindly as she could that I really was starting to look more and more like a librarian and didn't I want to do something about it?

Everyone this Thanksgiving has been drinking since late morning, and everyone but my mother, I'm sure, has slipped out for a snort of coke. It's now around one o'clock. Marie has been seeing a new man recently, but she's in a bad mood this Thanksgiving because her new boyfriend has lied to her about something, so she's been drinking more than usual. She's been distracted and sullen all morning, my mother says, not paying attention to the kids, who are running all over the house while my mother is trying to get Jules to pay attention to the gumbo he's supposed to be making. Marie's eyes, Mother says, have that buttery look they get when she's had too much to drink.

Jules, who is watching the football game, and Velvet, who is talking to Marie about her problems with the boyfriend, are also not watching the kids, and David has toddled over to the kitchen and is "interfering" (my mother's word) with her making the oyster dressing. She yells at him in a sharp voice, which tone Jules and Velvet pick up. They exchange knowing looks. Jules stomps into the kitchen and accuses Mother of not treating David the same way she treats the other grandkids. She retaliates, accuses him of not watching his son. He scoops up David, storms out, and claims he won't be eating anything for Thanksgiving, and she can just finish the gumbo herself if he's doing such a bad job.

Swamp Songs

Mother retaliates again by saying she's so upset now that she won't be eating anything either. Of course, both of them have already eaten quite a lot, as you can't make either oyster dressing or gumbo without tasting along the way, so their retorts are really just for show. And they will, of course, eat later. Meanwhile, the clouds of drama descend over the house, and they stop speaking to each other as Jules goes back to watching the football game and Mother to repairing the gumbo and making the oyster dressing she won't be eating.

Marie then says she can't eat either because her stomach is upset over the lies her boyfriend has told her, so it appears my mother is continuing to fix a meal for no one. There's always more food than anyone can eat when my mother cooks; I have learned from her that there should always be more than enough, that it's just not polite to not have enough for everyone to have third and fourth helpings, but this is ridiculous— the house filling up with the seductive smells of roasting turkey, oyster dressing, and gumbo, the French bread waiting to be heated, and no one claiming to want to eat it.

Marie tells my mother she has to run back to her house to get a change of clothes for her daughter. Velvet volunteers to go with her. Unbeknownst to my mother and brother, Marie and Velvet are, in fact, not planning to drive to Marie's house, but rather to Marie's boyfriend's house in Destrehan where Marie has decided to confront him about those lies.

Marie and Velvet take off, driving across about ten miles of swamp to get to the boyfriend's house. I can't help but think how swamp functions, in Louisiana, the same way the "woods" functions in fairy tales. Something bad always happens when you go into the woods. Either there's a wolf waiting to attack you, or a witch waiting to eat you, or parents who leave you there and don't come back. In Jane Campion's *The Piano,* which utilizes many fairy-tale motifs, the woods separates Ada's home with her husband from the place where her piano and her lover reside. When she crosses the woods a blue filter changes the light from warm to cool, and we know we are entering a taboo world. It is in the woods, in fact, where she is almost raped by her husband. In my mind's eye, when I reconstruct my sister's drive to the boyfriend's house, I see Ada tramping through the swampy woods of New Zealand to reach her piano and the man who would become her lover. The light turns blue, the cypress trees in the swamp grow beards, and their branches become grabbing hands.

When the two women arrive at the boyfriend's house they barge into the living room where he is drinking beer and watching the football game. Marie confronts the boyfriend with the lies. He becomes so irritated that he starts pummeling her. Her face, which my mother saw later, was bruised and swollen, her mouth cracked with dried blood. Velvet pulls her away from the boyfriend, but Marie, unfazed, stops on her way out to show herself to the boyfriend's mother, who is outside on the gallery drinking a glass of bourbon. "See what your son did to me!" she says, exhibiting her ruined face to the mother like some dark prize.

The boyfriend's mother looks up at her between sips of bourbon. "Well," she says, "you should know better than to talk to him when he's in a bad mood."

Marie and Velvet drive to the police station to file a complaint, then the police drive over to the boyfriend's house and arrest him, whereupon the boyfriend's mother calls my mother, who is sitting alone at the kitchen table crying in her wine and continuing to make the oyster dressing that she claims she is not going to eat. The boyfriend's mother shouts the story at my mother over the phone, and ends by saying she has a bad heart and that my sister has made it worse by calling the police and having them come over to arrest her son, that maybe she'll have a heart attack now and it'll be my sister's fault. My mother, who had heart surgery herself earlier in the year, retorts, "I have a bad heart too!" then slams the phone down. She and Jules forget about their differences as they wonder, during football commercials, where Marie and Velvet are.

This, as you may imagine, is the part where the swamp comes in.

You often can't see up or down or even around a swamp; flora grows so fast that a trail cleared a week ago near a swamp could be gone in another. And sex is everywhere, from the millions of mating insects and reptiles and amphibians to the choking abundance of the flora. Spanish moss drips like sweat from trees that cry out for sky. The entire Louisiana landscape seems sexual; from the slithering of the Mississippi to the spreading roundness of Lake Pontchartrain, to the still, shallow coastal bays and freshwater swamps, this landscape bristles with sex. But the swamp's way of seeming both inviting and dangerous reminds me of the eyes of my sister, those brown depths you cannot get to the bottom of that offer both seduction and torture. And so it seems, in an odd way, a suitable place for Marie and Velvet to have landed.

They are driving down the main highway from Destrehan to New Orleans, which is bordered on either side by swamp. Velvet has convinced Marie to let her drive. Neither woman is sober enough to be driving, but Velvet is "the worst driver in the world" according to my mother, even when sober. On this day Velvet has more than the usual trouble paying attention to the road; she keeps looking at Marie's wounds and saying, *Oh, my God, Marie, your face, your face.* Both of them know that damage to a woman's face is a serious thing in New Orleans. For Marie, not only will her ability to attract men be decreased for a while, but she can also forget about modeling lingerie in the French Quarter for an even longer while.

Velvet loses control of the car during one of these moments of looking at Marie, crosses over the neutral ground, and drives the car straight into the water on the other side. Except for I-10, which rises above the swamp, roads here seldom have guardrails to protect you from going off them into whatever lies beyond. Marie manages to have the presence of mind to roll down the window on her side of the car a crack before the car plunges into the water, an action that probably saved her life.

Marie does not know how to swim. She also has on boots and a jacket that weigh her down, and is emotionally and physically exhausted from the fight with the boyfriend. She told me later that she could feel herself sinking with the car to the bottom of the swamp, could feel the thick, brown water filling her lungs.

Velvet, despite her other flaws, does know how to swim, and manages to crawl out of her side of the car and swim over to Marie. After several tries, she gets her out of the car and pulls her to a floating cypress log, where Marie coughs up inky water and they both hold on until the police arrive, called by passersby who witnessed the accident.

The swamp is a drunken landscape if we think of the drunk's penchant for exaggeration—there's nothing subtle or classic or clear about it. Of all the bodies of water in south Louisiana, it is perhaps the swamp that most fiercely suggests the character of a people. There is a reason that swamps have gotten such a bad rap in the past, that they function in our collective mythology as places where awful things happen, where swamp monsters or progeny of incestuous relations live and wait to prey upon passersby. The swamp harbors the paradoxical: water as still as land, and land as moving as water. Chocolate-colored waters you can't see into hide alligators and fish, often hugely ugly fish—alligator gar, or grossly gigantic battered bass or catfish that have lived way too long. Cypress trees grow and survive in standing water where most trees would die, and develop appendages we still do not understand: cypress knees. Swamps are richly alive, despite the apparent stillness of their waters.

It is ironic that my sister almost drowned in a swamp. I'd been thinking about swamps for years, and how they symbolize for me what my family is. I have both loved and been afraid of swamps, the weirdly erotic beauty of them, and of the trees that grow in them. Not being able to separate the threat I sensed in their seductive strangeness from that of my family, I gave up and moved away from Louisiana. I moved away from that place where I worried the land and the family would make me too much like them, away from that place where I too could so easily slip from road to water, from hard-won sobriety to the waters of alcoholism, addiction, sexual obsession. I told myself I would not fall into those waters, would not go the way of so many in my family. I told myself I would stop doing drugs, would stop drinking, stop being so prolifically seductive; I would go to college, I would reflect, I would be different. The swamp, and my family, wouldn't get me. At least that's what I hoped.

No use telling me I'm mythologizing, romanticizing, or anthropomorphizing the swamps; no use telling me to call them "wetlands" and think of them as separate from my family, think of their much needed place in the coastal ecosystem. It wouldn't help: even Thoreau, that consummate naturalist, would fall into myth when describing what it was he loved about swamps. The darkest, most dismal swamp was a *"sanctum sanctorum,"* he writes in "Walking." It's in swamps he finds the strength and marrow of nature. In that place his farmer neighbors might call useless he finds a knowledge that nurtures his spirit in some way. Thoreau provides a way of seeing the inherent paradox in swamps, the twinning of destruction and nurturance that I understand as family.

And indeed I've found that the waters of my childhood fill my dreams under these moody Iowa skies where I now live, that all I can think about, living in the Midwest, is the South and its waters, how they've shaped me, how I love them, how I miss them. It's not for nothing that the genre of music we know as blues was born in southern lands filled with swamps and lakes and rivers. Something about these still or slow-moving waters encourages both song and reflection.

Marie and Velvet arrive at my mother's house hours after their rescue by the police, wet and bedraggled, Spanish moss and decaying matter from the swamp decorating their hair. They are wearing thin blue hospital gowns. They both collapse on the couch in the living room where the TV is blaring the last quarter of yet another football game.

When my brother sees Marie's face, his hands curl into fists. Despite the fact that there's not a commercial break on at the moment, he rises from the couch, stomps into the kitchen, picks up the phone, and calls the boyfriend's mother. He barks into the receiver, "Your son's dead!" then hangs up. He comes back into the living room and resumes watching the football game, though he has an angry look on his face, and his hands remain clenched; this is his way of letting the family know he cares.

Eventually, everyone eats gumbo and turkey and oyster dressing and finishes off the last of the wine. The next day Marie's waterlogged, uninsured car is pulled out of the swamp. She reports that there's a nest of about sixty snakes in it.

These are the stories that we live and tell here. There's usually a quality of too-muchness to the stories; everything seems related to everything else, everything touches everything else. In a landscape where water connects just about everything, and is sometimes the only way to get from Point A to Point B, stories rise that act like that water—there are surprising revelations, leaps such that you feel like you jumped a bank and have flooded the other side; it's not immediately clear where you're going, just that it's the same water you're on and that's all that matters, the force of water, the force of narrative that carries you along.

All during my childhood a painting by an unknown artist hung on the living room wall of my mother's house: a painting of an utterly destroyed building, and a staircase, intact, attached to the side of what was left of the building, went up to the height of the destruction and then back down again. It ended in what looked like a shallow lake. At the bottom of the staircase an old man with one leg and a cane, his eyes focused on the stairs, prepares to climb up. I could see the future of the man through the artist's eye; he would struggle up the stairs with his one leg, and then down, only to find himself facing the swamp, nowhere to go but back the way he came, if he had the strength. The one-legged man's eyes are full of hope, but what made the painting so powerful was the knowledge the viewer had: that the man's struggle would end only in more struggle to get back to the very place he had begun. Or, he could fall into the lake.

I used to sit for hours as a child and look at that painting, trying to understand the feeling that grew in me the longer I gazed at it. It was not unlike what I felt after a nightmare—both were frightening, but the nightmare left me with a feeling of emptiness, of fear uselessly spent, while this painting filled me with an indescribable fullness, like too much dark bread, something I couldn't quite digest. It was the same feeling I got as a child looking at the swamp in the fields near our house. I never felt anything or wanted anything from the waters of a chlorinated swimming pool other than to be able to see to the bottom, and to be cooled off when I jumped in. The swamps were different, though. You didn't want to jump in them because they were so muddy and full of half-deteriorated plants, and had things like snakes and turtles and alligators in them. Their water didn't cool you off; it was too warm. You didn't go to the swamp for recreation, at least I didn't, though my brothers often fished them. I went because I knew the swamp knew something I didn't, and I wanted that knowledge. The swamp was my intellectual superior. Perhaps this is what Thoreau felt when he called the swamp a sanctuary.

No one would talk to me about the swamp or the painting, and so I grew up talking to myself about them—I knew there were things going on in the family that I was not privy to as a small child: deaths, funerals, and the reasons behind them, the unexplained disappearance of my uncle, the way my brother was so silly and glassy-eyed, the reason my father didn't go to church with us. But none of this was discussed; like the painting, like the swamp, it was just there, and so we went to church with my mother where the priest talked about salvation, and to school where we learned math and acted in plays with happy endings, and went on vacations far away by motel pools that offered sun and swimming.

But the painting was always there when we got back. Where does that crippled man think he's going? I would ask my mother. She would shake her head and say nothing. No dictionaries or encyclopedias could explain that painting to me. I was seven, and all darkness was saved from me like a rich, brandied dessert. I looked to the swamp for answers but found only my own face reflected back at me.

Before moving to the Midwest I moved away from home and the painting, but not from Louisiana and its waters. I had one more swamp to cross. From New Orleans I moved to Lafayette to teach at the University of Louisiana, where I was closer to one of the largest freshwater swamps in North America, and the largest in the South—the Atchafalaya. But the university also had a small cypress swamp at its center, and for the three years I lived there I used to go to the swamp the way I had gone to that painting, the way I'd go to the swamp at home, like a willing Persephone, and look into it.

I returned to visit that swamp this past winter. It was dusk when I reached it, and the air was crisp and somewhat cold for Louisiana. Spanish moss, thick and tangled as my own hair after sex, curled down the stripped bodies of the bald cypress trees, covering one strangeness with another, exchanging one nakedness for another. I remember thinking, as I looked at the trees, that that's how I feel sometimes when I speak.

From farther away the swamp seemed populated with women, not trees, their bodies frozen into shapes of despair, or desire, or both—and I wondered what lusty god chased them here. I want to know the words of the prayer that saved them, changed them from women to trees, for I know they are trees. Weird sisters, who bare their root-limb knees, pushing them out of water muck to air as if to fuck the sky—.

Here, I thought, is my family's soul and nemesis, this swamp where our veins root, spread, and suckle the southern silt of it like a child who doesn't have a choice. Here have my siblings and I fed and grown to adulthood, here do our knees rise toward heaven, here do our bodies stand, obvious and rhymeless in thick, unmoving waters.

I stand next to the small swamp in the unreal, cool night air. The moon is almost full. It always amazes me that with the moon's light the swamp at night so clearly reflects one's face and all that one is, like a photographic negative: the body full with food and wine, the seductive hair, the whole history of drinking that is my heritage; the cypress trees and Spanish moss, the swamp lilies, the large night birds, the alligator bodies. The swamp is never so beautiful in the day as it is at night, and I drink in its beauty like milk.

Should I fall while drinking, I know I'll be with family.

Disappearing Bodies

FISHING FOR A BROTHER AND A LAND

It's 4:30 in the morning, and I'm driving with my brother Jules and his small son down Louisiana State Highway 300 in St. Bernard Parish, toward the small town of Delacroix, where we'll launch his boat and head off to fish the waters and marshes that make up the coastal wetlands east and south of the mouth of the Mississippi. These wetlands and much of the landmass that makes up the two parishes that border them, Plaquemines and St. Bernard, were created more than seven hundred years ago when the Mississippi shifted fifty miles east from its ancestral banks.

Delacroix is home to one of Louisiana's oldest and most beloved fishing communities, although if anyone other than a Louisianian or an avid fisherman has heard of the town, it's probably from the Bob Dylan song "Tangled Up in Blue," where he sings of drifting off to New Orleans "looking for to be employed" and winds up working on a fishing boat "just outside of Delacroix." It's unlikely Dylan would have found work doing much else but fishing in and around this town.

I'm in Louisiana because my mother had a heart attack and bypass surgery earlier this week. She's currently in recovery and doing well, so Jules and I are taking advantage of the good spring weather and excellent fishing conditions. Today we leave for open sky and the smell of saltwater and fish. We do not want to think today about my mother's veins, stripped from both her legs, to replace the failed ones to her heart. For the first time in a week we will not speak about that deep cut down her chest, the fluid in her lungs, her weight, her breathing.

Genetic, the doctor had said, on both sides of my family, weak hearts easily injured. "What does it mean to have a heart attack?" my young son asks me. "Does it mean that your heart attacks you? Or does it attack someone else?"

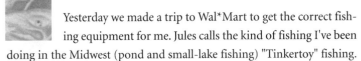 Yesterday we made a trip to Wal*Mart to get the correct fishing equipment for me. Jules calls the kind of fishing I've been doing in the Midwest (pond and small-lake fishing) "Tinkertoy" fishing.

"This fishing is different," he says, puffing himself up, proud that he knows something that I don't. He looks at my small pond reel in the Wal*Mart parking lot, then at me, and says, gently but firmly, as if he's a doctor telling a patient she hasn't long to live: "The fish will laugh at you, Sherry."

We purchase a heavy-duty reel, heavier line, and some sparkle beetles, locally made gelatinous artificials with glitter inside their bodies and a big red eye painted on the sides. We're going to be fishing for speckled trout, "specs" in local parlance, and redfish. Jules says they really like these sparkle beetles. I cannot fathom what the fish think they are, except that in the dark, often turbulent waters of the Gulf they might seem flashy: LOOK AT ME, LOOK AT ME, maybe something like the strippers in the French Quarter strip joints less than an hour's drive from here.

We head home to catch a few hours of sleep; we'll have to be up before dawn. As I lie down on my childhood bed and breathe in the close, familiar air of my mother's small house, I pray that this fishing trip will not end as the last one did.

Because the area we'll be fishing is located where freshwater and nutrients drained from the Mississippi meet the saltwater of the Gulf, it makes for an extraordinarily rich environment for a vast number of fish and shellfish. An ambitious angler could see blue and white marlin, tarpon, tuna, snapper, redfish, speckled trout, striped bass, large-mouth bass, sheepshead, flounder, catfish, crabs, shrimp, and oysters all in one day. Commercial fisheries in Louisiana are the most bountiful of the lower forty-eight, representing 25 to 35 percent of the nation's catch. Louisiana is first in annual harvest of oysters, crabs, and menhaden, and is also one of the leading producers of shrimp. Many would claim that south Louisiana offers the most dynamic fishing on the planet.

But it is also one of the most endangered areas in the nation, if not the planet, and though I've come to fish hoping to get some small relief from the worry over my mother's heart, it's hard not to think of the sickness at the heart of these waters. Louisiana is experiencing the greatest rate and magnitude of wetlands loss in the nation: 20 percent of the wetlands my brother and I will be fishing today are predicted to be lost by 2050 at the current rate of about twenty-five to thirty-five square miles per year, wetlands that serve as homes for more than half a million waterfowl, hundreds of thousands of shorebirds, and huge fish populations. In the past sixty years more than one million acres of Louisiana coastline have disappeared.

These are conservative land-loss projections developed by Louisiana State University and the Army Corps of Engineers, which show that Gulf waters will be one foot deeper at the Louisiana coast by 2050 and two feet deeper by 2090. Because 90 percent of the coast is less than three feet above sea level, an extra one or two feet will have a drastic effect: in fifty years, integral parts of south Louisiana will be open water.

One reason for this loss is that the Mississippi currently delivers less than half the sediment to the Gulf of Mexico that it did in the early

1900s. Prolonged maintenance of the river in its present location through artificial levees has contributed to the rapid deterioration of coast, as has the trapping of sediment material in upstream dams and reservoirs in Arkansas, Missouri, and the Ohio River basin. Draining wetlands to expand livable areas and digging vast networks of canals to facilitate extraction of oil and gas have also contributed to deterioration of coastal wetlands. When you look at this area on an aerial map you can see the straight canals marking it like long, unbroken scars.

The effect of this coastal erosion on wildlife is deadly. Coastal marshes are nurseries for young fish, including those we'll be looking for today, speckled trout and redfish. Cocahoe minnows, anchovies, and fiddler crabs spend most if not all their life cycles in the marsh. Shrimp also spend some time there. Oysters need the 25 to 50 percent salinity of a stable coastal marsh to survive. Wetlands and barrier islands not only moderate the effects of encroaching ocean salinity from the Gulf of Mexico, they also filter out many pollutants before they reach oyster beds.

The loss of wetlands is also dangerous to human life. As water replaces more and more wetlands and barrier islands, hurricanes meet with less resistance and encounter more shallow water, which the storm converts to often deadly waves. Nine out of ten storm fatalities are caused by storm surges, which can be fifty miles wide and up to eighteen feet high.

The rich coastal marshes we will fish today will be gone in my lifetime if nothing's done to heal this land.

Jules picked me up at my mother's house in Kenner at about four in the morning, and we loaded the drinks and ham sandwiches I'd made for us into the cooler on the boat. My nephew David is asleep in the backseat of Jules's truck. It's hard to sustain any kind of conversation so early in the morning, so mostly we drink coffee and stare ahead at the dark road.

Jules resembles our other brother, François. Dark and mustached with a strong jaw line and a smooth, muscled body, he's been lifting weights seriously for many years now. His neck and upper body seem slightly smaller than the last time I saw him, though. He was taking steroids then, which was a point of contention between us. I thought he looked grotesquely blown up, and was worried about his health. Now he looks more like the brother I grew up with, though older.

Jules and I are not close. The only person in my family I was ever really close to was François, and that was a strange and dark closeness. Whatever connection I had with François did not transfer to Jules, perhaps simply because he was so much younger: ten years. By the time he was old enough to be a friend as well as a brother, I had moved out of the family's home and to another state. The age difference is less important now that I'm in my forties and he's in his thirties, but Jules and I still seem worlds apart, though we share this love of fishing.

I stick my head out of the car window to feel the rush of warm, humid predawn air. There's nothing like the smell of south Louisiana air—a slightly sour, yeasty smell, thick with stuff you don't even want to know about, heavy and rich with life. It sometimes seems oppressive when you live here, especially in the summer, but to me it feels like an infusion of exquisite elixir when I return home after a long absence.

I worry about this place, its land and its waters, as much as I worry about the health of my mother and my remaining brother. I remind myself as I revel in the wind blowing my hair back that our ancestors, part of the great wave of French, Spanish, and German immigrants who came here for the free land, contributed to the current environmental crisis in Louisiana. For almost one hundred years my family owned and worked a small orange plantation along the Mississippi that began with a gift from the government. Homesteaders were given fifty arpents of land fronting the Mississippi, but they had to promise, in exchange, to build levees on their property. This is how the now hundreds of miles of unbroken, impenetrable levees that currently girdle the Mississippi got their start.

Because the early levees were neither high enough nor strong enough, the Mississippi continued to flood into the twentieth century. That is how my ancestors' plantation got flooded. I have tried to locate where our family's orange plantation was, but it has been reclaimed by the Mississippi, and all I can do now is look into the brown waters at the spot where the courthouse documents say it should be, and know that underneath those waters somewhere may still be the rotting remains of the plantation and their home, ripped from its roots by these waters. The cemeteries that hold the bones of most of my ancestors are also underwater.

Despite the loss of the plantation and the graves of my relatives, I know that flooding is a good thing for the land. Periodic flooding builds up the soil, adds a layer of rich sediment to the land it floods. When flooding is too strictly contained, as it has been by the building, in the twentieth century, of nearly unbreachable concrete levees, the land ceases to receive its annual rejuvenation of soil, and begins to sink lower and lower until finally the river itself is on higher ground than the land. This is the situation we have now. Well protected from the Mississippi by the levees, the land has sunk so low that it faces encroachment by the saltwater of the Gulf, which is licking higher and higher along the sinking coastline, like a relentless, insatiable lover.

The way we've locked the Mississippi into position through artificial levees, when its "natural" desire is to move and roam as it constantly searches for a shorter route to the Gulf, might be understood as a situation that's led the river to develop a kind of atherosclerosis, not unlike what led to my mother's heart attack. In humans, excess buildups of fatty deposits on the walls of the arteries gradually harden or calcify with time, and prevent the arteries from expanding and contracting as they should. The blood flow is restricted, thus the heart has to work harder to push blood through; blood pressure rises, and complete blockage results in a stroke or heart attack, as happened with my mother. In the case of the Mississippi, when flooding is restricted too much, the volume of water passing through any given point gets larger and heavier; what sediment there is often winds up at the bottom of the floor of the river, or just at its mouth, causing the river or the mouth of the river to rise, and eventually leading to a potentially explosive situation: a flood such as the devastating flood of 1927. The blocked "artery" of the Mississippi simply gives out. It's a classic recipe for a heart attack.

Disappearing Bodies

Jules has always fished, and I have taken it up over the past few years, but I had never gone fishing with him until last year. That trip didn't end well; he was doing drugs and selling drugs and drinking too much. Involved in an extramarital affair, aggressively silent about his life, he never gave me an opening to talk to him. He was guzzling beers the whole time we were fishing, even while navigating the boat. He hadn't bothered to purchase a fishing license, nor was he respecting the limits of fish you could keep. At one point during the trip both he and his friend who was with us started tossing beer cans off the side of the boat into the water. I went ballistic, and we didn't stay much longer after that. We rode back to the boat launch in a cold, hard silence that even the lovely warm and stinky Louisiana coastal air had trouble penetrating.

I never called or wrote to Jules, and he never called or wrote to me. Not only was he doing and selling drugs—cocaine, primarily—but he was providing our younger sister with drugs as well. And this had been going on, as far as I could tell, for about eight years, despite the fact that he had been a pallbearer at François's funeral. I kept pointing out to my mother that you cannot afford to own a brand-new Vette, a brand-new boat, and a new home in suburban Metairie and take trips to the Caribbean on a mechanic's salary. Mother kept saying that Jules was saving his money was all. I tried to do the math with her, but she had a block; she couldn't admit, at least not to me, that this son, *her son,* might go the way of François. Named after my father, François had been "his" son, Mother used to say. When Jules was born she told my father this would be her son, that she'd raise him the way she wanted, and there would be no beatings.

By that time my father wouldn't care; he pretty much ignored Jules, who, for all intents and purposes, grew up without a father. It was my father who was supposed to be watching him when, at five, he stuck the fingers of his right hand under the blade of the lawn mower when my sister was cutting the grass. My father was sleeping off a drunk when it happened. Jules lost the top third of his middle finger, and today what's left of his fingernail curves over the place where the tip of his finger should be, as if protecting some secret space.

As he grew up, Jules kept his distance from my father; he had always been more careful than François, and had managed to stay out of the arm of the law, for the most part. He told me later he wasn't going to be "stupid" like François, which meant he wasn't going to get caught by either his father or the law.

Jules *had* been a sweet, gentle child, everything my mother wanted after the roughness of François, and clearly he was, and is, her favorite child. He was painfully shy, and it was probably the social properties of liquor that snagged him. He began to drink hard as a teenager, and became the center of his group of friends, the one who always organized parties and other social events.

"Want a Coke?" Jules asks, reaching into the cooler in the backseat. He hands me the cold drink, and his scarred middle finger strikes me again as if he's five and it's just happened. I still have photos of him right after the accident, taken with my black-and-white Swinger Polaroid camera, sitting on the piano bench in the living room, his hand all bandaged up, trying to play the piano with the hurt hand, smiling.

The smell near the boat hoist awakens me from my roving thoughts—a more intense, saltier, fishier smell. We are in Delacroix, smack-dab in the middle of the coastal estuaries, bays and islands that offer some of the best fishing in the world. Smack-dab in the middle of the place that will most likely be open water in fifty years. This town is likely to wind up as drowned as my family's orange plantation. Many other fishermen with their boats are ahead of us, and we have to wait in line in the dark as each one is lifted off its trailer and into the water. Jules buys shrimp for bait at the store connected with the boat hoist. Hundreds of fishing camps line the thin strip of road that's gotten us here.

Remarkably, David sleeps through it all, and soon we're afloat and off. The sun is just beginning to rise; gorgeous marshland surrounds us. Blue herons, pelicans, flocks of laughing gulls, plovers, egrets, sandpipers—all manner of bird life fills the skies over the marsh. We will ride about twenty miles out to get to the other side of the bay. We see hundreds and hundreds of birds during the ride. I love the feel of the wind on my face. At one point Jules slows down and points out how wide the passageway is on either side. "It shouldn't be like that," he says. He knows nothing of the reasons; all he knows is that these waterways used to be thinner, there used to be more land, more places for fish to shelter. The land is disappearing, and with it the fish habitat. He points out some dead trees in the marshland to the east: "That's from when the hurricane brought too much saltwater into the area and killed the trees," he says, revving the motor.

Most healthy marshes are vibrant with many different kinds of grasses. These are depleted marshes, though, and contain mostly sea oats, oyster grass, and some mangrove. These marshes once produced a greater fur harvest than the rest of the United States and Canada combined. Today, not only is the land itself disappearing, but so is the wildlife it once supported so richly.

I like going really fast in the boat, even though I realize we're probably breaking some speed limit. It's this feeling of a rush that I love, and it's what I think I share with both my brothers. Now that I don't do drugs anymore, this is as close as it gets to that kind of physical high for me.

We don't start out using the sparkle beetles. We start out using shrimp, which are kept alive in a bucket of water in the back of the boat that has a pump aerating the water. We stop first at a marshy area where we'll cast toward the shore. I stick my hand into the bait bucket and pull out a wriggling shrimp.

"See that dark part in the head? That's the brain—stick the hook through there," Jules says.

I've eaten many shrimp in my day, but I've never handled them live. I pierce the first one with the sharp hook and try to remind myself that this is good, this is connecting me to my human role as predator, I'm killing the "angel in the house," as Virginia Woolf advised women they must do.

I get several hits, mostly small catfish, which I'm happy to let Jules take off the hook for me and throw back, as I've never quite learned how to avoid being finned by catfish. After about the fourth one takes my shrimp he suggests that if this keeps up I might want to change to the sparkle beetles, that the "trash fish" won't take them. A lot of people wouldn't consider catfish trash fish, but neither Jules nor I particularly like to eat them, and that's not what we're fishing for. I decide to stay with the shrimp for a while longer.

I tell him about my recent trip to Alaska, the extraordinary fishing in the state. I suggest he might like fishing there. He looks at me as if I'm crazy. Why would I go to Alaska when Louisiana is one of the prime fishing spots in the world? he asks.

Why indeed. I watch him out of the side of my eye as he puts his rod down and helps David, who has gotten his toy reel all tangled up. I'm surprised to see how gentle he is with David. He holds him, kisses him, and calls him "little buddy." I've never seen him like this with his children, and it occurs to me that maybe the divorce from Kathy he went through last year turned out to be a good thing, because custody arrangements have forced him to spend more time with his children.

I look out into the expanse of water and marsh that surrounds us, the huge body of stuff, so rich and full, yet so near disaster, and cast my wriggling, doomed shrimp out.

Speckled trout and redfish like rigs, Jules tells me, and he knows where they are. "Some people don't like the way the rigs look," he says as he slows the boat down and throws anchor near a deserted oil rig that rises like a skeletal castle out of the water. "But they're beautiful to me—and the fish think of them like home. If you go down to the bottom there's thousands of feet of shells down there that they piled to build the rig."

That, he says, and the structure itself create an ideal environment for the fish. This rig is called "the Wreck" because it is a wreck—a boat crashed into it, Jules explains, and the wreck has been left to stand because it provides such excellent cover for the fish.

Many boats are already circling the rig, and during the hour we fish here you can almost tell when you'll catch something: all you have to do

Disappearing Bodies

is look at the boats on either side of you and note if *they* are catching anything. If they are, then you probably will be too in a few minutes. The fish circle, predictably, around and around the rig, and we catch several specs here. We move on to other rigs, channels, and cuts, also good places to fish, with names like Black Bay, Red Eye Cut, and Pelican Point.

Speckled trout are beautiful fish, brilliantly spotted, with distinctive fangs on the upper front of their jaws. The insides of their mouths are yellow-orange. Not trout in the sense that a stream fly fisherman would understand trout, they are instead members of the drum family and are known elsewhere as spotted sea trout *(Cynoscion nebulosus)*. They are exclusive residents of the U.S. coasts and are one of the most familiar of Gulf fish. Annual U.S. catch of specs is between four and five thousand tons, though some research suggests that number is dwindling due to habitat destruction.

I ask Jules if it seems to him that the numbers of specs are dwindling.

"Nah, not really," he says, biting his line where a fish broke his hook and he's got to tie on another. "I think they're just hiding better." He sits down on the cooler to put on his new hook, his body brown, glistening in the sun.

"It is true, though," he continues, "that a lot of the marshes where I used to fish are gone. Too much water." He grabs a ham sandwich from the cooler and takes a bite equal to half of the sandwich. Mouth full, he continues, "So I guess the fish have moved to other places. Sometimes we have trouble finding them, but we do usually find them. Mostly at the rigs."

Environmental researchers believe that loss of grasslands and marshes as well as loss of food sources due to pollution are contributing to declining populations of specs, but I don't mention this to Jules because I have a fish on my line. I know it's a spec because of the way it hit. Hard. A spec's vicious and rapid first strike is meant to dismember its prey, although specs do not have much fight in them, and are usually not difficult to get in once you've got them really hooked. I lift the spec into the boat—it's a good-size one—remove the hook, and toss it in the separate cooler we have for the fish.

The next hit is a sheepshead, another familiar Gulf fish, easily recognized because of the six or seven gray bars on either side of it. Members of the porgy family, sheepshead are known for their prominent, strong teeth, which include powerful molars. Their front teeth look something like human incisors, but stick out a bit, like a sheep's. They like brackish waters and also like rigs and pilings. Unlike the spec, the sheepshead is a persnickety eater and will often nibble the bait off the hook before you realize they're there.

Jules shakes his head as I pull in the fish like a dead weight. Sheepshead are not streamlined, like specs, and their thick bodies make them a little harder to pull in. A flock of gulls wheels by.

"I hope you're gonna throw that back," he says.

"Why?" I know that sheepshead flesh is lovely, sweet and mild, perhaps one of the best tasting of the fish we'll catch today.

"Sherry, those fish are impossible to clean. Just look at how heavy the scales are—and do you see those fin spines? The base of those go deep into the flesh. It takes me about an hour to clean just one."

I throw it into the cooler anyway and smile over at him. He shakes his head and throws a line out.

"Well, I ain't cleaning it," he says, addressing not me, but the precise spot in the water where he's thrown his line.

I cast again, take up the slack, and wait. I realize with a start that though we've been out for several hours Jules has not been drinking. In fact, as I root through the cooler for a diet Coke, I notice there aren't any beers at all in the cooler, so he clearly doesn't plan to do any drinking, at least not on the boat. He looks over at me quickly, as I snap open the Coke can. It's as if he's read my mind.

"Yeah," he says, out of nowhere, as if I'd asked him a question, "I'm trying to stop drinking. Been going to AA meetings at lunchtime and on Friday nights. NA meetings, too. It's hard, I'm weak, I keep slipping, but I'm trying."

I look over at him. It is a rare moment when I'm struck speechless.

A spec hits the shrimp, and Jules is over at my side. "Keep the line up, Sherry. That's it, don't let it go slack, good, oh, he's a good one." He helps me pull a gorgeous spec on board, then sees that his own line has something on it. He reels in another spec, and we both set up our lines again and cast them out.

"Me and Velvet are going to counseling, too," he continues. "I'm really trying to work some things out about myself, about why I treat women the way I do and stuff."

I'm holding my breath; I don't want to say or do something to make this moment dissipate. "And," he says, taking a long sip of a root beer and casting out to a rising fish, "I been going to church."

I almost fall into the water at this point. It turns out he's going to a charismatic church, White Dove Ministries, located in Gretna, on the west bank of the river. In subsequent visits to Louisiana he will ask me to accompany him to the White Dove Ministries, and I will, despite my distrust of organized religion. And though it's not for me, I can see how it's helped him; the music, which goes on for forty-five minutes and includes saxophone, drums, guitar, bass, harmonica, and a forty-person gospel choir, is truly uplifting. And physical. The pastor, Brother Mike, looks a bit like Jules, and speaks with the same kind of thick New Orleans accent. He's got a thuglike humor:

"So. Ya think ya supposed to be havin' a good time on dis earth? Lemme tell ya, dis ain't heaven, it's earth, and it's supposed to be hard. Heaven is when ya die. And Jesus, well, he's gonna beat up on ya a little while ya here—kinda like a meat tenderizer, *bap bap bap bap,* and just when ya think ya can't stand it anymore, he turns ya over and *bap bap bap bap,* he gets ya other side." Jules takes notes in an Addiction Recovery Bible.

On the boat he tries to explain how he feels. A kind of sense of ecstasy. He struggles with the words, but I realize that he gets a kind of a rush from these church services; he could be talking about a cocaine high, except that he's speaking of it in spiritual terms.

"I feel it in my body, Sherry. I was never this moved at church when we were little."

We fish in silence for a while. I'm afraid to say anything at all. The sun burns bright and brilliant. We smear on sunblock, but I sense it's a useless activity. The sun will get us in the end. I decide to just enjoy it, the heat, the warmth, the dark smell of the Gulf, my brother's confidence.

"I kind of see what I been doing wrong," he continues. "I never thought it was wrong before, selling drugs in the house, with my *kids* right there, sleeping with another woman while I was married, and I never thought I was doing nothing wrong. It was all about me, but now it's not."

We reel in some more fish, and this time I've got a redfish. Jules unhooks a catfish, which he calls "Meow Mix," and throws it back, grimacing. I ask him what made him change.

He thinks a while, looking out into the water, casting and reeling in the sparkle beetle a couple of times before answering.

"Well, Velvet was the one who brought me to the church first, but I woulda never gone if I wasn't ready. I think it was the kids. I realized I had to be there for them. I didn't want to be like Daddy—I wanted them to have a father. One they could be proud of." He's silent for a while, casting and reeling, casting and reeling. He always was an impatient fisherman.

"Now that I'm not doing my drug deals I can hardly live," he says, taking off the sparkle beetle and putting a shrimp on his hook. "I lost the car, and now I'm living in public housing with a roommate because I can't even afford the full rent there. How the mighty have fallen," he says, grinning. "Managed to keep the boat, though."

David pretends to fish with his Mickey Mouse fishing pole, and for the most part is quiet. He sleeps for a while on the floor of the boat. We've slathered him from head to toe in sunblock, but I can see his skin turning red. We will all be burned red as redfish by the time we return.

We catch our limit of fish, mostly specs, some more sheepshead I've insisted on keeping, and the one redfish. Redfish are also a member of the drum family and are another beautiful fish, the upper body coppery and shiny, and on the upper flank, near the tail, a black ocellar spot. I love the spot—like some small dark stain or sin. Redfish are one of the largest drums, and though they are also a familiar fish they remain an

Disappearing Bodies

enigma to most. Sometimes they're everywhere and sometimes they're nowhere, and no one seems to know why. The habits of redfish are similar to those of specs, about which a lot more is known, but unlike speckled trout, it's become a protected fish by both the state and federal governments over the past few years. Some suggest that the craze for "Cajun-blackened redfish" has caused depletion of the species.

At some point David throws a cardboard apple juice box off the boat into the water. Jules chastises him, backs the boat up, and picks the box up out of the water. It's early afternoon, and the fishing has gotten markedly slower. Jules touches my shoulder and I grimace.

"You're burned," he says. "It's time to go back." We pull in the poles, lock them down, pull up anchor, and speed the thirty or so miles back to the boat lift.

I love the wind, the sun, the smell of the Gulf, but not having the fishing or Jules's talk to occupy my mind, I brood once again on the sickness of these waters. Louisiana has only recently begun trying to combat the land loss it's suffering. Until recently, the loss was not even acknowledged. We have always been first in coastal area in the United States; with well over two million acres of marshland (41 percent of the total marshland for the nation), perhaps we felt that we were sitting pretty. The apathy about land loss is so profound that it led one environmental law professor to comment a few years ago that if Texas annexed sixty-four square miles of Louisiana we'd probably go to war, but nobody pays much attention to the same loss from coastal erosion due to environmental disaster. Serious attempts to save the coast began with creation of the Coalition to Restore Coastal Louisiana in 1988 and the passage of Act 6 in 1989 and the Breaux Act in 1990, which authorized restoration projects that would create new marsh. Only since the 1980s has the Department of Natural Resources begun artificially creating crevasses that mimic natural crevasse formations in natural levees, which can't occur in artificial levees because of their strength, to try to combat wetland loss.

The Coast 2050 initiative was launched in 1997. It is charged with arriving at a vision and strategic plan for coastal restoration in

Louisiana. The approach is one that takes its energy from observation of the land-building process itself. Since river water, sediments, and nutrients built the wetlands centuries ago, the theory is that they can do so again if one restores as many natural water- and sediment-flow patterns as possible. The restoration would use a combination of natural forces and human engineering to reestablish the processes that built the coast long ago. Some say that a comprehensive program could restore and maintain 98 percent of the current coastal land, but it will cost billions of dollars and will require incredible levels of cooperation among government, businesses, and individuals. It's unclear if it will garner the level of support it needs to succeed, and even more unclear if the state and federal governments will invest the tremendous funds necessary for the restoration effort.

We are entering the no-wake area and will soon be at the boat dock. My thoughts wander to our mother. She is recovering from her surgery, but only time will tell if she will stay on the restrictive diet and accept the radically changed lifestyle the doctors are prescribing for her, where she must walk daily, despite her varicose veins and ailing feet. She won't be able to eat the food she loves. It won't be easy. Jules appears to be healing himself, but it's too early to tell if he'll be able to walk the walk too. His attempts at healing his relationship with Velvet will fail; they will be separated by the time of my next visit. He will continue to be involved with his kids, even coaching David's Little League team, but he will be drinking again, though not as heavily as he once did, and there won't be signs of drugs.

Two kinds of healing are going on with my mother and brother. For my mother, the surgical intervention made use of all the technology currently available, although the success of that intervention will depend on lifestyle changes, which she'll have to adhere to in the future. It's not unlike the way that rebuilding coastal land is futile if we continue to drain swamplands, to build unbreachable levees and canals. We have to change our lifestyles, too.

Jules's fragile transformation is due less to technology than to matters of the heart. He's using the latest psychological motivators from AA and Narcotics Anonymous, but it was a spiritual crisis that brought him to the moment of wanting to change. The coast needs, perhaps, both forms of healing. We need to bring all of our technological expertise to this crisis that also demands spiritual transformation. To be so profoundly alienated from the waters that provide us with food, shelter, and livelihood that we don't see or care how we are destroying it—this is a crisis of spirit, and as helpful as numbers are in showing the extent of the damage, I don't know that it's numbers that will convince vast numbers of the population to change their lifestyles.

What does it take to change? Having children? A brush with death, a look into the cavern of one's own soul, a renewed sense of faith and hope?

I'm aware that I could have easily gone the way of François. It was only a few years before his overdose and subsequent death that I had spent several months of my life shooting up cocaine. I remember the exact moment when I walked away from that life. Midmorning, midsummer. A muggy day in Hammond, Louisiana, where I was a senior at Southeastern Louisiana University. Depressed as usual from the high of the night before I stroll to a nearby park and sit down on a swing. Absentmindedly, I begin to swing. I look at my arms as they pull on the chains of the swing. I've forgotten to wear long sleeves, and bruise-colored pricks from the needle dot both of my inner arms like tiny forget-me-nots.

No one had to tell me that if I continued the course I was on I would be dead soon. I knew it in my bones, in my blood, in the skin and flesh of my arms. I felt I could imagine what it would be like to overdose. The ecstasy of it, the warm, electric feeling shooting through your body, more, more, more, the sense of something bursting, flooding, veins exploding, heart exploding, the sense of too-muchness, something heavy and hot flooding you, then a stopping sensation, your heart flooded, swollen to numbness, drowned, stopped.

The knowledge of your own destruction. It's something like a dark spot in your brain, in your heart, as tangible and heavy as the sour fish smell of the Gulf. I could either let that spot grow and take me over or I could slip through the sliver of an opening I could still see. I walked away from the swing, from my house, from my job, from much of my life at that time. I walked from the park to the room I was renting in downtown Hammond. It took me about thirty minutes to pack everything I owned into my car. I drove to Baton Rouge, about an hour away, where I stayed for a while with a friend who knew something about drugs and what they can do to you. I changed my name. I got a new job and commuted to Hammond two days a week to finish my English degree. I never looked back, although I never forgot, and can still conjure, more than twenty years later, the precise feelings of being high on coke.

Perhaps, among other things, it was the love I've always felt for my body that helped me to walk away. It was, I think now, a purely selfish act, an act of self-preservation. Perhaps this is how we need to think of the land here, as part of our bodies, not separate, and the act of saving it an act of self-preservation, not an act of generosity. We are creatures built for survival, and much as some of us would like it to be otherwise, it has not always been generosity that helped us to survive and prosper as a species.

We clean the fish at a friend's nearby camp. Jules filets them, even the sheepshead, and it doesn't take him as long as he said it would. I watch him hold the fish down and slit them open, his wounded finger gleaming with fish slime, and I feel content. I throw fish heads and guts to the garfish and crabs in the waters below us, then wash the blood off the wooden table we're using. We do this small thing together, our weak hearts pumping in unison, our pasts like shadows hovering over us, the smell of the fish everywhere, our hands working at the same purpose, the two of us, for the moment at least, holding it all off.

Communion

When I think of the food of my childhood, I try not to think of the Communion wafer, tasteless as cotton, brittle, as pale and thin as you can get and still have mass. A kind of anoretic bread, it reminded me of the fish food we sprinkled into the fish tank, except at least the fish food smelled like something. *Ecce Agnus Dei,* the priest would say, elevating the host into the air-conditioned air of the church, and I would wonder what kind of god would choose so bloodless a host.

The nuns explained we weren't to let our teeth touch it; we were to let it dissolve on our tongue or swallow it whole and hope we didn't choke on its pasty flesh. The wafer almost always got stuck to the roof of your mouth, though, like a stamp you'd licked first then tried to swallow. You had to use your tongue like a pry bar or plunger to get it loose: never did you get the sense it *wanted* to enter you. I took it on my tongue like a pill I had to take for my own good, and tried not to taste or think about anything when I swallowed.

I lived not to go to church, but to tramp through the swampy fields behind our house, pick blackberries till my fingers were dark with their juices, climb trees to read secret books about sex, catch crabs in the lake and later throw them into a pot of water scented with crab boil, or help my mother in the kitchen gather ingredients for a gumbo.

Throughout my life the rituals associated with cooking and eating felt more like Communion than the sacrament we took every Sunday in the church. I loved watching my mother cooking and baking as a child, and I have learned to take pleasure in those arts as I think she did. One learns the pleasure of cooking the way one does that of the body: slowly. First the patient kneading, then the loaves rising like lips to first kisses, reluctant and hopeful, and later the cool thickness of dough, responding to your touch like the thighs or breasts of the beloved. And the recalcitrant celery or green pepper or garlic that keeps escaping from the knife like a child running from the bath, the tomatoes that quietly and honorably allow themselves to be sliced, give themselves up to the cause, and the kitchen, all clean and virginal, the chopping board with its scars from other nights of chopping and cooking, the pots and pans all lined up and waiting like open hearts, and the smell of onions that rises out of the olive oil and sleeps with you at night, the smell of oil and flour browning, the sizzle of green peppers and green onions added just at the moment the flour and oil turn into a roux the color of rich peanut butter, the way the crawfish and shrimp and crabs turn orange as soon as they hit the boiling water—the transformations of cooking seemed much more glorious and miraculous to me than that of wine into blood.

We all loved the dark-rouxed gumbo my mother would serve up in large bowls after mass, with thick chunks of sausage and chicken, fresh shrimp and crabs from the Gulf, oysters like plump nipples, and savory broth that had communed with onions and celery and bell peppers, the holy trinity of vegetables in Creole and Cajun cooking. The broth was kissed at the end with Tabasco, blood of cayenne peppers that grew in the soil not far from our house, and the red sauce woke up our mouths and reminded us of our own body and blood. The family, fractured and fighting at other times, would come together in our love of eating; as we sat around the small kitchen table and spooned the gumbo into our mouths we were joined, almost whole, for those moments of eating.

In each bowl of gumbo we ate were the tangled roots of our birth-place: roux, a gift from the French; okra, a gift from Africa; filé (powdered sassafras root) from American Indians; peppers from the Spanish; sausages from the Cajuns; oysters supplied by Yugoslav fishermen; and fresh vegetables that come from the rich soil here: Creole tomatoes, garlic, and green onions. *Jardin loin, gombo gaté*, warns a Creole proverb: *Garden far, the gumbo's spoiled.*

New Orleans has always had a large black population—today it makes up more than 60 percent of the city—partly because of the long history of slavery here, and partly because the city, which was cosmopolitan and more European than American in many ways, was also open and accepting of free men and women of color. African Americans and Haitian refugees often found their way into the kitchens of the grand New Orleans restaurants, and with them came knowledge of stews and soups, spices, and new vegetables (okra, for example) to the cuisine. Later, when the Acadians, in search of freedom from British persecution, settled here, they brought their hunting and fishing skills, their skill with one-pot meals, and a love of pepper. Sicilians brought rich red gravies and a love of garlic.

I didn't realize, as a child, that so many cultures had contributed to the intoxicating taste of gumbo, but I did know, from helping my mother in the kitchen, that many ingredients went into the gumbo. I also knew that it had to be cooked a long time to make all those ingredients become part of some larger, more complex flavor. It is that slow cooking, a Creole tradition, that gives many of our dishes their unique flavor, a flavor that cannot be duplicated otherwise. It was a wonderful mystery to me, more interesting, even, than the mystery of the Eucharist, how all those flavors came together so beautifully to make that gumbo flavor.

As a child I didn't need to know all of this to know how intensely good the food was. *This,* I found myself thinking one day as I brought a spoonful of thick gumbo to my mouth, the roux-thick broth and a juicy, barely cooked oyster filling the spoon, *this* is the body of God. I swallowed the oyster whole; it slid into me, as warm and slimy as sperm, tasting like ocean. An unbroken secret or mystery, it slid into me as if it belonged there, had been a part of me once and wanted to be, again.

When I make gumbo for my guests in Iowa, they poke politely at it, removing the oysters and crabs to the plate the bowl sits on, to be discarded when I'm not looking. *I thought it was an eyeball,* one friend said about the oyster she threw out. *It looked too much alive,* another friend said about his rejected crab. In a state that is 98 percent white, and whose farmable land is planted with mostly corn and soybeans, it is no wonder that the natives—many kind people I count as my friends—would not have a taste for the wildly spiced, intense food of New Orleans, a food so rich in otherness and diverse ingredients.

I'm guessing that one reason my Iowa friends threw out the crabs in the gumbo was because they were still in the shells, and in order to eat them you had to pick the meat out of them. You had to get your hands dirty. The only person at my party who ate the crabs the way they should have been eaten was Irma, an American Indian friend. She sat down, broke the body of the crab in two, picked the meat out of the body, cracked the claws and sucked the meat out of them.

It *is* messy to eat boiled crabs, shrimp, or crawfish, our favored way of eating these delicacies. And it's not just Iowans who have trouble with this messiness. Gray, who was born and raised in Dallas, is just as picky about his food, despite having me for a mother. He is now sixteen and refuses to eat anything that has a shell on it or once had a shell on it. Both his father and I are from Louisiana, and grew up eating and loving seafood, but I think this love does not get passed down in the blood. You have to live in a place where water surrounds you, where it's almost part of your breathing, where everywhere you go there are mounds of crawfish and shrimp and crabs and the smell, raw or cooked, is everywhere because you are never far from a body of water.

That Gray was not raised in Louisiana has probably contributed to his lack of affection for crustaceans. We visited Louisiana a lot, though, making the eight-hour drive to New Orleans several times a year to visit family and gorge ourselves, his father and I, on the food we missed so much. Once, when Gray is about eight, on the first weekend in May, high crawfish season, we are driving from Dallas to New Orleans to visit my mother. This trip, though, we sidestep over to Breaux Bridge in the southwestern part of the state, where the Crawfish Festival is going on. I have been living in Dallas for ten years, and haven't had what I considered to be good crawfish in a long time. I know there will be some at the festival.

Every weekend of the year except December festivals related to food take place in Louisiana. In fact, several festivals are going on during any given week. During a recent trip in October I had my choice of thirteen festivals to attend over one weekend, including the Violet Oyster Festival, the St. John Parish Andouille Festival, the Italian Festival, the Bridge City Gumbo Festival, the Downtown on the Bayou Festival, the Louisiana-style Oktoberfest, the Mensaje Spanish Festival, and the Swamp Festival. The Crawfish Festival in Breaux Bridge is one of the best, though, for crawfish. Originally settled by and still populated primarily by Cajuns, Breaux Bridge has been declared by the Louisiana state legislature to be the Crawfish Capital of the World.

Crawfish, also known as mudbugs because they live in the mud of freshwater bayous, look like miniature lobsters. At their largest they are four to five inches long, and most of that is claw or head. About 90 percent of the fifty thousand tons of crawfish harvested in the United States are red swamp and white river crawfish from Louisiana. The red, most of which come from the Atchafalaya Basin, are heartier, larger, and usually wild. The white ones are milder in taste and are raised in crawfish ponds throughout the state, a crop that is often alternated with rice, another major Louisiana export.

There should be about two hundred thousand people at the Crawfish Festival, and lots of crawfish to eat: tons of boiled crawfish, crawfish étouffée, crawfish bisque, fried crawfish, crawfish pie, crawfish corn maquechoux, soft-shelled crawfish, and even crawfish jelly. There will be crawfish races, a crawfish parachute jump, live Cajun music, carnival rides, and a crawfish eating contest (the record at this contest is thirty-three pounds of crawfish in one hour). As I drive I'm filling Gray in on some of this information, hoping to get him excited about the festival, but when I look over at him during my talk, I see he's asleep. I hope he'll enjoy the festival, even if he doesn't eat any crawfish.

I'm mostly interested in having boiled crawfish. They will have been boiled in huge vats of saltwater spiced with abundant red pepper, Tabasco, and bay leaf. Potatoes, lemons, whole garlic, and onions will have been boiled along with them. Crawfish have a muddier taste than shrimp, not surprising since they spend their lives in the mud, and that's probably one reason we like them spiced up so much.

Once we arrive at the festival I try to interest Gray in a platter of crawfish, but he will have none of it. "Just some french fries, Mommy," he says, groggy from his nap in the car. "The crawfish are scary," he continues. "They look like little monsters, and they have those claws and they smell funny and you have to do too much stuff," he says, "to eat them." He looks like he's going to cry.

"Won't you just try one?" I ask. "I'll peel it for you."

"No! And I won't suck the head either." He wrinkles up his face. "That is *really* yukky. I just want a drink and some fries."

He's cranky because I woke him up abruptly from his car nap, and I can see he is not interested in being here. I decide the best thing to do is eat and get back in the car. He's still tired from the long ride. He can sleep at my mother's, I think, and he'll feel more comfortable there.

I stand in three lines, one for Gray's fries, one for drinks, and one for a platter of boiled crawfish. The air is full of cayenne and lemon and onion and crawfish, thick and deep like a fog. And Cajun music, that passionate music whose roots are deep in the swamps and bayous of this very place. The musicians here are not playing for tourists; these are hometown boys playing for family and friends. The insistent fiddle, the rollicking accordion, and the unrestrained voice of the singer rise and mix in the air with the smells of the crawfish. I recognize the song, "Les Veuves de la Coulée," a traditional Cajun song about widows from a coulée who go into town to buy some cloth for their daughters, "belles 'tites filles" to go to a party "chez Joe." I look in the direction where the music seems loudest. About a hundred couples are dancing. Big-bellied men and large-hipped women, laughing, and doing the two-step, utterly unself-conscious about their bodies and unrestrained in their movements. It occurs to me that that's what Cajun music is mostly about: lack of restraint. It doesn't matter that you don't have a pretty voice; the music isn't a pretty music—rather, its beauty is in its guts. The wild voice of the fiddle never fails to make me want to dance. It's like a kind of spice that gets in your blood.

The crawfish are warm, fresh from the vat. Steam rises up, and the pepper tickles my nose. Gray and I sit down at a long picnic table where we can hear the music. Lots of other people are also sitting at the table, each with a pile of crawfish, lost in the eating of them. Gray sits across from me with his pile of french fries, looking around as if he were in a freak show. When I start eating, his intelligent face looks on in what seems like horror as I, ravenous and unthinking at seeing the crawfish piled up all orange, fat, and warm, attack.

I crack a thick head off with a sharp twist, bring it to my mouth and suck the fat and cayenne-flavored juice out of it, making loud slobbering and sucking noises like everyone else around me. I peel one segment of shell from the body, then squeeze the tail, strip out the angry black vein, then pop the de-headed, de-shelled, de-veined thing into my mouth, toss the shell to the side, and start twisting another head off before the hot on the tip of my tongue has cooled, before the one in my mouth is chewed and swallowed.

It seems I've always done this like breathing, but the accident of Gray's gaze makes me think about it; he's never seen me eat crawfish. I realize I must look bad to him, like a glutton or some predator mother he's never seen before. He has brought a french fry to his mouth but stopped just before reaching his lips, frozen. This is a child who doesn't even like when his peas touch his rice, so I can imagine what he must think of this cracking and sucking. I reach over to pat his head and reassure him, but he cringes and wrinkles his nose again. He sneezes. My breath is so ripe and fiery with the crawfish and their spice that he backs up when I try to kiss him. And I'm sure my hands must smell like the crawfish; there's head-fat under my fingernails, and my fingers and palms are also sticky with crawfish juice. As I continue to eat, and the pile of emptied shells and sucked heads grows larger, he eats his fries, but becomes more and more subdued.

"You don't look right, Mommy," he finally says.

Later that evening we arrive at my mother's house only to be greeted by more crawfish. It's the season, and in honor of our visit my mother has bought twenty pounds from the neighborhood grocer, and invited my brother and sister over. "I hope we have enough," she worries. Gray is quiet but clearly morose as he watches my mother spread the newspaper out on the kitchen table and pour the little monsters out on them. I promise to fix him a peanut butter and jelly sandwich.

After my sister and brother arrive, we all sit around the kitchen table, and on cue start cracking and sucking. I think of Marcel Proust and his dainty madeleine dipped in his dainty tea, and how it brought him all those memories of home. It's sucking the head of a crawfish that does it for me. I sometimes think that the way we crack open crawfish or other shellfish is not unlike what we do to each other when we love, every tenderness also a violation, every birth a kind of cracking and breaking.

My mother picks out a big crawfish with huge claws and a smaller one with more petite claws, and makes them dance around the newspaper as if they're puppets. "See," she says to Gray, "here's Mr. Daddy crawfish, and here's the Mommy crawfish, *la tee da,* not very scary, are they?" Gray is even more horrified. He might have been scared of the crawfish before, but thinking of them as a mommy and daddy does nothing to encourage his appetite for them. He eats half of his peanut butter and jelly sandwich and goes to bed early.

If the way we eat crawfish seems an act of transgression and excess, eating oysters might be considered practically an act of worship in New Orleans. Not only do we put them in gumbo, but we fry them, sauté them, and have constructed elaborate dishes to honor them: Oysters Rockefeller, for example, invented at the turn of the century and named for Rockefeller because the dish is so rich. A thick, pungent sauce made with butter, spinach, parsley, scallions, and celery, spiced with white and red peppers, marjoram, basil, anise seed, and a good splash of Pernod, is broiled over oysters in their half shells. Oysters Bienville, another rich oyster dish, is named after the founder of New Orleans, Jean Baptiste le Moyne, sieur de Bienville. To make oysters Bienville you make a roux of butter and flour, then add green onions, parsley, garlic, heavy cream, eggs, dry sherry, chopped mushrooms, and shrimp, and season with white and red peppers. The sauce is poured atop the oysters on the half shell, topped with bread crumbs and freshly grated Romano cheese, then the oysters are baked.

Because these dishes are rather complicated and rich, we rarely prepared them at home, but almost always went out to a French Quarter or uptown restaurant to eat them. One pastime of the 1920s that still survives to this day is the oyster orgy, in which you spend a Saturday evening traveling from restaurant to restaurant, eating as many cooked oyster dishes as you can in one night. Oysters Rockefeller and oysters Bienville are always among the dishes one eats at these orgies.

South Louisiana is blessed with just the right conditions for oysters, which is why they are so prominent in our cuisine, and why we have such a love for them. Saltwaters from the Gulf mix with freshwaters from other bodies of water—lakes, rivers, and bayous—to give our oysters a lovely salty, sweet taste. Currently, there are about fifty oyster houses in New Orleans, and it is a rare restaurant in the city that doesn't carry at least one oyster dish.

My mother sometimes fried oysters or made a lovely, simple soup out of them and their liquor, milk, butter, green onions, and red pepper. The most elaborate dish she made was oyster dressing, for Thanksgiving and Christmas. My mother's version of this stuffing was a mix of chopped oysters, ground meat, pork sausage, bacon, celery, garlic, onion, mushrooms, green pepper, green onions, parsley, and stale French bread crumbs. It was seasoned with thyme, bay leaves, sage, and lots of red pepper. We could never afford to put a lot of oysters in the dressing, which is why she used the mushrooms, claiming they tasted like oysters when cooked into the dressing, and when chopped had the consistency of them. The aroma of the oysters cooking together with all the meats and seasonings filled the house during Thanksgiving and Christmas, and was still there the next morning, like the scent of a departed lover. When I make oyster dressing now, which I usually do on Christmas Eve night, I feel the complicated threads of connection with my female ancestors, who developed our family's version of this dish, and for a night I am filled with the happiness their cooking always brought me.

Most people who frequent oyster houses like Pearl's in the French Quarter go for the raw oysters. When I'm in New Orleans my mother and I always visit the Quarter and have one or two dozen raw oysters apiece. We make a sauce of ketchup, horseradish, lemon juice, Worcestershire, and Tabasco, dip the oyster in it, and then wash it all down with a beer.

It was my father, though, who gave me my first raw oysters and taught me to like them. I was about ten, it was a Saturday afternoon, and he was sitting, shirtless, on the front lawn with a big burlap sack of them, taking them out, one by one, sticking the stubby blade of the oyster knife into the lips of their shells—a quick twist and the shell would open. He'd stick the knife into the heart of the oyster, bring it to his mouth, and then kiss it off the knife. I sat on the front porch, watching him.

"Come here, sweetie," he said. "Taste this." He opened another one, scraped it loose from its shell, and offered it to me like that, off the tip of the knife. "Be careful," he said. "Don't cut your tongue."

I sucked it off the knife, trying to be careful, but the blade of the knife cut my tongue just enough to draw blood, and as the oyster slid down my throat I could taste my own blood and the sweet juice from the oyster mixing together in a sharp, rusty flavor.

 We didn't eat a lot of desserts as I was growing up because my mother did not like sweets. The one exception was bread pudding with Creole whiskey sauce, which she did make fairly frequently. She hated to waste anything, and the pudding was a way of using up leftover French bread, which we had with many meals. It goes stale quickly—like all intensely pleasurable things—but can be transformed easily into pudding. I would help her by breaking the bread into small bits. Sometimes I pretended I was a priest and the little bits were the host, the bread for Communion. *Dominus vobiscum,* I would say, as I tore the bread into a big glass mixing bowl. I would think about what the bread had been like when it was fresh, the crust brown and hard, but not too hard, the inside soft and white and cool, how you could squeeze it like a sponge. Now it was all stale and hard and not so good. I remember wondering if this was what it was like to get old.

While I was tearing up the bread, my mother would scald milk. Then she'd pour the scalded milk into the bowl, and I loved to watch the milk enter the bread, then transform the hard pieces into soft, moist morsels. I added raisins and peach halves while my mother beat eggs with sugar and cinnamon, allspice and nutmeg. We poured the mixture into a baking dish, and put it into the oven to bake for an hour. Soon the house would begin to smell of peach and sweet and cinnamon, like Christmas, like my mother's happiness. The smell would fill the house with goodness, with something that felt like grace.

While the pudding was baking, my mother would make a Creole hard sauce. She said it was also called a whiskey sauce because whiskey was a major ingredient. She mixed the whiskey with powdered sugar and vanilla, and beat it until it was creamy white and smooth.

We would eat the pudding warm with the sauce poured over it. The raisins would be swollen and full of the milky, bready juice: they would burst open in your mouth when you bit into them. The bread would be fruity, sweet and spiced, and the peaches were always a surprise when you bit into them. The whiskey sauce would warm me like an inner sun, like my father's face, my mother's perfume.

Much as I try to make my living in the Midwest palatable, to find beauty in this hardworking, plain place where oysters and crabs and crawfish and hot sauce and pepper are looked upon askance, sometimes when I close my eyes at night and think of where it is I now live, I see a huge, thin Communion wafer, big as Iowa, only rounder, floating above me, and I wake as if from a nightmare.

Ecce Agnus Dei, I hear the priest saying, but the land I think of when I say it is the land that birthed me, a crooked city carved out of the crook of a river, a land of wild food and weather, hurricane and heat that enters the food that grows here. This is the god I want: the god of roux that makes gumbo gumbo; the god of boiled crawfish and crabs, of bread pudding. I want a god who gave us noses and lips and tongues for a reason; I want my Lamb of God rare and juicy, thick with spice, its heavy scent rising to bless my hungry face.

Looking for Light

The huge trunks of the cypress trees, which stand four or five
feet asunder shot up to a height of fifty feet, entirely free from
branches, which then, however, spread out at right angles to
the stem, making the trees appear like gigantic umbrellas, and
covering the whole morass with an impenetrable roof,
through which not even a sunbeam could find passage.
—anonymous, the Atchafalaya Basin, 1842

Spanish moss hangs in disheveled, inverted triangles, lining the
top of the photograph and tapering off to crooked fingers that
point down to the waters below. Cypress knees dominate the bottom of
the photograph, rising out of the swamp like the incisors of some huge
beast. Both the moss and the knees appear black because the exposure
was set to capture the color of sun and sky beyond them. Seen through
what appears to be the open mouth of the swamp, the sun rises huge and
swollen, the color of a candle's flame. The sky is so red it almost hurts to

look at it, and though the landscape is lushly beautiful, one has the impression of something horribly wrong.

The photograph on the opposite page is taken from the same perspective, only farther back, so you can actually see the cypress trees on which the moss hangs. It is the moon that is rising in this photograph, not the sun. This sky is deep blue, and the moon hangs, a yellow disk in the sky, framed by the branches of a cypress tree. Again, the photographer has set the exposure to capture what is lit, this time by the moon, and so the cypress knees, the trees, and moss look like black cutouts pasted onto the photograph. Greg Guirard, the photographer, does not use filters nor does he manipulate his photographs, so I know the sky in the first photograph was really that red and, in the second, really that blue.

The challenge—some would say curse—of swamp photography is light. Swamps are often dark and difficult to photograph because the canopy of trees blocks the sun; when the sun does manage to shine through, its light is usually harsh. If the photographer sets the exposure for the sunlit areas, the unlit areas appear black on the film. Greg Guirard turns this potential negative to his advantage in these photographs where the shapes of trees, tree stumps, and moss haunt the photographs like depthless black ghosts.

Both of these photographs were taken at Lake Fausse Pointe in the Atchafalaya Basin (the name comes from the Choctaw *hachafalaia*, which means "Long River"). They appear in *Atchafalaya Autumn*, Greg Guirard's third book of photographs. Guirard is one of the most respected and locally beloved photographers of the Atchafalaya Basin of south-central Louisiana, an area threaded with rivers, bayous, backwater lakes, canals, levees, swamplands, woodlands, and agricultural lands. At 833,000 acres, the Atchafalaya is the largest southern swamp and represents the nation's largest swamp wilderness. The fish and wildlife populations, even with the current environmental problems from which the Atchafalaya is suffering, are staggering. More than three hundred species of birds can be found here, thousands of wintering ducks, and the largest wintering population of woodcock in North America. More than thirty thousand egrets, ibises, and herons nest in the Basin. American alligator thrive here, as do hundreds of species of fish, crawfish, crabs, and shrimp. Some reports put the Atchafalaya's fecundity at three and one-half times that of the Everglades.

There are other well-known photographers of this swamp, most notably C. C. Lockwood, whose book and film on the Atchafalaya garnered many awards. Lockwood is a photographer of the National Geographic type, however, and his photographs, while technically proficient, lack the introspective intensity of Guirard's work. The difference between Lockwood and Guirard is the difference between the objective but sometimes sterile prose necessary for an encyclopedia article and the hauntingly subjective lyricism of a poem.

The book I'm holding is a gift from Greg Guirard. We were introduced by an editor who believed Greg's photographs would complement an essay of mine the editor had offered to publish. I had long admired Greg's work, and knew two of his other books, *Seasons of Light in the Atchafalaya Basin* and *Cajun Families of the Atchafalaya.* I was pleased to have his brooding photographs appear with the essay. His photographs of the Atchafalaya are the ones that, for me, most clearly capture the spirit of that fertile and troubled place.

Until the beginning of this century the Atchafalaya Basin was filled with giant cypress trees, some more than one thousand years old. By the 1930s, though, landowners had logged every tree of marketable size. Today, only the huge stumps of those trees remain, jutting their immense cut bodies out of the water as a reminder of what was once and what may never be again. Bald cypress is one of few tree species (water tupelo is another) that can withstand and even thrive in standing water. Cypress wood is so long-lasting it's called the "wood eternal" because of its resistance to decay, which is why people still build houses and boats out of it. Buttresses and the knees that the root systems develop help the trees stand firm in the muck and water and get oxygen to the roots. But cypress seedlings need a dry period after they sprout to grow tall enough so that they won't be drowned by the waters during the annual spring floods. Due mostly to the construction of nearly impenetrable levees, the Basin no longer has dry periods that would allow a young cypress to reach a height such that it could survive in the water. The trees that have been cut down cannot be replaced, so the era of giant trees in the swamp is most assuredly gone. Barring an act of God, there will never again exist, in this place, a bald-cypress forest of such richness and age, a forest of such large trees. The national champion cypress tree, located in the Cat Island Swamp just north of St. Francisville, boasts a girth of almost fifty-four feet; a number of stumps in the Atchafalaya are at least that big. As a species of tree, only sequoia and coastal redwoods are larger.

All that's left in the Basin now are trees that were too young to be cut down during the era of unrestricted logging and the stumps of the great trees that rise as high as twelve feet from the surface of the water. This is why Greg calls the Basin the Land of Dead Giants. In his photograph "Sunrise with Cypress Stumps and Trees Near Bayou Benoit" the stumps appear as enormous dark clots. The slender cypress trees in the background, not many over fifty years old, seem fragile in comparison. The sun is rising, hopeful, in the sky behind the trees, but it seems almost transparent against the giant stumps. The water is a strange pink-orange hue. This photograph is as much about loss, keenly felt and expressed, as it is about the recording of beauty, and this is perhaps why I am drawn to it. Whereas other photographers might try to avoid the stumps—it is unusual to see a stump in Lockwood's published swamp photographs, for example—Greg cannot see the swamp without them. When I look at his photographs I am reminded of a line from Galway Kinnell's poem "When One Has Lived a Long Time Alone." The speaker of the poem lives "among regrets so immense the past occupies nearly all the room there is in consciousness."

For the past few months Greg and I have been exchanging work, letters, and phone calls. As I flip through his *Atchafalaya Autumn,* I realize that, aside from his photographs, I don't know much about him. He is a native son, this much I know; he was born and has lived his entire life alongside the west-Atchafalaya levee between Catahoula and Henderson, just minutes from the swamp. I know that he worked as an English instructor for almost ten years at the University of Southwestern Louisiana (now called the University of Louisiana at Lafayette), where I

Looking for Light

also taught for a few years, much later. I know that he has been a farmer, a cattleman, a carpenter and furniture maker, a crew-boat driver, a craw-fisherman, and a technical adviser for film producers. But none of this information tells me much about how he came to feel the loss of these trees so sharply. In the journal writings that accompany his photographs he writes that he finds himself mourning the passing of the giant trees of the Atchafalaya as though they had been relatives.

His photographs remind me of some things I do not want to be reminded of, yet I'm still drawn to them. I lived for three years near the Atchafalaya when I taught at the university in Lafayette. Those years, which might have been wonderful living so close to the Basin, fishing the swamp not far from the area Greg photographs, working in the heart of Cajun country, eating the food I loved, should have been wonderful. Certainly, there was happiness, but like the stumps that dominate so many of Greg's photographs, what went wrong is what dominates my memory. During those years I lived with an intelligent but troubled man who also loved the swamp, and with whom I often fished the Atchafalaya. The relationship, which had always been difficult, ended badly, with my having an abortion and determining to leave Louisiana. I left, heavy with a grief I thought would never dissipate, unable to look at the swamp without thinking of this man and the child we conceived but would not have. I had not returned to the Atchafalaya for seven years.

Greg's voice on the phone is soft, tinged with a Cajun accent. "Those urban swamps you talk about in your essay are not my swamp," he says, and I understand why he speaks of the swamp as his. If there is a landscape that has shaped Cajun culture, if there is a landscape that can be said to belong to a culture, to be so much a part of it that it does seem like a relative, it is this one, the landscape of the swamp. Although Greg and I are both Cajun, my Cajun grandparents left the swamp and moved to the urban center of New Orleans soon after my father was born. Greg's family stayed, and I would guess that he can trace his family's life on the Basin back a hundred years or more.

When the people we now call Cajuns left Nova Scotia in 1755 in a violent expulsion known as "Le Grand Derangement," many of them came to establish roots on the fertile banks of the Atchafalaya. They built a life here, learning to fish and hunt what lived in and around the Basin. They used cypress wood to build homes, pirogues, and houseboats, and they used the abundant Spanish moss to stuff mattresses and pillows. The cuisine we know as Cajun developed from their life around this swamp and the fish and wildlife that thrived here. One-pot meals, heavily spiced, such as the various forms of sauce picante, made with venison or rabbit; black-rouxed gumbos; and jambalayas made with crawfish, duck, and squirrel, for example, were easy to cook on the small camp stoves in houseboats and the many camps that still line the edges of the Basin.

Until recently, the Basin was relatively difficult to reach. Isolated and hard to make your way through unless you really know what you're doing, it was a great hiding place for Cajun conscript evaders during the Civil War. Swamp dwellers were virtually shut off from the rest of society until the 1920s when oil and gas were discovered in the Basin. Later, in 1973 when an eighteen-mile elevated section of Interstate 10 was completed, Cajuns were finally and irrevocably linked with the rest of the world.

Today the swamp itself is almost totally unpopulated, except for its edges. It is best understood as a tiny wilderness between the sprawling tentacles of the urban centers of Baton Rouge to the east and Lafayette to the west. William Darby wrote of the Atchafalaya in 1815 that it was a place of "awful lonesomeness," a place where "the imagination floats back towards the birth of nature, when a new creation started."

I have come to love Greg's voice, which is soft and slow and rich, like the swamp he has lived near all his life. I have also come to love his handwriting, large and sprawling, like the swamp before we built so many levees. He doesn't use computers because he doesn't get along too well with technology, he says. He writes handwritten letters and also sends me clippings from the local newspaper about the Atchafalaya. He tells me how his marriage of more than twenty years dissolved ten years ago, and writes about his new marriage to blues singer and sociologist Kathy Martin, who is from New Orleans. I'm not surprised he found himself drawn to a blues singer since I understand his photographs as I understand the blues: intense, exuberant, and moody songs of loss and light.

His photographs of the swamp suggest that he is someone who understands the kind of grief I took with me when I left Louisiana. I decide I want to see the swamp through his eyes. I decide it's time to go home, and it's time to meet Greg in person.

I make the visit a few months later, in October, a great time for seeing the swamp. I fly into New Orleans, pay a quick visit to my mother, then head out west over Interstate 10 toward Catahoula, where Greg lives. The drive takes about two hours. Just outside of Baton Rouge my car enters the elevated section of I-10 that spans the swamp, and I roll down the window and let the damp thick air into my lungs. There's water underneath me, water as far as I can see to either side, water behind, and water in front. The water, still and quiet, is dotted with small cypress trees, larger stumps, more trees, more stumps. From the highway I can see the occasional heron or egret rise up from the waters and fly slowly over them. I'm extremely conscious of how close the road is to the swamp, of how low to the ground I am. It's a feeling I get only in Louisiana, and it's a physical reminder that I'm home.

I get off the highway at Butte la Rose, just before the Henderson exit, which is the exit Ted, my former boyfriend, and I used to take when we fished the swamp. It is impossible to separate our understanding of a landscape from our memories of what we have done in that landscape, so of course my thoughts turn to Ted. He loved fishing with a passion I've rarely seen (and fishermen are a pretty passionate bunch), but he liked to fish without a boat or heavy equipment. It was a point of pride with him to catch fish in the most primitive way possible. We would fish off the levee near Henderson, mostly for small bass. It was Ted who taught me to love fishing, and it was in this swamp, with him, that I caught my first serious fish. Ted was uncompromising not only about how he wanted to fish. He played tennis, for example, with a small, old wood racket even though it put him at a distinct disadvantage. He refused to buy new clothes or new books, preferring to frequent the Salvation Army for his purchases. He was disdainful of bourgeois consumer culture, and I admired him for his principles, though eventually I came to understand that a man of unwavering principles is not an easy man to live with. As I drive along I-10 I think about how I loved fishing with him, how it was a time when we were deeply and quietly together, working to get food, usually for our dinner that night. How swollen we were with each other then, our hearts like two small fat fish on a stringer. Sometimes I think love is like that, a fish on a stringer, swimming in tight circles of meaning, caught at the mouth by the beloved.

I remember watching him clean the fish on the grass of the levee; he'd seem so hard and detached, scaling and gutting the fish alive, holding them firm against movement as he might hold my hand or head to kiss me. He would cut the heads off the fish last, and I remember the horrific image of them lying bodiless, hopeless, gills still opening and closing. Sometimes I can feel that cruelty in me, too, deep in hands and wrists, that my hands are as much capable of killing as they are of loving.

I look out of my open window at the swamp surrounding me and think that this is the way Ted surrounded me, this is how I allowed him to surround me, slow and thick and sure; all I could see was him and his world, his way of seeing the world, which soon became my world. I look at my own arms, gripping the steering wheel, keeping me on the road, and I remember his arms and hands, how they would be marked with blood and scales, black and gray fish guts and mess, how he would smell raw and strong like the fish, how I used to want to take him like that. He would open his hands, full of fish death, and it would seem we were all one, he and I and the fish. Once, turning to me with his hands smelly with fish, he said, "Cleaning a fish is like really making love with a woman, not just sticking it in." That day he had killed all we had caught and could have killed more, could have killed even what he loved; he could always do what needed to be done, face-to-face, mouth-to-mouth, hand-to-fist, the gesture of cutting the same as touching.

Looking for Light

Greg and I are driving in his old truck just before dawn to a place near Bayou Benoit where we'll put his boat in. He is a handsome man with a gray mop of hair and full beard. He's dressed in a long-sleeved blue cotton shirt stained with white paint, jeans, and sneakers. He has a worried, almost stunned look on his face, which I soon learn is a look he almost always wears. During the two days I spend with him I will rarely see him smile. He's not a talkative man, and I have to ask many questions to get him to say much at all. When he does talk, he hardly opens his mouth, as if he's a ventriloquist who doesn't want anyone to see his lips moving. I like him immediately. He's the kind of man you recognize right away as a good man in the most powerful sense of the word.

He's brought three cameras along, a Pentax 6 x 7 cm, a Fuji 6 x 9, and a 35-mm Minolta. The boat in which we'll be traversing the Atchafalaya is a sixteen-foot welded aluminum boat. He tells me that this was the boat used in *Shy People,* a film for which he was a consultant. He and his son were also both consultants for *The Apostle,* and he chats with me a while, as he launches the boat, about what it was like working with Robert Duvall. His voice, quiet and smooth, matches the swamp, and I think that if the swamp could speak it would have Greg's voice.

At sixty-three he's a tall bear of a man, still muscular from pulling logs out of the swamp, which is something he has done for years. During the days of unrestrained logging, cypress logs were floated from the swamp to sawmills. If the wood had not been cured by girdling the tree and letting it stand, the logs were likely to sink.

"Those loggers were really careless," Greg says, "because there's lots of beautiful wood at the bottom of the swamp.

"The logs, it's crazy, but they remain in a perfect state of preservation down there. Cypress wood is very dense and oily. It keeps termites out. When you drag those logs out, they're full of water and minerals. They make beautiful tables." His friend Roy Blanchard built a house out of cypress logs he pulled from the swamp, and Greg built a guest house out of salvaged logs, too.

It's dark out, and I'm grateful for the coffee and doughnuts we have that Greg asked me to pick up at Ti Sue's Bakery on my way in. "In 1973," he continues, "I quit my teaching job at USL. I made more money pulling logs from the swamp, picking up driftwood, and taking photographs than I had teaching.

"A lot of people do it," he says as we pull away from the boat launch, "but I'm the only one who will go into the mud to pull a log out."

The air is crisp but not too cold, the water the color of a nut-brown roux. On either side of us are stumps of the giant cypress trees, rising above the surface of the water. Younger trees surround them, and, rarely, a huge, thick-breasted tree. A good rule of thumb for judging the age of a cypress tree is that every foot of girth equals a hundred years. I see one tree that I guess to be at least five hundred years old. I wonder aloud why it hasn't been cut down.

"Hollow," Greg says. "Any time you see a tree that old, it hasn't been cut down because it's hollow, and it wasn't worth it—no lumber."

"What makes them hollow?"

"Fungus." Greg stops the boat and gets out his grandfather's level, which he uses to make sure the landscape is even when he shoots. He aims one of his cameras toward the big tree. "Fungus weakens the inside of the cypress, hollows it out, makes what they call 'pecky' cypress, with lacelike holes all through it."

The sun, which was just rising as we launched the boat, is soon fully in the sky. As we move along in the boat Greg begins to provide a running commentary on the quality of the light, a commentary that will not end until we leave the swamp and he puts his cameras up. It's either too bright or not bright enough or the sun's in the wrong place for a shot he really wants.

"The sun's not usually so bright," he complains. He is looking for "backlit Spanish moss," which means the sun has to be in just the right position in relation to the moss and where we are. He maneuvers the boat near a group of trees covered with Spanish moss.

"Let's get that tree between us and the light," he says, pointing to a large tree just to the right of us. He moves the boat to where the light is behind the tree and begins a series of shots from slightly different angles.

A fine level of mist covers the surface of the water. Fish jump out of the water on either side of the boat, and every now and then we pass a small fishing boat. We see egrets, blue herons, and tree swallows, guys crabbing.

After taking a roll or two of film in a few different places, he says, "Let's go somewhere else. I'll show you where there's still a few really big trees."

After we load the boat onto the trailer, we drive south in his truck for ten or fifteen minutes, mostly in silence, eating the apple crisps I bought from the bakery. We launch the boat at Lake Fausse Pointe, where Greg has shot lots of photographs for his books. This is also where his houseboat is located. He points out a bit of floating Styrofoam on the water. "See that?" he says. "I put that there. It's tied to a cypress log I'm going to come back and get."

As he navigates the boat in and out of stumps and trees, he talks to me about "The Bear," by William Faulkner, a story he rereads every year. What he doesn't say, but what I come to understand, as he talks, is that he is like the boy in Faulkner's story who desires "big woods, bigger and older than any recorded document." In the "shaggy tremendous shape" of Faulkner's bear with its one trap-ruined foot, Greg must see the shape of the wild but wounded swamp. He understands, like the boy, that men fear the unaxed woods, the bear's home, because it is wild. This is why they have to cut it down and parcel it out. As the boy is marked by the wilderness in Faulkner's story, so is Greg marked by the Atchafalaya and the ways in which men have marked it.

Greg first takes me to see his houseboat, a weathered, small flat-bottomed boat, pale blue in color. It looks like a one-room house someone has set on a raftlike structure. There's a front and back porch. It's tied up under a grove of large cypress trees that offers shade and cover. He lived on this boat while working on *Atchafalaya Autumn*.

"I stayed three to four days a week on the houseboat for several years, writing and photographing that book," he says as he helps me onto it. The boat has the feeling of not being lived in for quite a while, and Greg rumbles through, muttering something about rats and bedding.

The houseboat rocks gently in the breeze. Everything you'd need to live is here, a Coleman stove, a toilet, a bunk bed and sofa.

"Kathy and I come out here crawfishin' sometimes. She likes that." Greg has brought a video camera with him so that Kathy, who couldn't be with us for this trip, can see what he's seeing. We walk out onto the little porch in the back. He gets the video camera out now and pans the area.

"I caught a thirty-pound catfish from back here with Spam Lite," he says, while panning, almost smiling. "That's my secret for catching catfish."

He turns around for a few minutes and goes inside to check that everything is in order in the houseboat. He doesn't lock it, and sometimes people will help themselves to it as shelter. I stay outside looking at the thick chocolate-colored water, and the cypress trees with their witchy female shapes. I close my eyes. An exquisite feeling of being lost, of being so far away from anyone who might want to find you. I breathe in the smell of the swamp, the strange beauty of the trees. This is what wildness smells like for me.

A small splash in the water. I open my eyes and look down. Dark shapes circle the thick trunk of the tree closest to the houseboat. Maybe it's catfish. The last time I fished, in a small lake in Illinois, I caught a catfish. I was trying to fish Ted out of my system, trying to do this thing we always did together without him. I can remember that fish as if I had just caught it, stunned but young and strong, twisting for the life it would still have. It was thick with white meat and beautiful with its blue back and silver belly. The deeply forked tail, the fins that would stab me if I was careless. I remember stopping for a moment, holding the fish and thinking of Ted, caught and twisting for his damaged, intelligent, hopeless way of life, a twisting I can feel in my stomach sometimes like the prolonged thrashing of a creature that cannot speak its anguish into air. As I let the fish struggle its way off the hook back into the water I remember feeling my own lips slashed, heart marked, chest heaving for any kind of air. I wondered if Ted would have found beautiful the gymnastics I was performing to free my mouth of him.

I close my eyes again to blink away tears, and look out beyond the big tree with its circling fish. The sun is still low in the sky behind it, backlighting the Spanish moss draped on its topmost branches. Haloed by the sun, the moss looks silver and holy. I understand why Greg searches so for backlit Spanish moss. I blink again, and instead of moss I see Ted's wiry gray hair backlit by lamplight, a lamp in the waiting room of the Baton Rouge abortion clinic. He sits next to me in the room, irritated, detached, writing a letter to a friend. He's in shorts. It's October, and it's warm outside, even for the South, but there's something unnatural about it, as unnatural as I feel, body blossoming, breasts hardening, all bustle inside making the new person, and I with my plans sitting here counting out the last minutes.

Later, in an inner room the anguish of what I am doing couples with the drugs they've given me for pain, and I hallucinate: I'm somewhere else, away from the clinic, away from Ted's letter writing. I'm on the Atchafalaya the day of the new moon, I'm painted with the blood of my mother, there are drums and the wailing of children. I lie in the shallow water on top of roots and a bed of decaying leaves, and open my legs to a shadow—my own—black and metal glistening. The thing is done, and I lie in blood and water until the sun turns the sky red. Spanish moss hangs above me, in what looks like knotted threads of silver, just out of reach.

"Ready?" Greg asks, sticking his head out onto the porch. "Let's go see those trees."

We leave one boat for another, and as we pull away, I have the feeling of leaving something in the houseboat, some mean thing that needed to be left somewhere, this houseboat as good a place as any. In Greg's silence, which I'm grateful for at the moment, I wonder if there's something about a wounded landscape that draws out one's own wounds. It's not for nothing that nature writing is the genre of writing that is so deeply connected to reflection. There is something about being alone in a relatively wild place that nourishes reflection, asks for it, almost as if it were part of some call-and-response singing, the world around you the call, what you write in the journal the response.

Greg navigates slowly away from the houseboat and toward a grove of trees lined up in such a way that they form a passageway through this part of the swamp. He has that stunned, determined look on his face. I can imagine him sitting outside on the porch, or inside, with a kerosene lamp, writing and thinking. The journal he kept while on the houseboat gives a good sense of his day-to-day life on the swamp, but is also full of questions of our relationship to the wild. His is partly a journal about the ways we have wounded the world, and partly a celebration of the beauty of that world. The journal is also filled with information and recipes for meals he's fixed or what some swamper in another houseboat has shared with him. Despite the limitations of the houseboat, which of course has no oven, he sometimes cooked elaborate meals. On December 2, 1992, he writes that he had chicken and sausage gumbo and baked sweet potatoes. The week before it's squirrel and rabbit sauce picante, cooked over an open fire on the bayou bank. At Lake Fausse Pointe, January 4, 1994, he spends the evening shooting the sunset from behind big cypress trees. After the light is gone he writes that he went to the houseboat and fixed crawfish étouffée cornbread, and a salad of cabbage, carrots, apples, raisins, and pineapples. On January 15, 1994, he notes that he had a lemon Moonpie to celebrate having seen and photographed a gorgeous Virginia white-tailed buck swimming across the Atchafalaya River. And the day after Christmas he writes, "After sunset I travel the few hundred yards to the houseboat and begin to fix supper: cous-cous with sauce picante of rabbit, venison and pork sausage, biscuits with chicken and turkey jambalaya cooked inside, shrimp glacé, fried black beans and coffee."

The journal is also sprinkled with lamentations of shots he missed because he couldn't find the light he needed. At Lake Fausse Pointe, he writes: "Missed it again! At 5 A.M. the moon had set, the sky was perfectly clear, there were thousands of bright stars, and winds were calm. By 5:30 there was not one star visible; there was a slight breeze, no fog and a thickly clouded sky."

We are approaching a thick grove of big cypress trees, all of them spared by their hollow cores. I recognize the place immediately. Many of the photographs from *Atchafalaya Autumn* were taken here. Greg slows the boat down and steers us toward the trees, navigating so that we enter the heart of the grove and begin making our way through a passageway lined with large cypress on either side. He cuts the motor and we drift alongside the trees. A couple of them are astonishingly huge, certainly the largest cypress I've ever seen here or anywhere else. One of these giants that we float by, close enough to touch, has a trunk that seems as large as the body of a whale. As we pass by, it blocks the light of the sun for about ten seconds. I would guess that its trunk is fifteen to sixteen feet wide at the water level. I look up. Spanish moss glitters high in the tree's top branches, silver and beckoning, thick and tangled, curling down the bodies of the thick trees, moving against them in the breeze almost, it seems, lovingly.

"Look," Greg says, pointing toward the sky. A spider web, five feet wide, lit with sun and still wet with dew, is strung across from one tree's branches to another's, just above us, forming a patterned window to the sky. The strands are thick enough to be threads of Spanish moss.

I reach out to touch the bark of some of the older trees as we make our slow way through them. It's not a large area of the swamp, but it's large enough, and there are enough trees, hollow though they may be, for one to get a small sense of what this place might have been like before so many of the giant cypress were cut down. Even the cypress knees are different here, not just the fairly straightforward, knobby triangular shapes I'm used to seeing, but countless gnarled fingers of roots clustered together in what look like woody hands.

Greg stops the boat and begins to take a series of photographs of the trees that form the passageway down which we are traveling. I take a few with my Instamatic, then stop, not wanting anything, not even a camera, to come between my eyes and the trees. We stay here for almost an hour, moving between the trees so the light changes slightly and Greg can make different shots. He points out a small wooden platform in the water near us. It is almost invisible in the water.

"I built that," he says, "because I couldn't get a good shot of what I wanted from the boat." We angle around behind the platform, and when I look from behind I can see that this is where he shot the photograph I lingered over back home with the cypress knees and Spanish moss. From the level of the platform you can site the cypress knees at the bottom and the Spanish moss on top, and appear to be shooting from the mouth of the swamp.

"Phew, do you smell that?" A rotten smell, like decaying flesh or putrid garbage, rises up from a dark area in the water. "We've got some problems with the water hyacinths that root into the mud and then rot. Hydrilla, too. They wind up depleting the oxygen in the water."

The condition he's referring to is called hypoxia or "black water" because the water is dark in color where it occurs. The water hyacinth, an exotic that has become the predominant floating plant in the swamp, covers thousands of acres of the Basin in summer, and is a major player in hypoxia. Too many canals and bayous that distribute water out of the main channel of the Basin have been closed, resulting in stagnation; the water is unable to rid itself of dying plants and other organic material without circulation. These hypoxic areas are dangerous to fish and other aquatic organisms that cannot survive without sufficient oxygen in the water.

A flock of about thirty white pelicans flies above us, and we sit and watch for a few minutes. Greg talks about organizing tours of the swamp for the Delta Queen Steamboat Co. He tells me, between shots, that they saw seventeen bald eagles on one trip. "I found a dead pelican on a fisherman's line once," he says, "and measured it. Nine-foot wing span." He shoots some more. "My best experience on the swamp was the time I was in the midst of thousands of cormorants and pelicans—they were feeding and ignoring me while I was trying to photograph them. I loved how they were ignoring me."

"How about if we head home? I'm ready for some gumbo." I nod, and he starts up the boat. About halfway back to the launch we stop to watch another flock of pelicans. When Greg tries to start the boat up the engine coughs and won't turn over. The sun is high in the sky; it's early afternoon, and it's hot. Greg works on the engine while talking to me about the crawfish industry, one of his favorite subjects. I pull off my sweatshirt and lie back, exposing my face to the sun, enjoying the warmth.

"You know," Greg says, "thousands of women peel crawfish for a living here. Black, white, and Vietnamese. You can make a pretty good living at it when there are crawfish to peel. Men do it, too, though not as many. One man I know peels thirteen pounds an hour, and his wife peels eight. At $1 a pound that's around $20 an hour. There's a crawfish plant in Catahoula, it's a place to peel, but also to gossip." About thirty million pounds of red swamp and white river crawfish are taken yearly from the swamp, and even if only half of them get peeled, that's a lot of crawfish to process.

He squints at the engine and wipes his brow. "When there's no craw-fish in the Basin, like now, because there's not been enough rain up north, then they're out of work, too. Part of the year they can do crabs, but almost all the crawfish this year, because of the drought, came from ponds. Not much snowfall and rainfall in the Midwest this year, and that affects us." He squints again at the guts of the engine, twists a couple of screws, and tries to start it. Nothing. I think about the beginning of the lawn-cutting season back in Iowa and trying to start the lawn mower.

He bends over and fiddles some more with the engine. "The boat repair people are out of work, too," he murmurs into the engine. "So the fact that there's no crawfish affects more people than you'd think. But it's dying out. Kathy interviewed twenty crawfishing families, and only two of the kids want to be crawfishermen. There's not enough water to make it worthwhile. Last year the water was ten feet above sea level; it's usually eighteen feet. Can't catfish for a living, either. People used to make a living with crawfish and catfish in the Basin, but it's gone now. Catfish farms have the whole market these days."

He pulls a spark plug out of the engine, examines it, and wipes it off with a rag. "People want catfish the same size. So they got these ponds now, too. Crawfish, too—the ones out of the commercial ponds are more predictable. Sixty percent of the crawfish now come from ponds, 40 percent from the Basin. Used to be it all came from the Basin. Even the alligator hunters are affected. They used to get $54 a foot, so that for a ten-foot alligator you would get $540. Now they get $23 a foot." He's talking faster and almost nonstop now that he's talking about others.

"There," he says, and the motor comes alive.

Twenty minutes later we've loaded the boat up and are driving the levee road to his house. Greg has lived in it since he was two years old, with only brief periods of time away. The house was his parents', but the land belonged to his grandfather, Wade O. Martin Sr., who was an elected official for the parish and state, and who, it turns out, owned a sawmill on this property, just a hundred yards from the house. Through selling lumber for the mill he paid for the thirteen hundred acres of woodland he eventually passed on to his children and grandchildren. He was an experienced hunter and woodsman, and had a degree in agriculture, Greg says, and he was the most important man in his life. "He taught me everything I know about the land," he says. When I push him to tell me more, though, he seems reluctant to talk.

"Read my story 'The Land of Dead Giants,' he says. "It's all there. I'll give you a copy before you leave."

About nine hundred acres of the original thirteen hundred are left in Greg's family. His father is dead and his mother is in a nursing home at the time of my visit. What's left of the land now belongs to their children, and Greg has remained the primary custodian for it. The land, which was once farmland and cattle pasture, is now planted in trees—cypress, red oak, live oak, poplar, and fifteen other species. The trees that surround his house look very much like second-growth forest. It is hard to imagine it as farmland or cattle pasture.

"I planted all the trees," Greg mumbles, as he rummages about getting some food for his cats.

"Forty thousand of them," he adds, in a low voice.

"Forty thousand?" Stunned, I wonder out loud how long it would take to plant forty thousand trees.

"I plant about two thousand a year, every year, and have been for about twenty years." He's climbing a ladder to his roof to put some cat food up there for his cats. He looks down at me. "It's so the other animals don't get it." He climbs back down as his cats scamper up the ladder to the roof. His home, which used to be his grandfather's camp, is a moderate-size wooden house with a tin roof. It and the trees nearby are covered with Spanish moss. Even the TV antenna has Spanish moss on it. There is no lawn to speak of, but in addition to the trees, surrounding the house are a few sheds in various stages of disrepair, ladders, driftwood, water barrels, and a tractor. His nearest neighbor, Errol Verret, who used to be the accordion player for the Cajun music group Beausoleil, lives a mile away.

Inside, the house is simple but functional. There's a kitchen and dining area, a workroom with cypress tables he's making out of the recovered logs, a bedroom and back room with large windows looking out over the land, as well as two other rooms. His mother's house is attached to the main house via a screened-in back porch. A large tree grows in the porch through a hole in the floor and one in the roof. In his mother's quarters are beautiful pieces of antique furniture, china cabinets with lovely china in them, but the ceiling is falling in, and the smell of mold and dust is everywhere. It's clear this house hasn't been lived in for a long time. It is also clear that Greg is loath to let nature completely reclaim it, though its claws are deep into its sagging roof. The house hangs onto his like a peeling scab to a wound. I wonder about his relationship to his mother, but decide not to pry.

Before I leave Louisiana Greg will have taken me on a walking tour of his property. I will have seen almost all of the forty thousand trees he has planted, the forest that now surrounds him. I will have seen the low area he sometimes floods and turns into a crawfish pond. He will have introduced me to his longtime neighbor and friend Roy Blanchard, a man, not unlike many Cajuns, who once made his living crawfishing but now works as a maintenance man at the Holiday Inn on I-10. Before I leave I will also have spent time with two of his sons and their families. His sons are handsome and successful men who are cautiously affectionate with Greg, the way my son is with me. I will also have met Kathy, his talented and exuberant wife, and listened to some excerpts from her new CD, which will be out soon. If Greg, slow moving and reticent, is the epitome of the swamp, Kathy, intensely convivial and talkative, is the epitome of its urban sister, New Orleans, who has given up the urban life to live here with Greg.

I will have seen what he and Kathy call the Druid Tree, actually two trees—a red oak and a sugar berry—about four hundred years old, that have grown together to make one huge trunk that is partially hollow at the core. A tear-shaped opening, as big as a human, allows two people to enter the tree and stand together comfortably inside it. Greg and Kathy exchanged wedding vows inside this tree. Before I leave I will have walked inside the Druid Tree and felt the inner bark of it, been comforted by the close, earthy smell of it, the darkness inside so like a blanket or womb. I will have come to appreciate how appropriate it is for a man who loves trees as much as Greg does to have begun a new life in a shelter created by two trees so inextricably linked, to have pledged himself with his new wife having only these trees as witnesses. Before I leave I will have seen this land and these waters through Greg's eyes, and before I leave I will feel a new intimacy with this place that shaped my ancestors, these waters that harbor a knowledge of their deep past and my own recent past.

I return to Iowa, and a week later Greg calls to tell me his mother has died. As if to explain his composure, he tells me she was a domineering woman, that their relationship was not a good one. I wonder what will happen to her house, if he'll sever it from his, or empty it of her furniture and make it his own.

A few weeks later I receive a package from Kathy. Her new CD, *Catahoula,* is out, and she's sent me a copy. There's a photo of her on the cover. She's sitting in Greg's boat, smiling broadly, with the swamp in the background. She's holding their dog, a Catahoula cur, and some lotus flowers. The CD is called *Catahoula* because it's a mix, Kathy explains, of several kinds of music: blues, Cajun, folk, pop. Greg took the photo for the cover, and his image appears in the liner notes next to a song they wrote together, "Gumbo Man." Greg is actually smiling. Maybe he was listening to this song when the picture was taken, because there's no way one could listen to this song and not smile. It's got a Cajun–New Orleans feel to it, with Errol Verret, their neighbor, playing accordion. *I got a Cajun man,* Kathy belts out, *he likes to cook it up for me. He serves it up spicy, lord he serves it up hot, he'll use Tabasco by the cupful not the drop—.* The song is filled with slyly sexual references: his roux is "so creamy" it's almost too good to eat, and "when I get into his gumbo I can't stop, it fills me up so full, lord, I'm gonna pop."

Not long after I return to Iowa I read Greg's book *The Land of Dead Giants,* which is set in the Basin. It is the story of a boy's love for his grandfather, "Vieux Pop," who teaches him about the Basin, and how to hunt and fish and be responsible in the woods. Not long into the story the boy discovers that his grandfather was part of the crew of loggers responsible for cutting down the trees in the Basin. In a fit of crazed grief, the boy runs away from home, mindlessly kills a swamp rabbit, and throws it away. The rest of the story focuses on the boy trying to come to terms with the confusing deeds of a man he loves more than anything in the world. When Vieux Pop finds the boy hiding out in the swamp, he asks, "Do you pity the deer, Ti Frere, and the enchanted forest that has been converted into cutover swampland? Then pity me also. . . . I am a man who destroyed, with my own hands, the greatest and most beautiful thing I have ever seen with my own eyes."

The boy says, at the end, in a voice it is hard to distinguish from Greg's, "If I close my eyes I can see Vieux Pop building a pirogue, and tracking a deer through the dry November woods. I can see him stirring gumbo at the big woodstove, playing cards and making music with his friends. Every detail is clear and sharp, like the images in an old black and white photograph. And I'm still sitting there on the woodbox, half-asleep, dreaming of the giant trees that will never be again."

The story is clearly autobiographical, and helps me to understand how difficult it must be for Greg to have a beloved grandfather—the one who taught him to love the land and how to live on it—be responsible for cutting down so many of the giant cypress trees he also loves so much. I understand why he takes the loss of the giant trees so personally, why he feels such a responsibility to record their loss, and why it was so important for him to plant forty thousand trees. I understand why it's so important that he find some way to make use of the wastes of the lumber industry, to make art out of what was left behind.

In the end, *The Land of the Dead Giants,* like Greg's photographs, and maybe like Greg's life, is about remembering and forgiving. You find a way to live, despite whatever losses you—and the world—might have sustained. You forgive the ones, even if they are your relatives, even if they are you, who are responsible for those losses. You plant trees, you cook great meals, you marry a singer, you try to see, clearly, the world that surrounds you. You look for the quality of light that most illuminates those twins, beauty and loss.

And then you capture them.

The Sound of Planes

Once again I'm flying home to visit my mother. I have now spent almost half of my life living away from Louisiana, and have come to understand planes as umbilical cords of sorts; they provide the only reasonable way to visit this place that still has such an unholy pull on me. On a clear day like today, as the plane makes its final descent to New Orleans International Airport you can see the rough waters of Lake Pontchartrain, its body dominating the landscape like an insatiable, fat relative at a dinner table, and lower down, as if an afterthought, the Mississippi River, winding its way through the southern half of the area. You can see the gray scar of Williams Boulevard, running from body of water to body of water, and sometimes I think I can see my mother's small house on Williams with her backyard that rises like a jungle out of the swamp of businesses that have been taking over all the private residences there for the past ten years.

On maps, Jefferson Parish looks like a wide, childish *C* scrawled beneath the swollen body of Lake Pontchartrain to the north, reaching down past the Mississippi River and curving around in a sort of sloppy smile for about sixty more miles until it disappears into the Gulf of Mexico. Nestled in the arms of Orleans Parish, where one finds New Orleans, the antique jewel of the state, Jefferson Parish has no such jewel, but is, rather, home to Kenner, a city of just over seventy thousand where I spent most of my childhood.

The area we now call Kenner appears on early maps as "Cannes Brûlée" (Burnt Canes), and was so named because early French explorers noticed natives in the area burning cane to drive out game. The first plantations were built here in 1720, but by 1820 French, Italian, and German families had taken over the land, which became known as "Green Gold" fields. The families purchased truck patches and grew hundreds of different kinds of vegetables, including the incomparably juicy and sweet Louisiana Creole tomato. Kenner dominated vegetable markets until the 1950s, when more and more paved highways marked the beginning of the city's growth as a suburb of New Orleans. It was officially classed as a city in 1952. My family moved here in 1959, when I was five, and when few farms were left from that era. Kenner's course as an important suburb of New Orleans was sealed when, in 1970, I-10, linking New Orleans with Kenner, was completed. Easy access to New Orleans created rapid development of residential areas, shopping malls, and fast-food restaurants.

My mother lives at the north end of Williams Boulevard, the major north-south highway that runs through the heart of Kenner. When we moved to Williams Boulevard in 1959, it was a blacktop two-lane road; a farm owned by the Heberts, a family we rarely saw, occupied all the space across the street from our block, which was one of three blocks located just south of the shores of the lake. The nearest store was several miles away, and except for the three blocks of houses, there was nothing at that north end except large expanses of swampy land we called "fields," a patchwork of ditches, and Lake Pontchartrain, undeveloped at that time, whose levees rose at the extreme north end of the three blocks of houses. Today Williams Boulevard is a six-lane thoroughfare, and every inch of it is packed with restaurants and businesses.

My mother and her neighbor Mrs. Audrey—both widows with no children living with them—own the only private homes left on their block. Every other house has become home to a business: clock repair, jewelry repair, beauty shop, dog grooming shop, dentist office, snowball shop, seafood restaurant, insurance sales, etc. Williams Boulevard dead-ends to the north at the lake and to the south at the river. There's a levee for the lake and one for the river; the distance between the two levees is just a few miles. Take a left from my mother's house and you're at the levee for the lake; take a right, and soon after you pass the airport you're at River Road and the levee for the river. Thus was I raised between river and lake, with the airport in between.

The florist shop is the Malonys' old house, the family whose kids always seemed to have impetigo and runny noses. The jewelry repair shop is the old house of my brother's high school sweetheart, who eventually married him. The beauty shop is Mrs. Doris's old house; dead now, she was my mother's best friend. They both liked to read and they both loved music. Doris's hair was the color of dried blood; she wore it long and pulled back with a flat barrette. She used cigarette holders and named her son Shelley, after the English poet. She and my mother would have wine and escargot parties where they'd sit on pillows on the floor, burn candles, and talk about books and music. The few years Doris lived in Kenner were among the happiest for her. Doris moved to Ohio, though, after divorcing her husband, and died of lung cancer soon afterward. My mother has a photograph of her on her bedroom dresser, head held high, cigarette in hand. It's the only photograph she displays that is not of someone in the family.

In the block immediately to the north of ours, what we called the "second block," lived the Kavanaghs, an Irish American family, with their seven children, five of whom were the same ages as we St. Germains, so we became good friends with them. Their mother was five feet tall, weighed about three hundred pounds, and rarely left her bed. We used to go over to play canasta or rummy with the girls and their mother. Mrs. Kavanagh would be lying in the bed, her immense body filling it as I imagined the waters filled Lake Pontchartrain.

The Sound of Planes

In the third block lived the Guidreys, with their only daughter, Cerise. Cerise was two years older than me, and was half American Indian and half French. Her intensely sexual aura intoxicated her peers and frightened our parents. She wore tight jeans or cutoffs and loose shirts she left partly unbuttoned so that you could see her plump breasts, and she always seemed to have several boys around. They'd flutter around her, mesmerized, like moths to the flame of her body. None of us believed she was a virgin. It was hard to believe, in fact, that she had ever been a virgin. I remember wondering if it was possible to be born sexually mature. If, as the nuns would have us believe, Mary had given birth and still remained a virgin, I imagined the opposite might also be possible, that one might be able to come into the world already having lost one's virginity. Whenever I'd do anything as a teenager that seemed even remotely seductive, my mother would say, "You're going to grow up just like Cerise Guidrey!" This, in her mind, was the worst fate that could possibly befall me.

The two blocks that used to be home to Cerise and to the Kavanagh family are now commercial; the same small houses are there, spruced up, but signs for a chiropractor, quick shop, portrait studio, beauty shop, and other businesses have been slapped over doors that once led to homes where families used to live and work and play.

All of the original three blocks of homes remaining on the north end of Williams Boulevard are about forty years old. Small three-bedroom ranch-style homes that cost about thirteen thousand dollars when they were first built, most have suffered flood and hurricane damage over the years, and have had to be partially or sometimes completely rebuilt. The houses are built on pilings so they won't sink into the ground, but the land around them keeps sinking; people who live here have to have river sand or fill dirt brought in unless they want their yards to revert to swamp.

When I was a young girl I loved the wild growth that surrounded our house. Acres of open fields lay beyond it; ditches alive with crawfish ran in an almost unbroken line to either side of our block; Lake Pontchartrain was within walking distance, and good climbing trees grew everywhere. The fields gave me a taste of what wilderness might be like, and though I wouldn't have known to use the word *wilderness,* I'm sure that's what I developed a hankering for as a young girl. I knew nothing about wilderness; I just knew those fields. I dreamed of being a Campfire Girl, because I imagined they did wilder things than their cookie-selling counterparts, though my mother always said we couldn't afford it when I begged to join. My mother did read to me at night, though, about all those adventures I couldn't actually have. We read the classic adventure stories; I remember in particular her reading *The Swiss Family Robinson* to me, one chapter each Friday night. That's what I really wanted to do, be marooned somewhere and have to survive on my own.

I imagined the fields behind the house as some wildness I needed to tame, Lake Pontchartrain an ocean I would someday build a raft for and sail off on, the blackberry brambles and snakes preparation for the jungles I would explore when I left my parents' house. My skin turned, each summer, almost black, as if I were becoming the earth itself, because I spent so much time outside. My body craved the sun and the intense heat of the weather, a craving I can't seem to get back now that I'm grown. We lived without air conditioning many of the years of my childhood—something I cannot conceive of now—yet I never remember being miserable about the heat. It was as if my young body were yeast and the sun something that entered it as food, causing a frenzied joy and growth.

I loved the smell of the moist black dirt and grass under my nails; I loved the clay soil in the backyard, so good for making mud pies, and the thrill of catching a crawfish from the ditch, or of discovering a wildflower or snake or a new blackberry bush. The scratches on my thighs proved I was tough. There's a photo of me I recently came across that captures all I was in those early years. I'm eight and skinny as a cattail, I'm smiling, and my long, wild brown hair is pushed back with a headband. I'm standing in front of our house with no shoes on, the front part of my left foot wrapped in a bandage from where I'd stepped on something and hurt it, probably because I hardly ever wore shoes. My hands are down at my sides, but the fingers of each hand are reaching out,

The Sound of Planes

stretched till they look like they might break off from my hand; they look like small, fleshy rockets about to take off.

Tomboy, my mother would call me, curling my hair night after night, stuffing me into stiff petticoats and shoes that cramped my feet. I had a passion for the wild I don't think she ever fully understood, a passion for a place where beauty could not help you survive. And though I was hardly in the wilderness, Kenner, at that time, did seem like a frontier of sorts. For miles there was nothing but these three blocks of houses, a farm, and the undeveloped lake. As a child, my universe seemed mostly untamed. The fields behind our house and the lake were places of escape from the small house that offered no privacy or solitude. The fields behind our house have been "developed" now, and turned into apartment complexes. Every time I return home more apartments have sprouted up like tumors, until there's nothing left that now could be called a "field."

Although my mother claims to prefer the urban setting she now finds herself in, I still think that she liked the small pocket of almost-wildness that surrounded our home. She loved to walk the shores of Lake Pontchartrain, and she used to go outside almost daily to climb the mimosa tree in our front yard. She used to like to climb it in spring when its pink flowers belled out like fairy skirts—she'd take a book with her and read and daydream. When she climbed that tree it seemed like a small act of rebellion, which made me cheer for her and feel hopeful for my own future. She read to me on Friday nights; her voice, food and drink for my hungry spirit, fed me dreams of adventure. I think she must have dreamed of adventure and escape herself, escape from a life of seemingly endless dirty clothes and dirty dishes, difficult children, the certain emptiness of life with an alcoholic husband.

And, I have come to think, from the sound of airplanes.

Most people fly into New Orleans International Airport not realizing the airport itself is not in New Orleans but a few miles outside, in Kenner. Residents of Kenner are only too aware of its location, however, and that the city of New Orleans owns the airport. Disputes over issues such as noise pollution and traffic control are decided for the most part by the New Orleans mayor's handpicked airport board, a board that has the good of the city of New Orleans in mind when they make decisions, not the quality of life for residents of Kenner. The board has only one representative on it from Kenner.

It was in 1940 that Kenner was chosen as the site for what is now the international airport, but was then known as "Moisant Field" after a pilot of French Canadian descent who was reputedly a bit of a daredevil. Moisant was the first to fly between Paris and London and had come to New Orleans in 1920 to participate in an endurance flight. His plane crashed en route, killing him. In 1947 Moisant was the largest commercial airport in the United States. Although it's no longer the largest, it's still one of the busiest airports in the country. In 1999 it served 9,443,863 passengers. During holiday seasons, especially Mardi Gras and Jazz Fest, the volume can be dizzying, with airlines booked to 100 percent capacity.

Wherever you live in Kenner you are not far from the sound of the planes taking off and landing. At first the sound was horribly jarring to me. The year we moved to Kenner, I was always putting my hands over my ears as the awful *aacchh,* which sounded like the heavy breathing or snoring of some angry god, would commence. It was worse outside, and I would often run in from my swinging or mud-pie making or tree climbing or blackberry picking to escape it. The thin-walled house muffled the roar only slightly, though I could put my head under my pillow, which helped.

The sound shook the walls of our house gently but meaningfully, reminding us of how fragile we were, and of how little power we had; we were poor, we lived where planes flew right over us, there was nothing we could do about it. The walls of the house trembled with the passage of

The Sound of Planes

every plane, and the windows rattled horribly the way they did when we had gale-force hurricane winds. Years later when I read D. H. Lawrence's story "The Rocking Horse Winner" about a little boy who believes his house speaks, no one had to explain to me how it was that a house could speak. With the help of the plane, our house muttered in low, guttural tones, an intermittent but recurring reminder of who we were and where we lived.

The sound of the planes also served as a reminder that we were in the twentieth century, the age of technology. It seemed to mock my attachment to an imagined wildness, and though I didn't understand this fully as a child, the planes, so serious, so unambiguous—they sounded like they knew what they were doing—made me feel foolish. I made paper airplanes, lots of them, as a child, and flew them both inside and outside. Some of them worked, some of them didn't, but none of them flew as high as the ones above me; none went very far at all, actually, and none made the sound the planes overhead made. I used to wonder if you had to make that awful sound to succeed in anything.

The sound of the planes was a sound like the rattling and coughing of the air conditioner my mother never turned off. It was like the weather or the water that surrounded us: a presence that seemed as omniscient, as omnipresent, as the God the nuns were teaching us about. With you when you were playing in the yard, with you when you were swinging a bat, with you when you were singing a song, with you when you were walking to school or walking home from school, with you when you were helping your mother cook, with you when you were eating, with you when you ran away from home, which you did, though you didn't get far because you would end up at the lake or the river, with you when you went out on a date, with you when you sat in cars and kissed your boyfriend for the first time, with you, with you, *with you,* like an irritating, smothering kind of lover.

I got used to the sound, of course, as you get used to anything if you're around it enough, as I got used to my father's drinking and my parents' arguing, which I used to also shut out by running to my room and putting my head under my pillow. Sometimes their arguments would coincide with a plane taking off or landing. They would shout louder to make themselves heard over the plane's noise, and then there would be two sounds to try to shut out.

It was as if we were squeezed onto a strange island, to the north the lake, to the south the river, to the west empty plantations, ghostly and decaying, to the east the specter of New Orleans. And above us, the sound of planes. The road in front of our house went to water in both directions, and the sky was claimed by a terrible presence that, finally, like the lake at one end and the river at the other, you had to accept, though there were ways that we tried to rebel. Much of the life my mother built for us in Kenner was built, I think, in opposition to the sound of the planes and what that sound represented.

My plane has landed, and I'm walking through the concourse to the baggage claim where I'll get my suitcase and make arrangements to pick up my rental car. As you walk through the New Orleans airport a dank smell of long-air-conditioned air assaults you, not pleasant to the uninitiated, but familiar smelling, to me, nonetheless, and thus comforting. You know you're home because the smell of moisture, of decay, of old air from air-conditioning vents that are not cleaned out enough because they are always in use tell you so. The smell of the air in the airport is not unlike the smell of the air in my mother's house, though the airport's air is central, and my mother still lives with loud, rattling window units.

I walk through the concourse, which has developed in much the same way Williams Boulevard has. It's filled with bars, restaurants, and shops selling pralines, chicory coffee, Tabasco sauce, boxes of tourist beignet mix, King-cake mix, jambalaya, red beans and rice, gumbo and shrimp-Creole fixings. You can even get frozen crawfish tails here to take back home, at about twice what it would cost you outside of the airport. There's a Bag a Beignet shop, a Jester Café, a French Quarter Café, a Praline Connection, a Creole Express, a PJ's Coffee and Tea Shop. You can buy hotdogs made of alligator meat, muffulettas, po'boys, and bread pudding. The airport is also packed with nonfood items for sale: New Orleans T-shirts, alligator pencils, voodoo dolls, Mardi Gras posters, beads, masks, and other Mardi Gras paraphernalia. There's a bookshop and a music shop, both of which focus on local music and books.

It takes me about twenty-five minutes, once I get my bags into the rental car, to reach my mother's house. It's only a few miles from the airport and would take less than ten minutes if it were not for the airport traffic and innumerable traffic lights that infect Williams Boulevard.

In the one and one-half miles that make up Williams Boulevard just south of my mother's house, I drive past an explosion of commercial growth: a Popeye's Fried Chicken, a Wendy's, a Burger King, a Potato King restaurant, a Shoney's, an Office Depot, a Spee Dee Oil Change, a Super Cuts, a Fisherman's Cove restaurant, a Jade Palace restaurant, a Texaco, a First American bank, an Asia Gourmet restaurant, an Imperial Garden restaurant, a Casa Tequila restaurant, a Tokyo Japanese restaurant, a Pizza Hut, an Office Max, Hanna's Boutique, a Golden Corral restaurant, an Albertson's grocery store, Trauth's Lake House restaurant, a car wash, and the office of a spiritual adviser, among many other establishments. Finally, after about seven red lights and heavy traffic, I arrive at my mother's, one of very few private residences on the street since I turned onto it from the airport.

Her house, the house in which I grew up, is small and low to the ground, part brown brick and part wood. The wood is covered with vinyl siding that has greenish brownish mold on it from the dampness of the climate. The front door, painted dark brown to match the bricks, has no storm door to protect it from the elements, and so is slowly rotting away. Like a wound that won't heal, the wood veneer has peeled off over the years in fleshlike strips, revealing raw wood underneath the stained brown of the outside. My mother, who lives on my father's retirement pension, cannot afford to replace the door.

It's summer now, and a magnificent specimen of plumbago, about five feet tall and twenty feet wide, is in full bloom, its richly petaled pale-blue flowers lighting up the small house, concealing the ugly brown brick like a great caftan. An avocado tree, about twenty feet high, shades the north side of the house. The lawn, an intense green, also begs for the eye's attention. It is St. Augustine grass, a hardy, vigorous grass that always needs to be cut, and that I usually cut when I visit. Everything surrounding my mother's house that is not green is blooming: the hibiscus broadcasts shades of coral and pink and red; there are white calla lilies, purple hydrangeas, the sweet pink of azaleas, and the cool, cool blue of the plumbago. A polyphony of disheveled, beautiful color.

The concrete steps that lead up to the front door are pulling away from the house. Because of the shade the plumbago affords, huge roaches live in that nice, cool concrete crack, hanging out there until someone opens the door and they can scuttle in. I look down as I approach, and see them moving about, dark and sure of themselves, in the space between the steps and the house.

My mother greets me as usual, with a brightly colored caftan on, her blonde hair curled and pulled back off her head in a flat barrette like the one her friend Doris used to wear, and long, dangly earrings. She's recovering from the heart attack she had last year; she's lost sixty-five pounds and looks healthier than I've ever seen her; her skin's glowing and bright, her voice strong. "I can breathe again," she says, "and I feel so much better." She's on the Weight Watchers program, and has been walking every day, mostly in the Esplanade Mall a mile away, just off Williams and down West Esplanade, a wide boulevard that follows an even wider canal that runs the width of Kenner. The mall is a fairly new development; when I was growing up, that area consisted only of swollen grounds and open fields.

At sixty-eight my mother is still a handsome woman who possesses that curious mix of the girlish and the mature one finds in many older southern women. She has the angular, strong Germanic face of her father, and "bedroom eyes," eyes that seem to flirt with the photographer in almost every picture I've seen of her.

If my mother is handsome now, she was a strikingly beautiful woman when she was younger. The photographs of her when she was dating my father, and later, when they were first married, seemed to me, as a child, photographs of a movie star. Here, at twenty, in a photo taken in Waveland, Mississippi, she poses in shorts and a white camisole, revealing her midriff, tight and tan, a colored scarf tied gaily around her head and pulled to the side. In another photo from the same era she's dressed to go to a ball in a strapless gown; she's turned away from the camera, revealing gorgeous, swan-shaped shoulders. Long, black lace gloves match the black lace that lines the yellow taffeta of her floor-length gown.

My mother's house is an odd mixture of low and high: the living room, the room in which we spend most of our time, is carpeted with worn gray carpet that smells musty because water seeps in during heavy rains. Heavy dark-blue curtains hide postage stamp–size windows. A small fifteen-year-old air conditioner wheezes through one window during all seasons. An oversized ceiling fan, too big for this room, sweeps its blades as if it means to clear-cut everything; it feels like the early gusts signaling a hurricane. There is an old flowered sofa and love seat, a rocking chair, a television set. The wall is covered with art prints, mostly from modern painters—Picasso, Manet, Van Gogh, and Degas. There are also watercolors from local Louisiana artists. Where there aren't prints there are photographs of family.

And everywhere, bookcases, bookshelves, and books: books of poetry, history, novels, philosophy, popular culture, books, books, and more books. My mother has never thrown away or given away any book she has ever bought. As she kept buying books over the years, she eventually ran out of room for them. They are shelved three levels deep in makeshift bookcases that line the living room floor. There are bookcases in the kitchen, bookcases in the halls, bookcases in all the bedrooms, and books stacked in piles all over the floor in her bedroom and in the bathrooms. In the living room, next to the chair she sits in when she reads, is always a stack of about ten books she's currently reading. Thousands of books are stuffed into this tiny house.

My mother's voice gave breath and life to the first poems and stories I heard, and I am indebted to her for the great love of reading that was her enormous legacy to me. She read to me before I even understood what words were, and continued even when I could read myself. She gave me books for every birthday and holiday, inscribed and dated in her beautiful, flowing hand. She got me a library card as soon as I was old enough and took me often. I felt nurtured by her untutored passion for books and the worlds one might find in them. Not only did she love to read books, but she also loved the look of them, the feel of them, even the smell of them. No book ever made it into our house without my mother putting her face to it, riffling through the pages and inhaling. As a kid I used to think there was something about the way a book smelled that indicated to my mother whether it was a good book or a bad book. My nose was not as sophisticated as hers; books smelled either "old" or "new" to me. But I think she was able to detect subtle scents of inks, of the particular genus of trees that went into making the paper, even the smell of the place the book had been for the past few weeks. With used books, her nose could detect traces of smoke and sweat, perfume, wine and coffee, the almost lost aromas that gave her, I think, a sense of intimacy with the book's previous owner.

She would take me to book fairs each year, where we'd wander congested aisles of books impenetrable as jungles, and come home with boxes of books. We never missed the New Orleans Symphony Book Fair. She'd bring home, every year, literally dozens of boxes from the fair, which infuriated my father, who rarely read anything. After we were all in bed she would sit on the sofa in the small living room and read, drinking tea, her feet propped up, and the basket of clothes to be folded, which was never empty, next to her. The house was a mess; it stayed that way most of the time. She read, and read, and read, often listening to music when she read, a habit I have picked up from her.

She read recipe books from cover to cover; she read novels, collections of stories, collections of essays, anthropological books, poetry books, from Rimbaud and Baudelaire to Sexton and Plath, classics, especially Russian classics; she read history books, especially Louisiana history, natural history books, collections of letters, you name it, she read it. She has a library to rival any Ph.D. I know today, though she has only a high school education.

At night when the children and even my father were all in bed, I'd sometimes get up for a glass of water, or to go to the bathroom, and I'd see her in the living room, just the yellow glow of one lamp like a halo, lighting her rapt face and the book she was reading. If I interrupted her, she would look up at me, slowly, with a faraway look that gradually melted as she recognized who I was and tried to translate what I had said to her.

As well as books there was always music as I was growing up. The "library" of her house, the room that used to be the living room before our garage was closed in, is lined with stuffed bookcases from floor to ceiling, but also houses her stereo system and extensive music collection. Before we had a good sofa we had a good hi-fi. She listened to classical music, blues, jazz, and piano music. She also played opera a lot.

When my father would come home from work, if she was listening to opera, he would walk straight over to the stereo, lift the needle, remove her record, and replace it with something else, usually country music. Maria Callas's *Oh sarò la più bella . . . Tu, tu amore?* might be interrupted, midcry, by Hank Williams singing, *Your cheatin' heart, will tell on you, you'll cry and cry. . . .*

My mother didn't like country music, but she did love the blues, and Dinah Washington was a favorite. I knew if she had on "What a Difference a Day Made" not to try to talk to her. Sometimes she'd be cooking and listening to music at the same time, and there would be a sadness in her face, as when she talked about the boy she almost married instead of my father, and sometimes she'd cut her finger while chopping up onions or garlic, and then there would be music and the smell of something cooking and the sound of planes and my mother's blood, all in my eyes and in my ears like some terrible infection.

Today when she opens the door to welcome me, rollicking piano music pours out of the house like water rushing over a levee, flooding onto the streets of this neighborhood where she has lived for forty years. Sometimes I think my mother's intense love of music, like her love of books, developed as a strategy, not entirely conscious on her part, to *not* hear the noise the planes made. When the planes flew overhead, she would turn her music up so loud the whole house shook, and I couldn't tell if it was the planes or the music or, more likely, some alliance between them responsible for the shaking. It is from my mother that I learned to like my music loud. When I moved out on my own, I bought the largest, loudest speakers I could possibly afford. During moments of sadness, nothing, not prayer, not drinking, not sex, can console me as much as good music, turned up so loud that even your skin seems to be a membranous drum whose sole responsibility is to transmit sound.

Mother loved soft music, too, especially piano music, and late at night when no planes were flying she'd sometimes play Chopin's *Etudes* or *Nocturnes* while folding or ironing clothes. Useless to play them during the day because she could never turn the volume up high enough to hear them without interruption over the noise of the planes. If she was in a good mood it was Dr. John or the Neville Brothers or Professor Longhair, some good and sloppy New Orleans music. That's what she listens most to now—New Orleans music. Though my mother has lived in Kenner for most of her life, she has never fully accepted that that's where she lives. She was born in New Orleans, and loves everything about it—the food, the music, the politicians, and the excesses. She likes to say she lives in New Orleans, not Kenner. When I told her recently I wanted to write about Kenner she looked at me puzzled, and, it seemed, worried for my sanity: "Why," she asked, "would anyone want to write about Kenner?"

My mother stayed home most of the years I was a child. She took care of the children, and cooked. She became a good cook, like her mother and grandmother before her, and she passed on her love of good food to her children. She was inventive, as she had to be, because my father's salary was not really enough for us to live on. We all went to Catholic schools, but I know sometimes the tuition did not get paid, and the piano, the most valuable piece of furniture we owned, was almost repossessed several times. She didn't see a doctor or a dentist for ten years. The money that might have kept her from losing her teeth in her midthirties went, instead, for the school tuition and piano lessons for the children.

Sometimes we ate oatmeal or pancakes for dinner because we didn't have any meat. Sometimes we had red beans and rice every night for a week, my mother scavenging the refrigerator for something new to put in them to make them taste different—more onion, tomato, green pepper, more red or black pepper or thyme. Or just more hot sauce on the table. Today when I smell red beans cooking, their creamy onion-pork smell filling the house, I think of her, and that smell enters me like her love and her sorrow.

That's not to say there was never any happiness. During the early years of their marriage my mother and father did go out sometimes, to parties, or out to eat, or to bowl. She would come to our beds to kiss us goodnight before they left the house, stockinged, girdled, and lipsticked, hair curled and sprayed stiff. Her perfume, thick-tongued, velvet, and sweet as heating milk, would waft over me like a drug. Perfume was something my father always gave her for Christmas—she would never have spent money on it herself. I think she must have felt attractive when she wore that scent—my father clearly liked it on her since he gave it to her year after year—and maybe that's why she always seemed happy when she was wearing it. Or maybe the essence of pleasure for her resided mostly in her sense of smell; it represented a singularly exhilarating way of knowing the world. That would suggest why she so loved breathing in the bouquets of books, and why she is such a good cook.

Mother says they never intended to stay in this house; it was meant to be a "starter" home, but somehow they were never able to save enough money to move anywhere else. She offers me a glass of wine, we sit on the sofa in the living room, and I make a comment about the heavy traffic on Williams. She sighs.

"I know, I know it's bad, but I'd rather have the traffic than what was here before that: nothing!"

She reminds me of how hard it was raising five children in such a relatively isolated area. They had only one car, which my father always took to work in Arabi, an hour away, and no store was within walking distance.

"It's so different, now, Sheryl," she says, rescuing a stray hair from her barrette and softening it back. "There's so much more to do now. There's

River Town—you know, by the river end of Williams?—you should go there. There's a Mardi Gras museum and an aquarium, and the tourist buses from New Orleans are stopping there now. And they're calling the lake end 'Lake Town,' it's so built up, fishing piers, boat launch, the Pontchartrain Center, and now the Treasure Chest Casino."

The sound of a plane flying overhead. I smile weakly.

"How about some dinner?" she asks once the plane's sound has faded.

After eating a dinner of grilled chicken and vegetables—Weight Watchers style—we go for a walk down the block to the snowball stand that used to be the Kavanaghs' house, where she gets a diet strawberry snowball and I get a Creole cream cheese–flavored one.

We walk back home, sit in the aluminum porch swing in her backyard, and eat our snowballs, looking out at the yard. My mother's backyard is small, but it is thick and rich with plant life. It's as messy with flora as her house is with books.

I notice that the rosemary bush, which used to be seven feet high and almost as wide as the shed, is gone.

"You're the one responsible for the rosemary's death," my mother says, scooping out a spoonful of the strawberry snowball, bringing it to her mouth, and sucking it in deeply.

"How? It was fine last time I was here. I just pruned it back a little." I slap a mosquito that's been sucking on my arm. A blossom of blood stains my arm.

"You pruned it too hard. It never came back. But look at the sweet olive, isn't it doing well?"

We sit and talk and swing and eat our snowballs, and the planes pass overhead like always. We have learned to stop a sentence when the plane gets above the house and finish it when the sound goes away. Thus do the planes function as punctuation, semicolons of sorts, in our conversations. The pause the noise forces on us can actually be a positive thing, as every adult child comes to realize that in order to maintain a good relationship with your parents certain subjects are better not brought up, and sometimes it is better to think twice before saying something.

The Sound of Planes

The noise of the planes is an interruption that also provides time for moments of quick reflection: *Do I really want to say this?*

I look out to the south end of the yard. The bay leaf, almost hidden by fern and elephant ears, is a good two feet taller, I think, than it was last summer. Azaleas cover that whole side of the yard, their pink blossoms like colorful spiders. My neighbors in Iowa would give their right hands to have lush, giant azaleas like these. None of my mother's are fertilized or mulched; all she does is sometimes water them when it hasn't rained in a while. Banana trees, from some cuttings I gave her years ago, line the west edge of the yard, hidden behind the shed, growing small bunches of fruit she says will never make it to full ripeness before winter sets in. A large holly tree dominates the southwest edge of the yard; she tells how it started out as just a small gift plant someone gave her. Spider plants and devil's ivy grow wild underneath the holly tree, the progeny of house plants she had set out that escaped their pots.

There's lots of canna, and some mint. She's always had mint, which she has put in iced tea for as long as I remember. There's a pecan tree on the east side of the lawn. I get several pounds of pecans, wrapped in bright green and red netting, from my mother every Christmas along with stories of how she had to save them from the squirrels. The avocado tree towers over the north end of the house. "I just threw a pit out of the kitchen window one day, and it took root," she tells me, scraping the last of her snowball into a spoon. Her tongue and the roof of her mouth are stained bright red from the snowball syrup.

She's proud of the fecundity of the yard, the way things just take root and grow so lushly without much work on her part. She trusts that the land will take care of you, believes that out of mess can come good stuff, and that too much control, if not necessarily bad, is not always good. But there's a darker side to letting nature run unchecked, and she reminds me of it now.

She puts down her empty snowball cup, gets up from the swing, and walks around to the back side of the holly tree. "Look at this, Sheryl, can you believe it?" She's pointing at the wisteria. It weaves all along the back fence, in and out of the banana trees, all around the holly; on the other side it threatens to smother the azaleas; some thin green tendrils have even entered the shed. It's everywhere in the yard; I don't know how I couldn't have noticed it.

"It poisons the ground," she says. "Your father and I planted it years ago. I had no idea this would happen.

"It's like something from outer space," she says, furrowing her brow. "I've tried to kill it I don't know how many times. It just won't die." I can see she's really worried. She can't do the work that needs to be done out here. I finish the rest of my snowball, pull a rusty hacksaw out of the shed, and start hacking away at the knotted, woody veins of it where it's threatening to strangle the azaleas. I soon realize this is a much bigger job than I thought. This hacking will only make the wisteria come back more vigorously in a week or so. But my mother looks on, as I hack, pleased. It seems to her that I am doing some good. I look around at the impossibility of the project, then promise I'll finish the job tomorrow morning.

It's getting late. The sun, huge and orange and low in the sky, is bleeding into the horizon. A breeze. More mosquitoes.

"You know," Mother says, looking up at the sky, "it's hard to keep things from growing here. On some summer nights I swear you can see the wisteria uncurling its tendrils across the fence or the lawn, or that you can hear the banana leaves unfurling. They must love the heat and humidity." She fans herself with her hand. If she loves New Orleans and is proud of her status as a native, she's never grown to love the heat. It affects her more deeply, I think, the older she gets, and I wonder if I will grow to have ever less tolerance for the heat when I'm her age. We are standing close to each other, and I can smell the salty, musty smell of her, the smell of the sheets in her bedroom. I move a few steps away, sit in a lawn chair, and focus my gaze on the back of the house, on the rear of the air conditioner in her bedroom, which sticks out from the house like some kind of mistake.

The sound of a plane overhead again. The leaves of the pecan tree brush above us. I'm sweating from the few minutes I spent hacking at the wisteria. I lick my lips and can still taste in my mouth the last of the cold, sweet snowball. This, I think, is home: this unchecked wildness that is my mother's backyard; the sweet, icy coldness of a snowball; the hot, humid weather that coats your skin like some slick animal; and the sound of planes.

Mother starts talking again, as the sun sets and we begin to have to fight off mosquitoes in earnest, about the development at the lake. I'm not paying much attention because the whole idea of development at the lake is painful for me to consider. I'm thinking about mosquitoes, and examining the squashed one on my arm. I remember as a child the "mosquito truck" spewing its fog on summer nights, and us kids running behind it all the way to the levee, laughing and playing in its funny-smelling clouds. I still remember the sweetish chemical odor of the fog and what fun it was to disappear in it.

I force myself to pay attention to what my mother is saying. She's really keen on the casino, which offers five-dollar lunches, has lingerie and Tupperware shows, and features bands she really likes, including local New Orleans bands. She and her women friends, who no longer cook now that their kids are gone, go down there often to eat lunch or dinner. She doesn't gamble, ever, she assures me, although her friends do; she just likes to go to the events they sponsor.

The sun is gone now. It's dusk, and the crickets have begun singing, a lyrical humming. "You should go, Sheryl, up to the lake. They've turned the area outside of the casino into a kind of park. They have boiled craw-fish Friday nights during spring and summer, and drinks and bands. Go tomorrow and see. There will be a lot of people."

"Okay," I say.

"Really. You should go up, take a run up there. I take my walk out there, too, when it's cool enough. It feels safer than it used to, with all the people." She moves the swing back and stretches her feet out the way a child would as she swings back and forth.

I'm glad my mother's happy. There's nothing more painful than a mother's sorrow. It is like a weed in your heart, a weed with a root so deep and so thick and so twisted that you cannot dig it out without taking the heart with it.

She's going on about how good it is now that there's a big grocery store just a block away, that her bank is just a few blocks away, that the mall is less than a mile, and this casino, just three blocks away. I close my eyes and feel the coolness of the oncoming night settling over my body like a soft, light shroud.

The next day I dig up what I can of the wisteria and poison the rest. It takes me all morning. I plant some of it in a pot to take home with me. If it survives the trip home, it won't be as invasive in Iowa. Our cold winters will keep it in check, if they don't kill it. I take a nap in the afternoon, and that evening, after it cools down, I put on my running shoes and jog up to the lake. I'm planning to try to ignore the development my mother's been talking about, and run on the broken-down old road I remember that winds around the lake to the west, toward the pumping station my friend Michelle's father used to operate, and where Jefferson Downs is now located, the racetrack that has also added to the development here. My father worked a second job for several years at Jefferson Downs, a job that helped pay for piano lessons and Catholic schools.

I run north for two blocks past the snowball shop, a Shop 'n Go Deli, Lucky Lee's restaurant and bar, Kenner Eye Care, Nicoll's Limousine Service, a dentist office, and the Finish Line, an off-track betting establishment. The neutral ground for the last few hundred feet before the levee to the lake is planted with palm trees and pampas grass. On either side, weeping willows, a few hibiscus and plumbago. Just before I reach the levee, a sign with the image of a mermaid on it announces that Pontchartrain Center is to the left, and parking for Treasure Chest Casino is to the right. Another sign announces that the Hilton Hotel is now open.

As I round the levee and look out toward the lakeshore I see new wooden gazebos, a large expanse of manicured lawn, and five or more wooden fishing piers. Trucks are bringing in load after load of earth to expand and build up the shoreline. Trash cans dot the area with brightly colored signs on them: an American flag and *Kenner: America's City.* Several boys are fishing off the piers. To the east, the garish lights of the Treasure Chest River Boat Casino. To the right, a new playground with

The Sound of Planes

swings and tunnels and slides. A new lighthouse and concession stand. A sign announces, "Laketown Improvements Phase I Complete. Phase II: Concession Area, Shelters, Lighthouse, Walkway, Pier Additions." On the lawn they've created in front of the casino looms a huge tent with a big crowd stuffed into it, and a band tuning up. Hundreds of people are lined up for the five-dollar crawfish being dished out in another tent; others are in the beer or snowball lines. Kids and dogs are running around everywhere. Those who aren't in the tents or in line have spread out on blankets and lawn chairs, sucking on crawfish heads or eating snowballs or drinking sodas or beer, waiting for the band to start.

I frown and run the opposite way for a while, toward the less developed area. The lake used to be wild and quiet. I could come up here to think, to reflect; it was mine, I think as I run, and my tennis shoes hit the pavement in rhythm with that refrain: *mine mine mine.*

The band cranks up, breaking my rhythm. It's the Little River Band, an Australian group popular twenty years or so ago. I turn around, almost without thinking, and run back toward the tent so I can hear them better. People are laughing, swaying, dancing on the grass. Smells of cayenne, crawfish, beer, and the sweetness air takes on when there are a lot of children running around. Smells of gas and oil and fish from the lake.

Would I really rather this place stay unchanged? The truth is I don't know. Despite the increased commercialism of this area, there's no denying the lake is cleaner than I've ever seen it. I stare into its waters as I run along the pier toward the sound of the band, and see lots of dark shapes moving underneath the surface. It looks clean. No gray foam, no stinky debris. When I was growing up, as isolated as this area was, the water was horribly polluted. There were always dead fish and crabs littering the shore, and you couldn't see anything moving underneath, only an oily sheen reflecting whatever was in the sky.

"It's a long way home," the Australians belt out, "a long, long way," and as I run in and out of kids and dogs and kites and blankets and newly planted grass, past the casino, back down the levee, back down the six-lane Williams Boulevard, alongside the houses with their lights advertising hair salons and florists and beer and food and medical services and insurance and jewelry and clock repair, back toward the airport, back toward my mother's house, I have to agree.

A plane starts its long, deep whine across the sky. At least one thing hasn't changed. As much as I'd like to think it was the natural world that shaped both me and what I understand as home, the plane reminds me that technology probably had just as much of a hand in it. And maybe it belongs here as much as my mother's gloriously overgrown backyard, her pecan or avocado tree, or even the wisteria.

I approach my mother's house and slow to a walk. I'll circle the block a few minutes to cool down. It's hot and my breath is labored. I'm not used to the heat and humidity anymore. I walk past our front lawn where my father first gave me raw oysters, where my brothers and sisters and I used to play and fight, and I feel a sharp emptiness in my gut. This place has changed not only by addition but by subtraction, too. The absence of my brother and father creates a chasm so huge no amount of plant life or commercial development could ever hope to disguise it.

When I get to the back of our house I peek into the backyard, newly cleared of most of the wisteria. All I left was a bit growing on one side of the fence. It's blooming and beautiful, but contained now, thanks to me. I wonder if the role I have come to play when I visit my mother—a sort of gardener—has something to do with my own need for control. I enjoyed cutting down the wisteria, imposing my will on it. That pruning and shaping will give more room to the other plants in my mother's backyard, and she's happy I did it. But I also pruned the rosemary bush, and it died.

It's hard to know how much to cut away. Some days I can feel my mother and father inside me like a jungle, vines and roots and flowers and plants everywhere, a mess of organic matter, like my mother's backyard. Some days I want to luxuriate in their tangled undergrowth; other days its vibrant confusion scares me and I want to clear it all out.

I'm back in front of the house again, cooled down but exhausted and thirsty. My mother will have a tall glass of iced mint tea ready for me. I'll open the door to her house, drink her tea, lie down on the sofa that smells of us all, revel in the cool air-conditioned air and even the sound of the planes. I'll close my eyes and wonder where I'll plant the wisteria when I get home.

Whips and Unruly Women

Every touch is a modified blow.

—E. Crawley

It's summer in Iowa, and Gray, who is now seventeen, has been
pacing my bedroom, listening to my phone conversation. I've
just this moment hung up.

"What do you want, Gray?"

"Mom, how come you never seem happy when you talk to Paul?" He
stops pacing, folds his hands, and glares at me from across the room. I
am an enemy ship in a computer game, and he will send volleys of word
bombs to blow my head off the screen if I don't respond.

"I'm not unhappy when I talk to him," I say, getting up from the
chair and forcing a smile. "It's just that he's tired when we talk—England
is six hours ahead—and it's usually late there when we speak. So I guess
I pick up on his tiredness. And he's working in archives all day; it's hard
work. He's not always in the best of moods."

Gray examines me with a look not unlike the one I give him when I know he's told me something patently untrue. He's confessed to me in the past that he's worried I'll never find happiness with a man, and I know the gruff attitude he sometimes uses with me masks a deeper worry. It is a wound kept ever open by what he must surely perceive as my inconstancy with men. He's seen me with a myriad of partners, and even then I've been careful not to expose him to them all.

"Whatever. I'm going to Will's. See you later." He's out the door, down the steps, front door slamming before I can say, *Be home by eight.* On his way out he knocks down a photograph from the bookcase at the top of the stairs, which of course he doesn't stop to pick up. I walk over to it, check for cracks, and set it back on the shelf. It's a photo of Paul and me taken a few months ago in Louisiana. We're standing in front of my mother's house the morning of Mardi Gras. I'm wearing a traditional Cajun Mardi Gras costume with a screen mask and capuchin, and Paul's face is painted blue and red. He's wearing my mother's purple hat, and we both have on enough Mardi Gras beads to strangle.

Paul and I have been living together for about a year. He arrived in America last year from England to take a teaching job. A mutual colleague introduced us, and within a few weeks we were seeing each other every night; within two months he had moved in with me. It seemed a natural progression in our relationship: we both loved literature, jazz and classical music, good food and wine, and we both loved good, hard merrymaking in bed. I couldn't get enough: cooking, eating, and drinking with him; lying in bed at night; reading and listening to music; in the mornings making love. He is passionate—and opinionated—in his love of music and fiction, and I was inspired by his passion. He was born and raised in Liverpool, and the mix of gritty Liverpudlian street spunk and the sharp intellect one might expect from a Cambridge graduate drew me in. I recognized in him a fierce—and sometimes maddening—type of Brit: arrogant, domineering, cuttingly witty, and brutishly honest, qualities I found refreshing. Midwesterners are often nice to the point of ridiculousness, and the various interesting ways in which one might use the tongue are not much appreciated in Iowa. As is often the case, though, what attracts you most to someone may become the very thing that drives you crazy later.

Those months, however, were exquisite in the ways first months always are: the wonder and seduction of the strange lips of one who is newly in love with you, the growing familiarity of a warm and particular body next to yours at night, the intimate gestures, the patience one has with the other before the first argument, the bewitching mix of lust and affection that marks the beginning of a relationship.

Gray was eighteen months old when I left his father, who immediately began living with another woman, a colleague from his work. They have now been married about thirteen years and have had two more children. Gray has gone back and forth between his father and me virtually all of his life, in the early years staying the school year with me and the holidays with his dad, in the later years the opposite. His father has remained in the same city, Dallas, for the past twenty-five years; during the same time I have lived in four states and three countries.

There were men before Gray's dad, of course—some of whose names I don't remember—men I didn't want to get serious with because, I told myself, I had to do well at university and I was working full-time. Who had time for a relationship? But sex, well, that was another matter.

And yet it's not that easy: I thought I loved most of the men I slept with, for sex has ever been confused in my mind with love. Certainly, I loved some more than others. Derek comes to mind first, a tall and reedy scientist with red hair and freckles, a big heart and sexy imagination. With him I lasted longest—seven years—and we're still close friends. The others run together like river water hemorrhaging to the sea—hard-drinking men, fishing and camping buddies, older men, younger men, men with skin as black as rich oil, farmers, lawyers, cold academics, warm intellectuals. Even a woman, sweet and beautiful and loving. I left her, too. I left them all, sometimes, I suspect, to avoid being left. I am the

Whips and Unruly Women

queen of leaving, both my homes and almost everyone who has ever loved me. In the past ten years I've bought three homes and sold two. I've planted trees in the yard of every house I owned, in the same way I planted myself in the heart of every partner I ever had. I planned to stay.

A few years ago when I broke up with a Ghanaian man to whom Gray, who was about eleven, had become attached, my son stormed around the living room: "Mom! He's from another culture! Can't you be more understanding?"

I explained my reasons for the breakup, or as much as I could reveal of them to an eleven year old, reasons that, of course, I thought were logical. His only response was, "They're going to call you 'Run-around Sheryl'!" A few years later, more cynical, he would joke when I picked him up from the airport for his summer visit, "So, have you met any more future ex-boyfriends yet?" It's an understatement to say I know he'd be happier if I could settle into a relationship.

And despite my track record, it's something I wish I could do. I'm sure it would mean growth for me to be able to share my life with someone. Perhaps that's why I want so much for this relationship with Paul to work despite the fissures already apparent. I believe I'd lay my body over those fissures, pluck out my eyes, sew my lips shut to make it work. This time, I've told myself, it won't be my fault if it doesn't.

Still, I probably work less at it than I think I do. If I don't actually leave men, I scare them away with unorthodox behavior and my seeming lack of boundaries: too much openness, too much of a willingness to go anywhere, no matter how scary. In some ways this makes it easier for them; I become a sort of Medusa, and they are eventually relieved when I send them away instead of turning them to stone.

I don't want to do this with Paul. I wipe a bit of dust off the photograph I've just replaced, and turn around to examine our bedroom. It's a large converted attic; half of it is devoted to the master bedroom, while the other half serves as Paul's office. His side is bare now, papers and laptop gone, but the rest of the room is in complete disarray. In one corner a thick blue towel lies crumpled, still damp from my bath this afternoon. My workout clothes are in a heap next to the towel. A black bra is draped on the chair where Paul usually works. My dog has piled his toys up in the middle of the room where he sleeps now, one paw over a plush bear with half the stuffing ripped out. In the late-afternoon sun, dog hairs glint like strands of gold all over the carpet. A few piles of books lie on the floor next to my side of the bed, and empty water and wineglasses decorate the night table, shining like faux jewels in the sunlight.

I've learned not to leave clothes around when Paul's here because he picks them up and washes them in hot water, shrinking them. When he's here he makes the bed every morning. I haven't made it since he left for London six weeks ago. I suppose one good thing about living with him is that when he's here I'm somewhat neater.

Just across from the unmade bed is a bathroom whose trash basket is overflowing with female paraphernalia. I've been having a monstrous period for the past three months, bleeding like a woman miscarrying anew every day. The havoc this has caused—despite my precautions, the blood seems to have stained something in every room of the house—was, before Paul left, one cause of tension between us. Can't say that I blame him. It's not pretty, and who wants to have sex with a woman whose body is so out of control? I'm scheduled next week to have surgery: a uterine fibroid will be removed, and I'll have an endometrial ablation, which should stop the bleeding. I've come to think of this unending period as an act of rebellion on the part of my body, as if it were trying, without success, to purge itself now and forever of some poisonous thing at its center.

More simply put, both house and body are a mess, and the seemingly unstoppable river of blood is only the most vibrant and disturbing symbol of a disorderliness that may lie at the core of my being. My hormones are not only out of Paul's control, but they're out of mine as well; I'm embarrassed at how tenderly sensitive I've become, and how truculent. In some odd way all this bodily upset over which no one has control may be the potently silent source of many of the arguments Paul and I have.

And they are many: daily—no, hourly—bickering punctuated by more murderously spirit-chilling arguments those months before he left. He doesn't like my hair, long and wild; I don't like his, severely cropped.

Whips and Unruly Women

He doesn't like my collection of female singer-songwriters or Latin or Cajun music, or much of my popular music, and an argument often ensues when I try to listen to them in his presence. We fight about money and who spent more for dinner, gas, or anything, really. He would have us iron sheets; I have never ironed a sheet in my life. The arguments have now moved into the physical sphere. One night, not long before he left, during a particularly vicious round I pummeled his chest over and over shouting that I hated him. During another argument he grabbed me so hard to prevent me from leaving I had a bruise on my arm for a week.

Since he's gone he phones every other night, though, distracted, sounding depressed, but ending every call with an "I love you," and sometimes, "I'm looking forward to seeing you." I respond in kind, but underneath it all, I'm a hurricane of emotions, filled with love, despair, and anger.

He says he's always been a neat person. In contrast, I've always been messy: I was born into a chaotic landscape, and I come from a family of messy people. Some of my siblings can live for long periods of time in fertile, volcanic, voluptuous messes that defy logic or reason. Things stuffed everywhere, under beds, between mattresses, things piled up on top of things, floors unswept or unmopped for months at a time. My family—our overflowing bodies and desires as well as our dramatic, intense personalities—is as tangled as a tropical forest or swampland. We don't defy the mess of water and land that nurtured us, we reflect it.

Interestingly enough, my siblings have also had trouble staying with one partner. One sister has been married four times, although she's been with the last husband quite a long time now. My youngest sister has had a series of partners that could rival mine since the death of her husband several years ago, and my brother's also been through a few since his divorce. None of us have followed the example of our parents, and though I don't know the figures, I imagine we are not that unusual for our generation, which seems to be characterized by restlessness.

My mother says we all love drama and that's why we have such problems with relationships, and she is certainly partially right, but I think the colossal magnitude of our failures goes way beyond a genetic predisposition for the dramatic. Some of it may have to do with being southern; it's not just southern *fiction* that begins in failure and moves forward from there, from passionate failure to passionate failure. It's almost as if we sense that we are by nature and culture ridiculously tragic, and so we move through the world seeking to confirm that nature. Some of it has nothing to do with where we're from, but is rather generational: we are the television generation, and we learned from those hours we spent in front of the television that if you tire of a program you have only to change the channel. Things are bound to be worse for my son's generation, nursed by the ease not only of switching channels via remote, but also of surfing the Internet and clicking through documents. Maybe it's too simplistic to suggest a direct connection between the ease of changing channels or web sites and the ease with which we move between partners and places, but the connection is an intriguing one to consider. For me it's an anguished movement, though, which may be why I'm drawn to write about that place where I was born and in which I lived longest. Writing is a way of returning, of somehow still being there.

I look around again at the chaos in the bedroom. Even I have a tolerance level, and today is the day I've decided to clean it up. I gather up the clothes and towel and put them into the clothes hamper. I take the glasses downstairs, dust the bookshelves, pick up the books, vacuum the floor. I even make the bed. It doesn't take that long, and I wonder again why I let it get like this. I wish I could clean up my relationship with Paul as easily as this room. I do miss the son of a bitch. Although we seem to argue constantly, there's a vibrant edginess about him that I like. He can be generous, too, as when he loaned me a large sum of money to pay for surgery that my dog needed.

I flop down on the bed and turn on my side. On the floor next to the dresser sits my capuchin, the traditional hat of a Cajun Mardi Gras costume. It's the one I'm wearing in the photo Gray knocked down. It looks sort of like a dunce's hat covered with gold and purple material. Another quarter yard of cloth is gathered and attached to the bottom back edge, extending from ear to ear, so that it covers the neck and cheeks. I bought it, and a matching suit, in Eunice on the way back from the Tee-Mamou Mardi Gras in Louisiana. It was Paul's first visit to Louisiana, and I had hoped the trip might shore up our relationship, that he might come to understand me better by seeing the world into which I had been born.

My journal is sticking out from underneath the capuchin. I pick it up and flip through it. Pages and pages detailing arguments with Paul. I'm vexed that I've written down only the bad things. I seem to bristle particularly at his attempts to control me: here he's ordering me around as if I were a child, here he's demanding to know what I'm doing, seemingly at every moment. Here he's dominating conversations, dismissing me with a sharp movement of his hand when I try to speak.

Nothing, of course, about my own part in these arguments, my stubbornness. I have always had a contrary nature; no one has ever been able to tell me what to do. When I was a child I taught myself to cut with scissors—upside down. I would squinch three fingers into the small opening meant for the thumb, while my thumb would wiggle around in the larger one meant for several fingers. No matter how hard my mother tried to show me the right way to cut, the way that made more sense and worked better and was more comfortable, I refused to do it her way.

Nothing in the journal about my own need to be in control, about how hard it is for me to compromise. I want things to be the way I want them to be, a habit of one who has lived a long time alone. Old journals would reveal that my solution when things don't go my way is to leave, or threaten to leave.

I flip back to the beginning of the journal, spring of this year. The first entries have to do with our trip to Louisiana, and as I read I remember again how excited I was to be going home for Mardi Gras, how I nurtured the hope that Paul and I would grow closer.

The New Orleans carnival was a vibrant part of the rhythm of our lives as I was growing up, a cycle of celebration that shaped my siblings and me as surely as the weather, the land, and the bodies of water surrounding us. I have fond memories of Mardi Gras in New Orleans, but as I grew older I became more curious about the Cajun Mardi Gras, about which I'd heard tantalizing bits and pieces through the years, though never, oddly enough, from my father, whose mother, Celeste Fontenot, was Cajun. My father was not proud of his Cajun blood, and never taught us French, although it was the first language he learned. Many from his generation were made to feel ashamed of their ethnic roots, so much so that the language and culture almost died out in the middle of the twentieth century. The fact that his mother was both Cajun and a deaf-mute was a double blow to my father's pride—and he didn't bother teaching us much sign language, either.

Celeste was born and lived much of her life in Ville Platte, a small town in French Louisiana a stone's throw from Mamou and Basile, two towns that have some of the most vital Cajun Mardi Gras traditions today. There, maskers travel on horse or converted trailers from house to house in search of ingredients for a gumbo that will be served later that evening. This *courir*, as it is called, is in the tradition of the medieval *fête de la quémande*, a ceremonial begging ritual in which revelers travel the countryside begging and offering a performance in exchange for gifts.

A Mardi Gras *courir* in Ville Platte has been going on for many years, but my grandmother would not have participated in it because until fairly recently women were not allowed to mask and ride with the men, who dominated the runs. In fact, the male riders were so aggressive and wild they often scared the young girls of the houses they'd visit. My grandmother, as a young girl, probably hid inside and peeked out behind curtains when the Mardi Gras visited their home.

Celeste moved to New Orleans when she married my grandfather, and though she would return to visit Ville Platte frequently, my father never took us to visit the relatives there. A shatteringly thorough silence about that side of the family prevented any of the children from really getting to know our rural relatives or much about their culture. I felt this silence even more keenly after I moved to the Cajun mecca of Lafayette, about two hours west of New Orleans, to take my first teaching job. There I began to be exposed, on a daily basis, to students and colleagues who were full-blooded Cajuns and had lived in French Louisiana all their lives. The local National Public Radio station played almost as much Cajun music, it seemed to me, as classical music. Cajun restaurants were on every corner; Cajun music and food festivals took place every spring. Even some television programming was in French.

I remember clearly lying in bed one night in Lafayette listening to a Cajun music program, struggling to understand this particular brand of French, and wondering how anyone could really like this music with its wailing, whining singing and shrill, insistent fiddling. This culture I didn't understand was, by blood, my own, and I didn't have a clue about what that meant.

I would come, in the years I spent in Lafayette, to love the music and the culture. I would find that these people—my people—possessed joyous, raucous spirits. Lovers of drink and dance, wonderful cooks and outdoorsmen and -women, whenever they spoke, whether in English or in French, their speech was buoyant and musical. I bought a house in Lafayette, near the university, a house made of cypress, that wood so impervious to rot. I planted cypress trees and river birch in the backyard, an oak in the front. I learned Cajun French, and published a translation of a book-length poem about the Cajun diaspora.

Four years later, disappointed with the disparaging attitude toward education in Louisiana and a university system that didn't give even cost-of-living raises to faculty for three years running, I left to take a better-paying job at a private liberal arts college in Illinois. I also left a painful relationship with a man as prickly as Paul, and for the first time sent Gray to live during the school year with his father.

When I visited Lafayette last year I drove by that house where I'd come home to my Cajun ancestry. The river birch towers over the back of it, its cinnamon bark cracking and peeling in beautifully intimate patterns, as I knew it would. The cypress and oak are almost as tall as the apex of the roof of the house, and the oak has spread its branches over one half of the front yard. I reached my arms around the river birch's shaggy trunk, breathed in the birch-air, celebrated and mourned the roots it had grown that I had not.

Something falls out of my journal onto the floor—a few old photographs of my grandmother. I bend to pick them up. The photos show a happy, affectionate woman, clearly in love with her husband. In photo after photo, she's smiling brightly, leaning on his shoulder or sitting on his lap, even when they're considerably older. In early photographs she's pert and fashionably dressed, good looking in a sexy kind of way. One large photograph taken in the twenties shows her with my grandfather and a group of friends from her deaf-mute association. They seem to have been having a picnic and are clearly cutting up. Some of the women have pulled their dresses up; my grandmother has rolled her pants up to her thigh. She's holding out her bare leg, which my grandfather is supporting, for the camera. She has a man's shirt and tie on, which is probably my grandfather's, as he's in his undershirt. Her eyes have a mischievous glow to them. This is clearly a woman who, at some point in her life, had been gutsy and somewhat unruly.

In another photo—she is older and plumper—she's opening a bottle of champagne in front of the house my grandfather built for them in New Orleans. Another one shows her during a rare snowfall in Louisiana, grinning, snowball in hand, getting ready to throw it at the photographer, probably my grandfather. On the back is written, "Snow. Celeste throw snow's ball at 2501 Gallier Street."

The most recent photo, from the sixties, is of her in the hospital with my grandfather, who is on a respirator. She's leaning over him smiling and hugging him, even though he looks as if he will die any moment. And in fact, he does die soon afterward. I don't have any photographs of her after his death. She has never lived alone; she and Albin were married more than fifty years, and before that she lived with her parents and twelve siblings. That aloneness after his death must have been unimaginably difficult. Frail, elderly, increasingly unable to read lips, she will try to survive on her own with her only child's help. My father is only a few years from his own death at this point, though, and so deep into his drinking that he'll often forget to drop in on his mother to check on her, forget to take her to the store for groceries, forget about appointments to take her to Ville Platte to see her siblings.

A few years after Albin's death Celeste will become ill with a heart condition and spend her last hours in a hospital. There, the nurses and doctors caring for her do not speak sign language. They tie her arms

Whips and Unruly Women

down to prevent her pulling out her IV, which effectively takes away her voice. When my mother visits her, Celeste signs over and over, hands tied down, the letter A—a fist with the thumb pointed up, the sign for *Albin*. She dies with both hands clenched, thumbs up, her body, in its last moments, forming the name of her husband.

Is this what it means to be with one partner for a lifetime, that they enter you so fully, become so much a part of you that it is their name, only their name, that you want to say at the end, their name in your hands, their name on your lips, your body shaped with only their name? I wonder whose name I will say. Who will have my name on his lips, in his body, at that moment? I slide the photographs back into the journal.

It's frightening how fate can sometimes converge, or conspire, with dreams, fears, or desires to push you in a direction you might never have gone. Last year, around the time I was thinking about my grandmother and about the Cajun Mardi Gras, I became suddenly and permanently deaf in one ear, victim of something doctors call sudden sensory-neural hearing loss, a poorly understood phenomenon that is, evidently, not all that uncommon. My condition is not related to my grandparents' since theirs was congenital, but I had a lot of time to think, as I struggled with a considerable diminishment of hearing, about this new, unwanted connection I now had with them. I began to sense that the silence my father had passed along to me about them could easily become a more literal one. If I had lost the hearing in one ear, why not eventually the other? I needed to open my ears, and my heart, to everything that was around me while there was still time.

My mother and father argued a lot during their thirty-odd-year marriage, and it is no doubt their relationship soured me on wedding anyone, at least when I was younger. I never saw them kiss, and don't recall any affectionate moments between them, though there must have been some when I was a kid. What I recall most is the rancor, the stiffness and tension, the disagreements, the way my father made light of the marriage with his more or less public affairs. I didn't want that; I wanted a more meaningful partnership. I also saw how my mother, an intelligent, creative woman, was so often overcome by housework, how dominated she was, in some ways, by the institution of marriage, which in the fifties meant the gritty work of taking care of several children and keeping a house. It was, needless to say, not a glamorous life, nor did it seem to me as a teenager and young woman a life that made up for its lack of glamour with the rewards of affection or desire.

I was thirty before Gray's father and I married, but no matter; I soon became the type of woman I most detested: a bourgeois, sofa- and curtain-buying, credit-charging woman. We lived in the suburbs of Dallas, where my nice spouse worked long hours and we both gained weight and we never had sex and we argued, and even though there was—and still is—affection between us, I didn't like living like that, either.

When I think of a male as family I think *father, grandfather, uncle, nephew, son.* Never do I think *husband.* Gray's dad and I were married just over two years, such a short time I wasn't able to fully come to terms with what it meant to have a man as a husband. *Husband.* Hus-*band, bind.* A word that has buried within it in the very sound of binding. From Old English *husbonda,* house dweller. To husband: to manage carefully, to cultivate, one supposes, that wilderness, the wife. The OED says of *wife:* "Old English *wif* 'woman': ultimate origin unknown."

Like my grandmother, my mother had only one husband. And through all of his shenanigans, my mother never divorced him, though they did separate near the end of his life. She lived alone those last couple of years while he lived with a drunk, thick-bodied woman—we figured she was his drinking buddy—who disappeared when he went into the hospital. It was my mother who came to his bedside while he lay dying, driving the long drive from one end of the city to the other, talking brightly to him as first his speech went, then, slowly, almost everything else, until he was reduced to little more than a cowering animal that couldn't seem to let go of what little was left of his life. And it was she who, at the end, kissed those parched lips that had betrayed her, whispered in his ear that she forgave him, that he could go, it was all right, he could go, just go now, go. And he did.

Whips and Unruly Women

I don't know that I could find such forgiveness for one who had wronged me so much, and I recognize a strength in my mother I may never have. Yet if it is so hard for me to forgive, why have I chosen to live with a man whose tongue is so sharp, whose way of being with me often feels like a kind of violation?

A few months ago I asked my friend Deb to tell me what she thought my worst flaw was. She laughed and said, "Oh, Sheryl, it's men. If there were ten men lined up for you, you would go through them and say, oh, I'll take *that one,* and he would be the absolute worst one for you." She hastened to add that she loved Paul—he's so outrageously and interestingly a bad boy, how could she not? "And," she added, "you like prickly men, don't you?"

My journal records that Paul and I left Des Moines on February 22, 2001, a day with below-zero temperatures, the ground encased in layers of snow and ice that had been there since November. It had been, and continued to be, the coldest winter anyone could remember in twenty years in Iowa, and we were happy to be escaping to better climes. My mother had said to me on the phone, the day before we left, that she hoped Paul didn't mind a messy house, that she hadn't had time to clean up properly. I told her not to worry, and asked Paul to focus on her book and music collections, not the state of the house.

Because of a long flight delay, by the time we arrived at my mother's house, which would be our home base, it was almost midnight. After seven hours in airports we were emotionally and physically exhausted. If the place was messy I doubt either of us would have noticed. At any rate, I was thankful Paul didn't say anything about it. We had a cup of my mother's oyster soup and a glass of wine, and talked to her a little about the Cajun Mardi Gras, with which she was not familiar, having always spent Mardi Gras in New Orleans.

It's not that unusual for urban Creoles of my mother's generation to remain relatively ignorant of the traditions of a rural culture just a two-hour-drive away. Although Cajuns and Creoles have intermarried,

Cajuns who have remained in rural areas often think of New Orleans as a city of sin and decadence (they are not so wrong in this respect) and criticize their Mardi Gras celebrations for having too many tourists and being too commercialized. Many New Orleanians, while they may like Cajun food and music, often think of Cajuns as backward, "simple" people, and often know nothing of their Mardi Gras celebrations.

There was now a women's Mardi Gras, I told my mother, in the rural community of Tee-Mamou that took place the weekend before Mardi Gras day. This all-women run had been taking place without stop for about thirty years now, and that was the one Paul and I would visit the next day. The women, many of them conservative Catholic housewives and mothers, became, for that day, something other: tricksters, beggars, outlaws, spreaders of disorder. My mother smiled at this: "I can identify with that," she said, spreading her hands out at the piles of books and papers on the dining room table.

The Mardi Gras were "controlled" by *capitans,* captains who had braided burlap whips made expressly for that purpose. My mother furrowed her brow when I told her about the whips, but I had read up on them and was ready with a quick history. I explained that during the Roman celebration of the Lupercalia, costumed men beat women with animal pelts to ensure fertility. European traditions from the medieval period often involved public whippings of both men and women during carnival, and in Germany women would pull a plow through the streets as men cracked whips above their heads. So, I finished, there's a long history to this whipping stuff, and anyway it's all play—no one really gets hurt. My mother didn't seem convinced, but she perked up when I showed her a book of the beautiful masks and costumes of the Tee-Mamou women, and was even more interested when I talked about how they ran around collecting ingredients for a gumbo, since gumbo is her specialty.

After sharing another glass of wine with her I was talked out, and Paul and I tumbled into bed. I fell immediately and deeply asleep, dreaming of masked women who had whips in their hair.

The next morning I woke early, refreshed. I lay in bed and stroked and kissed Paul awake, hoping a good beginning to the day might keep

Whips and Unruly Women

us from arguing. I walked around my mother's lovely, messy backyard, drinking her strong coffee while Paul showered. I made us a couple of bagels with cream cheese for the trip, and we were on the road by six, driving west, past Baton Rouge and Lafayette, toward Tee-Mamou. *Westward ho, toward the whips!* I thought to myself.

When Cajuns settled southwest Louisiana they settled three major geographical areas: in and around swamplands and coastal areas, along major rivers, and in the prairie grasslands. We were driving through the prairie grasslands, the landscape where my grandmother spent her youth. These prairies had never been immense unbroken lands like the ones Lewis and Clark documented in the Midwest. These had always been separated from each other by bayous and major streams that supported forest growth on their edges.

In our sleepy struggle to get out in time, I had left the map at my mother's, but I figured I could still find this place where the run would begin. My friend Barry, a Cajun folklorist I knew from my time in Lafayette, had given me directions over the phone a few weeks earlier, which I'd memorized: the Tee-Mamou run would start at the Frugé Barn on Highway 1123 (a gravel road) off Highway 97 about a quarter mile north of a restaurant called DI's. At eight the Mardi Gras—which is what you call the costumed participants—would begin their run.

After about an hour we stopped at a McDonald's on I-10 because Paul was hungry and didn't "fancy" the bagel sandwiches I'd made. He got an Egg McMuffin and coffee, which he sipped quietly as I drove. I didn't get anything since we had the bagels. So far, so good: no arguments. I wanted to keep it that way.

"So how long have these 'runs' been going on?" he asked.

"Barry says the *courir* was found in most French sections of Louisiana in the nineteenth century," I said. "It was evidently a pretty rowdy celebration, though. Some towns decided to suppress it in the early half of the twentieth century. I would guess that the shame associated with all things Cajun in the first half of the century also contributed to its lack of popularity."

By eight we had driven for about two hours, and I thought we were probably not far from where we should turn off. I had to stop at a couple of gas stations for directions, though, which irritated Paul because we lost time. He used the second stop to get another cup of coffee.

"Do you know where you're going?" he asked a few more miles down the road.

"Yes," I lied. "Tee-Mamou is between Bayou Nezpiqué and Bayou des Cannes in Acadia Parish." This was true, but what I didn't say was that without a map I didn't know the precise location of either of these bayous.

I felt the irritation in Paul growing, a tension like a presence, getting thicker and thicker. Just then we passed a number of rusting trailers and dilapidated homes with clumps of peeling paint and broken-out windows, undeniable evidence of the heart-stopping poverty of much of rural Louisiana. Partly because of a tradition of devaluing education, partly because of depressed wage rates, almost 19 percent of Louisianians live in poverty. It distracted Paul for a moment.

"Bloody hell," he said. "Do people really live like that?"

My mother had told me that Celeste's family had been "very poor," and I now had the landscape to fill in the picture of what that might have meant. I focused on the road ahead. Empty: no cars, no horses, no people anywhere, only these broken-down homes. In the brown calm of the landscape, in the midst of placid crawfish ponds and rice fields and gutted homes, it didn't seem much like the place for any Mardi Gras celebration I would recognize. I began to wonder if I'd made a mistake dragging Paul out here.

A few minutes later Paul looked over at me, his patience having run out.

"You're lost, aren't you?"

I didn't answer but instead made a quick turn onto a road whose sign indicated it was 1123, even though it wasn't a gravel road. When I made the turn Paul spilled some of his coffee.

"God's truth, Sheryl, can't you be careful?"

"I'm sorry, Paul. You should've kept the top on your coffee cup."

"Bloody right you're sorry. Now I don't have any more coffee. What are you going to do about that?"

Whips and Unruly Women

"I said I'm sorry. Do you have to speak to me like that? I didn't do it on purpose. We can stop somewhere and get more."

"Oh, right, that's rich. Do you see any little cafés out here in the middle of nowhere?" He sighed loudly and glared out onto the road. I knew better than to respond.

The road I'd turned onto didn't seem to go anywhere but to more crawfish ponds and falling-down houses, so I turned back and retraced our route.

"I can't believe this. Where're you going now?" Paul sighed again. Out of the corner of my eye I saw him throwing something out of the window.

"What are you throwing out?"

"The bloody sandwiches. I spilled the coffee on them."

"They were wrapped in plastic. How could the coffee have penetrated that? And anyway, it wasn't that much coffee."

"Right, Sheryl. Just leave it."

"That's all there was for me to eat. You had breakfast. That was my breakfast. I can't believe you threw them out."

"Just leave it, Sheryl, leave it. It's your fault the coffee spilled."

"Paul," I said. Now I was angry.

"Keep your voice down, Sheryl. I don't want to hear it. Oh, and thanks for ruining the day."

There was nothing I could say that wouldn't fuel the fight, so I shut up. We continued in a strained silence up 97 and a few minutes later finally saw a sign for DI's Café. The Frugé Barn would be just north. And sure enough, a gravel road snaked just past DI's. By this time I was speeding, and Paul was gripping his seat. I turned left onto the gravel road.

In the midst of the tentative greens and dull browns that marked the end of winter and beginning of spring, a riot of color. From a distance it looked like giant bouquets of moving flowers or strange multicolored animals clotted together in a large field, dark heads swaying wildly in the wind. Nearby, a barn, and next to it a converted cattle trailer painted yellow, red, and green, with *Tee-Mamou Mardi Gras* hand-printed in large colored letters on the side. As we approached we could see a number of costumed figures standing around it; some were already inside. A police car with *Sheriff Acadia Parish* painted on its sides was parked next to the trailer.

"There they are!" I yelled.

"I see them," Paul replied dryly.

We pulled off onto the side of the road and made our way toward the trailer. As I looked out on the mass of dancing color, I tried to focus in on some elements of the costumes, which were of wildly different materials, but so similar in shape as to seem like a uniform. The suits were all made from similar pajama-like patterns, loose and large, with different material—one had red crawfish all over a black background, another had a red right pant leg and a yellow left pant leg; another suit was made out of various shades of purple; another was bright red; yet another was made of stripes of green, gold, and purple.

Their masks were all full-face screen masks. The principle behind looking out of a screen mask is the same as looking out of a screen window. You can see out, but it's difficult for others to see in. Most of the Mardi Gras didn't have their masks on yet but were holding them in their hands. I was close enough to make out the details of some of them. A few had used Spanish moss for hair, eyebrows, or beards. Several were covered with brown fur and were clearly trying to look like animal faces. One mask had plastic insects all over it.

I glanced at Paul. He was examining the women and their costumes as closely as I was, a somewhat bemused expression on his face.

The male captains, some young and some old, were not costumed or masked, but dressed casually, mostly in jeans and T-shirts. They were all holding the thick braided-burlap whips, which, I learned later, they had made themselves. Soon after we had gathered around the trailer one of the captains yelled, "Okay, Mardi Gras, let's go!" and the costumed figures who had been loitering around gathered up capuchins, masks, and beers, kissed children and husbands, and ran onto the trailer.

As soon as they were all stuffed—there is no other word to describe how tightly they were packed in—onto the trailer they began to stomp their feet and beat on its sides, shaking it so much that it tipped from side to side and I wondered why it didn't turn over. They yodeled and yipped at the top of their lungs. I felt infected by their immediate, pure rowdiness and joyful unruliness. The air was filled with an electricity that made the hair on my skin rise.

I looked over at Paul again. He had thrust his hard and compact body into the small crowd of onlookers, and there it stood out, tense and tight as a fist. He was smiling, but keeping himself at a distance from me.

Several of the women were already drinking. One woman had two cans of beer in her hand, both of which she would drink before they reached the first stop. If not for the tension with Paul, I would have been unrestrainedly happy, like a kid the night before Christmas. Something fun was going to happen, everyone knew it, rules were going to be broken, everyone knew it, and the excitement and impatience in the women's as-yet-unmasked faces shone out to me like beacons of light. I don't think I would've felt this had we been at the all-male Mardi Gras run. Something about there being all women charged the atmosphere in a particularly satisfying way for me.

The sheriff got into his vehicle and the onlookers into their cars. The caravan began to move: first the sheriff, then the trailer carrying the Mardi Gras, then a trailer carrying the musicians and captains, then the few cars of those of us who were following. Our windows were open, and we could hear the Mardi Gras yelling and cutting up in the trailer. We moved slowly through the countryside down the same empty roads we had just driven, past the same crawfish ponds and rice fields and farms and broken-down houses where maybe some of these Mardi Gras lived. The noise and rowdiness of the caravan cut through the landscape as a punk guitar riff might move through Barber's *Adagio for Strings*, rendering the space and the land strangely surreal.

Eventually, the caravan pulled into the yard of an isolated ranch-style farmhouse. The owners were waiting on the front porch. We parked and jumped out of the car. Paul walked quickly, far ahead of me to one side of the driveway; I followed, stopping on the other side. The head captain walked up to the owners.

"Les Mardi Gras demandent la permission pour visiter ta maison," he asked in a loud but polite voice.

The owners nodded assent, and the Mardi Gras, who had by now donned masks and capuchins, yipped and yodeled. They ran off the trailer in a burgeoning mass, which various captains attempted to herd into a sort of meaningful clump. Like a conductor, the head captain then led them in their Mardi Gras song, which they chanted while slowly approaching their hosts. They're supposed to appear as supplicants, but something about the tension in their bodies as they moved forward to the hosts, like cats stalking prey, added a menacing note to the procession. They emphasized in the song that they were beggars, not evildoers, but the fact that they felt the need to stress it suggested they knew their appearance might evoke fear.

Their song began by claiming that they came from England—"On vient de l'Angleterre, O mon cher, O mon cher"—which seemed strange to me at first because this tradition is obviously French, not English. I wondered if they simply wanted to indicate how far they'd come. Or not. Maybe, I thought, it was the demands of rhyme: *Angleterre* might be there because it rhymes with *cher*, a word that appears at the end of a line in almost every verse. My friend Barry would suggest to me later that it's about being other: how *other* could the French be than English?

So the song starts out with a lie designed to set the mood for the tricking and deception that will go on the entire day. The rest of the song has to do with a bottle the singers claim to have that they drink down to the dregs by the last verse. At first it's full, then only half full, then, "Only the dregs are left, O mon cher, O mon cher," they sing. "And we don't drink the dregs." Given that they will drink an incredible amount during the day—it may be that the altered state of consciousness drinking brings on is necessary to feel completely free to be so *other*—it makes sense that drinking and begging for drink dominate the lyrics.

As soon as the song was over, musicians with guitars and accordion struck up a two-step, and everyone started dancing on the front lawn of the house. Mardi Gras danced with themselves, with the owners of the house, with captains, and with spectators, swirling in and out of the oak, pecan, and magnolia trees that dominated the large yard. The unrestrained pleasure of the music and dancing mingled in my gut with the pain of the tension with Paul. My stomach churned, and I felt both happy and sick.

A tall Mardi Gras with a mask made out of Mardi Gras beads grabbed Paul, who doesn't care for dancing, and forced him to dance with her. Another one, with a mask and beard made of green potholder yarn, pulled me onto the grass to dance. Mardi Gras are not supposed to talk when they have their masks on, so the dance was a strangely silent one, all gesture and movement, like a silent film. Her potholder-yarn beard brushed against my face as we danced, and I noticed as we moved in and out of the mass of suits and masks that most of the masks sported beards. I learned later that beards are so prevalent on these masks that the Mardi Gras are sometimes called "Les Barbue," the Bearded Ones.

The beards suggest a male element, of course, and gender switching is part of what's going on with them. But they also suggest a sort of female wildness, an untamed and uncultivated element. In Greek myth presexual women were almost always understood to be wild, and were often represented as various sorts of animals. They, like their teacher, Artemis, preferred roaming about the forests without any men around. Watching these Tee-Mamou women, some of whom must have been grandmothers, dancing without restraint, it was clear that this day was also about going back to a wilder time without supervision or the responsibilities of family.

When the dance came to an end, my dance partner switched over to another Mardi Gras whose mask bore a nose made of women's nylons. It was stuffed, but drooped down, looking for all the world like an uncircumcised penis. A bell was tied to the very end of it, as if to mock the organ even more. Most of the masks had prominent noses, large and either up-turned, down-turned, or noticeably crooked. Tongues also seemed important: felt tongues, satin tongues, plastic tongues, even a plastic alligator that served as a tongue. One green felt tongue had ants and a flower glued into it.

Another mask sported huge plastic nostrils, a hideous open mouth and lolling tongue. In fact, several of the masks with the long tongues like this one reminded me of classic Gorgon masks. Some ancient myths tell of a band of Libyan women who wore those masks partly to frighten off men or others that might be too curious about their mysteries. Eventually, the mask was used as a symbol to frighten anyone off from anything; Greek bakers, for example, would sometimes put one on their ovens to keep the curious from peeking in and causing their cakes or loaves to fall. It's a mask that has ever been identified with women, though, especially Medusa, a mask that projects aggressive female sexuality and energy.

After the dance the Mardi Gras yipped and yodeled again, and dispersed throughout the yard. Some of them began to beg. One got down on her knees in front of me, pointing to her empty hand and asking for a "petit sou." I shrugged my shoulders, at which point the Mardi Gras grabbed the car keys out of my hand and ran away with them.

The Mardi Gras who weren't begging were running around the lawn cutting up. One grabbed hold of the whip of one of the captains and tried to wrest it from him. She wasn't strong enough to get the whip away, though, and he whipped her hard, the braided whip flying in the air over and over like the tentacles of an octopus. Eventually, she jumped up and pulled the cap off his head, shrieking with laughter, and ran away. He followed, cracking the whip behind her.

Another climbed a tree where she sat looking down at a captain brandishing his whip. He yelled at her to get out of it. She refused and he started to climb up the tree after her. A woman wearing a suit made of camouflage material tackled the captain, bringing him down. Four other women ran over and jumped on top of him as well, hollering and chortling. He tried to whip them all but had a hard time, and wound up falling to the ground, doubled over with laughter. Another captain came over to help him out, trying to whip all the Mardi Gras and yelling at them to get off. Next, three large women attacked one of the captains and brought him down. They sat on top of him, laughing and pummeling him, one on his neck, another on his groin, and another on his ankles. A young boy next to me exclaimed with glee, "Look! They got the man with the whip!"

Whips and Unruly Women

From somewhere out of the crowd, Paul sidled up to me, took my hand, and squeezed it. "You know they'll go home and fuck well tonight," he whispered.

I smiled, took his hand, and tried to relax. The bodies that had been dancing not so long ago were now wrestling. It occurred to me that what made the whole drama so thrillingly sexual—aside from the exaggerated tongues and mouths and noses of the masks and the intense physicality of the roughhousing—was the presence of the whips. The undeniable, real possibility of harm. I wanted to say this to Paul but didn't, fearing any remark at all, however innocent, would become a catalyst for a fight. *Thwap, thwap, thwap* went the ineffectual whips, and I wondered if some of the women wore padding to protect themselves from injury. *Thwap, thwap, thwap.* I remembered an old friend confessing to me that he and his girlfriend had begun to "experiment" with whips. His girlfriend, he said, "loved it."

Paul seemed relaxed and smiling, but underneath the smiling face I thought I could also see his *other face* contorted into a snarl, that Mr. Hyde face he wears when I've done something to displease him. I looked away.

It's true I've often been attracted to men who are temperamental, but I wonder now if the emotional stinging that results from that trait might not function as a sort of psychic whip. It seems to me that sex by definition always has something transgressive about it, even when you want it to mean nothing but love. Any entrance into one's physical being, whether wanted or not, is a kind of violation.

Still, sometimes I long for the sex I imagine long-married couples must have, a comfortable sex that doesn't involve the presence of whips, either real or psychic, some coupling that's rather like sliding into your favorite easy chair. No easy chair for me; I've moved from partner to partner as these women move from captain to captain, wearing my own slightly different mask with each one, participating in constructing the whip that will bind us together. The difference between my relationship with Paul and these women's relationship with their captains, though, is that they're laughing. Paul and I rarely laugh; when he lashes out with his tongue and when I respond in kind it's not meant to be playful.

Eventually, the head captain called for the Mardi Gras to get back onto the trailer. Some resisted, and a few had to be dragged or carried onto the truck. At the next house the pattern of asking permission to enter, singing the song, dancing, and cutting up was repeated. The air smelled like grass and crawfish and beer, and with the quarrel between Paul and me on hold for the moment, I felt better.

After some dancing, the owner of the house emerged with a chicken cradled in his arms. The Mardi Gras yelled loudly, surrounding him. He thrust the chicken into the air where it flailed about, then hit the ground running along a crawfish pond and into a field where all the Mardi Gras followed, yelling. They chased it around the house over and over, into the street, into the ditch alongside the house. Many of them fell down during the chase. Paul and I both laughed. Finally, one of them caught the chicken, and there was great rejoicing.

As the day went on the play, and the whipping, escalated, probably because the women were drinking so much that they were feeling freer. The teasing and tackling got harder, and the whipping seemed in earnest, but everyone continued to drink and laugh. And they left each house with something for the gumbo, whether it was a chicken, onions they'd pulled out of the host's garden, green peppers raided from the kitchen, flour, salt or rice given freely, or in one case crawfish stolen out of a nearby pond. At every stop Paul and I found ourselves being tricked or teased in some way, and as the day went on our truce felt a little more solid.

At one of our last stops I remember looking around and noticing that almost all of the women were either sitting in the limbs of a tree or climbing trees. It struck me that the association of women, especially unruly women, with trees is an old one. The stories of many Greek female figures are intertwined with them: the apple tree was sacred to Hera, the olive tree to Athena. Most famously, the mountain nymph Daphne actually prayed to be turned into a tree to escape Apollo's designs on her. Ovid's rendering of the moment Gaia granted her prayer, the same moment Apollo reached her, is exquisite. As he takes her in his arms her feet root, arms turn into limbs, skin toughens, and voilà: tree. The earliest sources about the relationship between women and trees, though, lay in Sumerian myths about the rise to power of the goddess Inanna, the hero Gilgamesh's sister. Inanna was said to have a special tree—a huluppu tree—growing in her "holy" garden. In the tree lived a serpent, an *Anzu*-bird (a bird associated with disorder), and the "dark maid Lilith." They had all built their home in the huluppu. She had to call on her brother to help get these three creatures—all associated with some sort of chaos—out of the tree. After getting rid of them (Lilith is said to fly off to "wild, uninhabited places"), Gilgamesh makes Inanna both a crown and a bed out of the tree, two symbols of the powerful and complicated intimacy among women, trees, and disorder.

In later Christian narratives it's Eve's association with trees (and the snakes that live in them) that supposedly causes us to be thrust out of the Garden. As I watched the Tee-Mamou women climbing trees, the whip-brandishing captains mostly unable to control them, I couldn't help but think of the Garden of Eden story. The chaos that Eve brought there these women bring to the lawn of a house. The whips curling around the trees where the Mardi Gras perched looked like twining snakes.

Near lunchtime, at one stop alongside an old cemetery, the unmistakable smell of gumbo entered me, as full and thick as the memory of a sweet, lost love. The rich scent of nutty roux, chicken, sausage, onions, and peppers wafted over the motley group like a blessing. In a closed-in porch that doubled as a kitchen a man stirred a huge cauldron of filé gumbo over a fire. The cauldron was about four feet deep and three feet wide: the communal gumbo to be eaten later that afternoon. Paul and I left before it was time to eat, but I carried the smell of that gumbo with me all the long ride back to my mother's.

The thought of food brings me to my senses, and I sit straight up in my bed, dropping the journal on the floor. Gray should be home soon, and it's time to start cooking supper. I hop out of bed and bound downstairs, trying to get the thought of gumbo out of my head. It would take several hours to make, and I don't have that kind of time. Instead, I'll make some puttanesca, my favorite pasta dish, which will take about half an hour.

When I cook I am filled with a foolish hope. The words *recipe* and *rescue* have long been confused in my head—I'm like my mother in that way. Whenever things got really bad, her solution was to retire to the kitchen. And shouldn't combining various elements skillfully in a recipe count for something? You're assured of success with a tried-and-true recipe in a way that you aren't in the world outside a kitchen.

If I can't succeed with men, at least I can make something good to eat.

In the kitchen now, I pour some fruity olive oil into a pan, mince a few cloves of garlic, and sauté for a few minutes. A sprinkle of crushed chiles, a can of anchovies. Sauté until the anchovies melt. How could anyone be sad with the aroma of olive oil, garlic, and anchovies in the air? Next, two cans of whole tomatoes. I put some water on to boil for the pasta, call Gray at Will's, and tell him to be home in half an hour.

Calamata olives and Parmesan cheese, out of the fridge. Some photos from the Louisiana trip are still on the refrigerator door. I put the olives and cheese on the counter and take the photos down. One is of the backyard of a stop the Tee-Mamou women made. It was the gumbo house. At the center is a statue of the Virgin Mary with Mardi Grad beads around her neck. Two women are sitting on the grass next to the statue, resting their heads—masks and capuchins still on—against her. This was my favorite image from the day. Gumbo in the air, drunkenness and revelry all around, and in the midst of it this moment of rest with the Virgin, decorated in Mardi Gras beads.

I have a small Mary statue in my study, next to my collection of voodoo dolls and statues of Greek snake and bird goddesses. My Mary is also draped with Mardi Gras beads, as is one of the snake goddesses. I wonder what the Tee-Mamou women would think about the company my Virgin keeps. I've had to hide my voodoo dolls, a collection to which my mother often contributes, in my study because Paul doesn't think they're anything one should display. That should be private, he says. He said nothing about my mother's collection of voodoo dolls when we visited, though. She has so many she keeps them in a large wicker basket in her living room, as if they were shells, or candy, something one could help oneself to if necessary. It's not that we believe the dolls could help us with anything. My mother's a fairly committed Catholic. But they're beautiful and interesting in a fierce sort of way, and anyway it's better to hedge your bets about that sort of thing. You never know what kind of help you might need.

I wander out into the living room while the sauce is cooking down, sit on the sofa for a moment, and look at the other photo. It was taken on Bourbon Street in New Orleans on Mardi Gras day itself. The day is both painful and absurd to remember. Painful because Paul and I had a number of vicious arguments that lasted almost the whole day. Absurd because we carried these arguments out while dressed in our costumes. The worst occurred when I parked the car downtown and locked the keys in it. Though I managed to get them out about twenty minutes later by breaking into the car with a coat hanger, the incident infuriated Paul. His response infuriated me, and so we remained much of the day.

What I loved most about Mardi Gras day was walking around in the Cajun Mardi Gras costume. I loved being so hidden; the gutsy women from Tee-Mamou seemed a part of me, so much so I remember feeling as if I were wearing a crowd of women. As I walked down the streets of New Orleans, I felt them with me, and by extension my grandmother.

In the photo there's a massive crush of people on the street. If you squint and look at the picture you could almost imagine it is a sort of polluted river where thousands of multicolored, tragically misguided salmon have come back to spawn. I remember the smells: beer, rotting seafood and fruit, piss, and vomit. The smells sweated from the street itself, a sort of body odor I recognize as belonging to the French Quarter. A sweet, raunchy, familiar smell. A large man in a blonde woman's wig, covered from neck to ankles in Spanish moss, walks past at the far end of the photo. On the opposite side of the photo, a fleshy man dressed only in a G-string hung with beads strolls by, the beads swinging as he walks, revealing his penis swaying along with the beads.

If you look closely you can just barely see in the background a balcony where two giant papier-mâché women, clothed in only G-strings and pasties, tower over a huge clump of costumed men and women. A large banner above them proclaims, *Tetons et Derriere.* I remember what happened after I took this photo: a woman in the street pulled up her shirt, and someone from the balcony tossed her a strand of beads. Then one woman on the balcony convinced a man on the street to drop his pants. She hurled a fistful of beads at him.

On the next balcony was a naked papier-mâché male about eight feet tall with an erect penis extending about four feet out from the balcony. The penis was hung with about twenty pairs of beads. We took a photo of this, too, but I don't know where it is. Paul and I glanced into one of the open doors to the numerous bars and strip clubs that lined the street. A young man in briefs and beads danced on top of the bar, touching himself. A male customer waved some money; the dancer bent over to take the money and let the customer fondle him.

I remember watching all this, then feeling claustrophobic because of the crowds, trying to walk on either side of the street to avoid them. Each side was lined with overflowing black plastic bags of trash, though, some of which had been kicked open. Plastic cups, shrimp and crawfish shells, fish bones, and other bits of unrecognizable food and trash spilled out onto the street, whose paving we could hardly see because of all the trash. We walked ahead anyway, smashing the beads and shells and cups and trash under our feet. A couple dressed as roaches, complete with antennae and wings, bumped into us and mumbled apologies.

This, I think, fingering the photo, is my city. Vulgar, overflowing with drunks and exhibitionists, stinky with the smell of vomit, of things rotting. This is the place I wanted to show Paul so that he would know me better.

I go back into the kitchen to finish the puttanesca sauce. The water is boiling. I put the pasta in, call Gray again, and tell him to come home *now*. I stir the sauce that has cooked down to a thick consistency. I throw in about a cupful of the olives, a handful of capers, a little red wine. I chop up some parsley and throw that in, too. I grate the cheese, set the table, pour a glass of wine, and put on some jazz—Sidney Bechet. I sip the wine while I wait for Gray to come barreling in the front door.

I wonder if Paul has been as shaped by the landscape of England as I feel I have by that of America, if part of our difficulties might lie in the ways in which our different temperaments have been molded by where and how we grew up. There's no wilderness to speak of in England, while some argue that an important part of the American temperament might have been shaped by our struggle with wilderness. England has lovely parks and gardens, cultivated areas where humans have clearly won out against wilderness. It's a relatively small island that has been inhabited for so long it's no wonder just about every stitch of it has been manicured in some way. Much as I've enjoyed the vibrant culture one finds in England, especially London, I've always felt a release returning to America, flying over our vast, not completely tamed continent. A feeling of air, of breath, of hope: still some almost-wild spaces.

I must seem a wilderness to Paul, my unmanageable hair, my unsubmissive, intractable spirit, my perverse and seemingly irrepressible bleeding, my general messiness something he is drawn to and struggles with, knowing it will never fall under his dominion. An English garden I will never be, though what metaphor might express what I am I cannot quite tell.

Medusa? My tongue can sometimes be as sharp as his. If I were not such a knotty, exacting woman, I would have stayed with one partner for longer, right? Or so Gray likes to remind me. And I have to admit I've been drawn to the figure of Medusa for most of my life. For many years I've dressed as her for Mardi Gras, tying rubber snakes in my hair with sparkly pipe cleaners. I have a Medusa mask as well that I keep on the wall in my study. I have snake pins, snake earrings, snake necklaces, none of which I wear much, but I'd be unhappy if I lost them. A small Gorgon statue, decorated with Mardi Gras beads, guards one of the bookshelves in my study. I did my dissertation on Medusa, and my first book of poems was written in the persona of Medusa, though the voice was mine. We had so much in common: I was divorcing Gray's dad at the time and scaring away every man I met, or so it seemed. I imagined she must have had a hard time with men too; every time she looked at one she turned him to stone. I imagined she might have been unhappy about this, that she might have wanted a relationship, but something about her nature prevented it. And we both had C-sections, of sorts: Gray was cut out of my womb, and Medusa's son, Pegasus, emerged from her neck when Perseus cut off her head.

It occurs to me now that one reason I might have liked the women's Tee-Mamou Mardi Gras so much is that in some crazy, mixed-up way the whole thing was so Medusa-like. Their wildness, their ability to stop the captains not with their gaze but with their often very substantive bodies. And the flailing of the whips: the whips belonged to the captains, but it was Medusa's spirit, her snakes that they made me think of. The dream I'd had the night before we left for Tee-Mamou, of the masked women with whips in their hair, was really a dream, I see now, about Medusa.

I've always been attracted to her, and yet it's not just the appeal of Medusa's wild-haired, unsubmissive, powerful visage, or the appeal of a Gorgon face one might put on to keep the crowd away from one's most hidden self. Or even that her gaze, which turned men to stone, might more profitably be seen as the gaze of the poet: the vision that stills life into art. There's something else, even now, especially now, that makes me feel connected to her.

I pour the bloodred puttanesca sauce over the pasta. Blood. Medusa had special blood. When she died Athena drained her body of it. The blood from one side was healing blood. The blood from the other side of her body had the power to kill, and Athena kept them in separate vials. The only blood I know of that might be said to be healing blood is menstrual blood, and Medusa is perhaps the prototype for the menstruating woman whose gaze was said to sour milk and beer, ruin crops, absorb the power from weapons, etc. So am I, after all, just a pawn in an older, larger narrative, the story of the ever changing, uncontrollable body of woman? If so, all may end well: even though Perseus cuts off Medusa's head, it still retains its power to transform anyone who looks at it into stone, even, eventually, Perseus, who, in my favorite version of the myth,

Whips and Unruly Women

thinks the head has lost its power, looks at it, and is turned to stone himself.

If only one could see the truth of oneself before one dies. When I look at myself my vision seems dimmed somehow, though, like my damaged hearing. It's your own voice somehow that warps and dulls your understanding of yourself. It's easier to imagine or invent a truth for anyone other than yourself.

And what if what you see when you look in that mirror is something that scares you, almost turns you to stone? If only there were one who could look with you. One who could love you through all of it, your frightening face, your bleeding, your masks. See through it to some passionate, cowardly, pulsing thing at your core that you cannot even see yourself. *If someone could love me as I am,* I wrote in one of my Medusa poems, *I would take off my face, I would undress my snakes, peel back their raw skin, change them into red tulips.*

The ribbed penne, sturdy and beige against the blue bowl, the dark, glistening olives, the green specks of parsley, the red pulp of tomato, the scent of garlic-kissed olive oil, and underneath it all, like a held bass note, the invisible ingredient that gives the sauce its startling richness and structure, like a deep, sexy kiss you hadn't expected: anchovy, that messy, smelly fish I love.

Puttanesca. *Of a harlot or a whore.* Some say the dish got its name because prostitutes used to make it to seduce customers with its aroma, which most could not resist. Of course, Paul would say, it's a dish you would love.

Gray's bike crashes against the front porch. I set the puttanesca on the table and pour him a glass of spring water. If I can't give him, or myself, an uninterrupted life with one man, or one place, I can at least give him stories of other women—his grandmother and great-grandmother—who stayed with one man and in one place, stories of the place I was born and stayed the longest, and the hard truth of what I seem to be.

Bechet's saxophone slides into the beginning bars of "All of Me," open and bare as a naked woman, rich, intimate, sophisticated. The smell of the puttanesca is like a drug, the one glass of wine goes to my head, Gray is at the door, and I feel, for a moment, at rest in the writhing mess of my thoughts, at rest for a moment about my restlessness.

Maybe I should stop searching for an overarching narrative. Maybe for me each beloved is more like a poem; maybe my story is lyric, not narrative. A necklace without beginning or end. Of a harlot or a whore. Anchovies. My blood all over the house. Medusa. Celeste. Cypress, birch, oak. Fisting his name. Olives, garlic. My name. Whips. Husband.

The front door opens, a rush of warm air: *Home, Mom. What's for dinner?*

AFTERWORD

Bring Me a Dream

I sometimes wonder if Louisianians' deep love of and apparent need for masking and deception does not have environmental as well as cultural roots. Certainly, the physical landscape of Louisiana is deceptive: the Mississippi's shifting course over the years periodically transformed land to open water and vice versa, so that even land that had existed for several generations could be eventually masked by the river's flooding. The surface waters of slow-moving bayous, swamps, and the Mississippi—all an inscrutable brown or gray color—provide a mask for what swims underneath. Alligators float along in sluggish bayous looking like logs, while lush flora during all seasons provides deep cover for birds and reptiles. Crawfish thrive and hide in opaque waters only inches deep. Because waters surround, permeate, and penetrate the land, natives have had to learn to live with not being able to see to the bottom of things, with not always being able to tell where the edges of things are. They've had to learn to live with a physically ambiguous landscape. And though the people may sometimes take off their masks, New Orleans itself never does—levees, pumps, and canals make the mortar and concrete illusion of a city possible in all seasons.

In addition to the masks the land itself wears, Louisiana's state tree, the bald cypress, is one that appears costumed. The Spanish moss that decorates the cypress was called by the French *barbe espagnole* because it reminded them of the beards of early Spanish in Louisiana. The Spanish, in return, called it *perruque à la français,* the "French wig." Not only does our state tree appear to be disguised with beards or wigs, depending on which nationality you are, but in swamps or flooded areas it also grows appendages that look disturbingly like woody human knees. A tree with human-looking body parts that appears to disguise its "baldness" with an epiphyte that looks like a beard or a wig is the perfect tree for a people who love to disguise themselves.

One might say that the culture of masking took root and thrived in the landscape of south Louisiana as the nonnative nutria have, without the deleterious environmental effects of the staggering populations of nutria. It found both a people and a physical environment well suited to it.

This culture of masking has taken a peculiar turn in my family, one that's well illustrated by an event from my childhood. It's summer, 1962: my cousin Denise and I are spending the weekend at our Maw-Maw's house. Denise is nine and I'm eight. It's late, about two, and we're curled up together on the sofa, watching a horror movie. Both of us have short, chopped-up hair, our scalps almost bald in places. Earlier in the day Denise had discovered Maw-Maw's scissors while rifling through a junk drawer, and decided to play beauty parlor. Maw-Maw says we look like refugees. Next to us on the sofa sit our Barbie dolls, which have also suffered the refugee haircut. Earlier that day, before the haircuts, we had dressed them in their sexiest outfits and made them prance around while we played the Chordettes singing "Mr. Sandman" over and over on the record player. Maw-Maw says "Mr. Sandman" is my song because it came out the year I was born.

Pretending the Sandman might bring our Barbies some dream guy soon becomes boring, especially since neither Denise nor I have a Ken doll. That's when Denise went looking for the scissors. Our dolls are now as scary looking as some of the characters in the movie we're watching. Their naked heads seem peppered with doll-size bullet holes.

We're watching the end of *Up Jumps the Devil*, a movie in which a satanic character keeps sneaking up behind other characters and scaring them, literally, to death and into hell. Every time the devil character jumps, Denise and I jump. We crowd closer and closer as the movie moves to its horrific climax and the house sinks deeper into darkness. When the station goes off the air, we are too terrified to walk over to the TV and turn it off. Its static is all the noise that punctuates the sleeping house and its weird white glow all the light there is. My heart is beating hard.

I can tell Denise is terrified, too. Her eyes are huge, wary as a prey that knows it's being stalked, and the way the TV lights her face makes it seem unnaturally white. With her clumped-up hair and bits of bald scalp showing, she looks more like a zombie than a refugee. When I think, now, of the way Denise's life would unfold—she would become a junkie and prostitute, dying young, like my brother, of a drug overdose—it is always this image to which I return: her haunted, refugee-child face, transfixed in a hissing, otherworldly light.

But back then, Denise is just my cousin, someone I like to hang out with, and the only warm body I have, at the moment, to keep the shadows at bay in that house. Because our grandparents' house is a shotgun house, we know we'll have to walk through every room to get to the back bedroom we're sharing. We get up cautiously from the sofa, hold hands and creep, pressed up against each other as if we are one entity, out of the living room, past the dining room, past the front bedroom where Paw-Paw sleeps, into the kitchen, to the doorway of the bathroom hall. Just as we take our first steps into the hall, the bathroom door opens, and a weak light appears behind it. A tall figure, face and hair hidden by a black veil, walks into the light, turns, and starts to move toward us.

Denise and I both scream and immediately turn around, trying to get back through the doorway to the kitchen. We stick in the doorway and fall down, kicking, screaming, and squirming, but unable to move forward. In her fright Denise bites my arm, drawing blood, and sucks on it between screams like a confused vampire.

"What's going on?" Paw-Paw growls from the front bedroom.

Denise and I continue to scream and flail. A light comes on in the front bedroom, and Paw-Paw appears in an undershirt and boxer shorts. I dare not look back at the black figure.

"Someone," Denise shouts, her mouth bloody from my arm.

"In the bathroom," I sob, managing to crawl out from under Denise. I stand up and run to Paw-Paw, throwing my arms around one of his bare legs.

"Teresa, what the hell are they talking about?"

I put my hands over my eyes and look through my fingers back toward the bathroom, peeking between Paw-Paw's legs. Maw-Maw is standing in the light from the bathroom. She's dressed in black and is in the process of dropping a black veil from her face.

"I was just brushing my teeth," she says.

She walks over toward us and pulls us away from Paw-Paw and into her. I look up at her. A soft, inscrutable smile plays across her face.

"I put the veil on to keep my hair from getting wet." When she picks me up, I bury my head in her dark hair. Her skin smells like roses.

"You two have been up too late; you've got the devil in your eyes. Whose idea was it, anyway, to watch that movie?" she asks.

Later I will remember it was her idea, but at the moment I just want to revel in the knowledge that she's not the devil. She takes us into the bathroom, washes off my arm, and puts a Band-Aid on it. She tucks us into bed and puts "Mr. Sandman" on the record player. "Sleep tight, the Sandman's going to come sprinkle sand in your eyes," she says, closing the door. I remember sleeping fitfully that night after the song was over, listening to the groanings of the huge window fan until morning.

I was so relieved that the black figure turned out to be Maw-Maw that I didn't think too much at the time about the implausibility of her explanation for the black veil. As I thought about the incident over the years, though, I came to believe that she had probably scared us on purpose. Maybe to teach us a lesson about staying up late or maybe because she couldn't help herself. A woman born and bred in New Orleans, she knew the value of masks and dark stories that acted like masks. She used to tell us about a bogeyman who lived under the bridge down the block from her house. He was always drunk, she said, and did horrible things to boys and girls. If we went by the bridge he would grab us and take us under the bridge, and our parents would never be able to find us. For years I believed this, and wouldn't go near the bridge. I had a vivid imagination, and used to have nightmares about what, exactly, a bogeyman might look like—like the troll in my Billy Goats Gruff storybook, I finally decided, dirty and old with black teeth and a warty nose—and what, exactly, he would do to you. My mother laughed when I confessed my fears. "She just doesn't want you straying too far," she said. "That's why she tells you that."

Maw-Maw also used to tell all the female grandchildren not to look in the mirror too much or we'd see the devil's face. "That was to keep you from becoming vain," my mother would say. I was too young then to know what being vain meant, but her warning stuck with me. I used to be afraid to look too long in mirrors for the fear of eventually encountering some other unwelcome face there. The odd thing is that in a strange way she was right: wait long enough, and you'll see, as you age, your own mortality staring back at you.

When Gray was five, we lived on the upper floor of an old house with big windows in all the rooms. I didn't bother to get curtains or blinds because I figured we were so high up no one could see inside. But at night the windows turned into dark mirrors. I remember Gray saying to me once, as if it were a momentous discovery, "Mom, it's frightening to see your face reflected back to you in a window at night," and I remember thinking, yes, it would be frightening, especially for a child, because it suggests there's something scary about yourself, some dark side you don't quite understand or even recognize.

Gray and I used to have a bedtime during this same period: after he'd taken his bath and brushed his teeth, we'd crawl into his bed together with a couple of books, one of which was always a collection of poetry. In the early years it was a fat children's poetry anthology with vibrant, full-page illustrations. I'd read him a few poems, then sometimes we'd look at the pictures and talk about them. One poem that particularly delighted him was about Halloween. Next to the poem was a colorful enlarged illustration of the traditional Halloween witch's face: green, warty, black teeth—a sort of female version of what my bogeyman looked like. Every night before turning out the light, I'd say the same thing: "Good night, sleep tight, the Sandman's going to come and sprinkle sand in your eyes!"

One night, after reading him a poem, I turned to the page with the familiar witch illustration and pointed to it. "Ooh, what's that?" I asked.

Gray didn't hesitate. He looked at me with his beautiful, clear eyes and said, "Sandman, Mommy, that's the Sandman."

Later as I lay, sleepless and anguished in my bed, I tried to imagine what it must have been like for him night after night as I kissed him, leaving him with the thought that a monstrous being was going to swoop down and put sand in his eyes. Crazy things went through my head: I remembered how I had thrown sand in a boy's eyes in first grade because he had teased me, how the boy had been taken away in an ambulance and showed up at school a week later with a patch on his eye, which, in my memory, he wore the rest of his life. So that is what I am, I remember thinking, a Sandman child and now a Sandman mother.

In calmer moments I would marvel at how expertly we can project a horrific face even when we don't want to.

Maw-Maw used to sing a song to my mother as a child about a letter bordered in black. The refrain was "Your dear old mother's dying, your dear old mother's dead."

"Can you imagine she would sing this song to her children?" my mother asked me, more amused than angry.

Yes, I told her, I can. If she can dress herself as death's lackey to scare her grandchildren, I can imagine her singing a song about a mother's death to her children. Our family seems to have a need to show the face of the ruined one, as if somehow we are not whole without displaying that face others keep to themselves. I think of my mother telling me the story of the one-eyed face of my great-great-grandfather, of my brother pressing his grimacing face into the window of my boyfriend's car, of my sister showing her beaten face to her boyfriend's mother. I think of my grandmother Celeste wanting to have that photograph of her husband, Albin, on his deathbed, tubes in his nostrils and down his throat. I think of my father displaying the headless body of the choirboy at Christmastime, of the effigy he made with my mother's wig head, of his own monstrous face at the end, as orange and bloated as a rotting pumpkin. I think of Denise's and my refugee faces, of the heads of our ruined Barbie dolls. I think of how my face must have appeared to Gray the first time he saw me devour crawfish. Of the Sandman face in his poetry book. Of how, in writing this book at this moment, it feels as if I'm donning Maw-Maw's black veil.

Not just my family but the culture in which we were raised loves to celebrate the darker areas of the psyche—note our jazz funerals, the blackly comic rituals of the "whippings" of the Cajun Mardi Gras. These celebrations of ours may come, in part, from the fact that we are surrounded by waters we love whose surfaces vary in color only from brown to purplish or greenish black: ditches, canals, bayous, shallow lakes, swamps, even the Mississippi, so slow moving and filled with sediment by the end of its travels here that it is truly inscrutable. We emerge from the wombs of dark waters, we are fed from the breasts of dark waters, and dark waters form a large part of the landscape we spend our lives on; is it any wonder that we have transformed that inscrutability into ritual?

Masking, dancing, drinking, drugs, and even eating are all forms of "getting high" here, which expression, in a land that is mostly at or barely above sea level, suggests a condition that is fiercely literal. I know that the singular shape of my own desires has been energized by the strong personality of this place that gave birth to and nurtured them. I also know that my own sense of writing is deeply tied to this particular place, the Deep South. Although Iowa is where I live now, it feels wrong to write from there, from the center of the country, as a midwesterner. Nor, although I've traveled to its extremities, can I write from its "edges"—the East Coast or the West. I am at heart a bottom dweller, and must write from that muddy bottom.

To write from the bottom, the place where the river that drains much of the country finally empties itself into the Gulf of Mexico, is to write first of all with a profound sense of the power of water. New Orleans author Kate Chopin had her heroine in *The Awakening* give birth to and destroy herself in water. Though that novel is a century old, the metaphor of water as birth-giver and destroyer and shaper of lives is still a powerful one.

Writing from the bottom also means, for me, writing from a place where I'm almost drowning; I'm fighting my love of the sensuous— food, drink, and pleasure, all of which tempt me from the essential work of writing, and all of which eventually find their way into the writing. Most writing that comes from this area, in fact—works by authors such as Anne Rice, John O'Toole, James Lee Burke, Brenda Marie Osby, and Robert Olen Butler—privileges the sensuous, all the ways in which one might speak to the body.

Those of us who write from the bottom are distracted regularly by the weather, which threatens destruction with each hurricane season. As a result, we often have a highly developed sense of the dramatic. If you are writing from the bottom you are possibly living in a dysfunctional family and have a highly evolved sense of tragedy and, out of a need for survival, humor. Perhaps your prose is as lavish and twiney as the flora that flourishes in this semitropical climate; perhaps it is as full and rich as a river or swamp at night. Perhaps your writing is too sexy for mainstream America because you were raised on sex and you can't help but see it everywhere.

You are probably more comfortable with dirt, with lying, with corruption, pollution, scandal, violence, drugs, and alcohol than much of the rest of the country. You have lost a brother, a father, a mother, a whole family to some tragedy, the telling of which may seem stranger than fiction to those not from here.

A friend from Wisconsin who attended graduate school in Louisiana used to always complain about how dirty Louisiana seemed: the streets, the sidewalks, the yards, the houses, and public buildings. I would look at him blankly when he complained. "The dirt is interesting," I would say, and then it would be his turn to look at me blankly. I finally understood the shock Louisiana must have been for him when I moved to the Midwest and was myself shocked by the scrubbed homes and unlittered streets of rural mid-America. I missed the dirt. There was nothing to transform, at least nothing I had been trained to see. The blinding clean surfaces did not inspire me as much as the muck I'd grown up with. I think one of the reasons the swamp is such a powerful symbol for me is that it has come to represent a kind of dark mirror for my family, a mirror I've had to teach myself not to fear.

For my mother, the Sandman is flesh and blood: he is the one who replenishes the river sand under her house every few years, keeping it in touch with the land. For her, the Sandman brings a kind of soil that represents a stubborn hope. The land may sink and wash away, but she will not retreat to higher ground.

If she asks the Sandman for anything, she asks him to bring the dream of a home that will hold its own come hell or high water.

ABOUT THE AUTHOR

Sheryl St. Germain is associate professor of English at Iowa State University in Ames, Iowa. She is the recipient of many awards, including the William Faulkner Creative Writing Award for the Personal Essay, a fellowship from the National Endowment for the Humanities Institute on the Environmental Imagination, and two National Endowment for the Arts fellowships. She has published four collections of poetry as well as *Je Suis Cadien,* a translation from the French of the poetry of Jean Arceneaux. Her poetry and essays have been published widely in numerous journals and anthologies.